D1525473

Developments in
housing management
and ownership

Developments in housing management and ownership

edited by
Ricardo Pinto

MANCHESTER UNIVERSITY PRESS
MANCHESTER and NEW YORK

distributed exclusively in the USA and Canada by ST. MARTIN'S PRESS, New York

Published by Manchester University Press
Oxford Road, Manchester M13 9NR, UK
and Room 400, 175 Fifth Avenue,
New York, NY 10010, USA

Distributed exclusively in the USA and Canada
by St. Martin's Press, Inc.,
175 Fifth Avenue, New York, NY 10010, USA

British Library Cataloguing-in-Publication Data
A catalogue record for this book is available from the British Library

Library of Congress Cataloging-in-Publication Data
Developments in housing management and ownership
      / edited by Ricardo Pinto
          p.   cm.
      Includes index
      ISBN 0-7190-3713-1
      1. Public housing—Great Britain—Management. 2. Housing,
Co-operative—Great Britain—Management. 3. Housing authorities
—Great Britain. 4. Home ownership—Government policy—Great
Britain. 5. Housing policy—Great Britain. I. Pinto, Ricardo, 1966
HD7333.A3D475   1995
363.5'85'068—dc20   94-43135

ISBN 0 7190 3713 1 hardback

First published in 1995
99 98 97 96 95   10 9 8 7 6 5 4 3 2 1

Typeset in Joanna
by Koinonia Limited, Manchester
Printed in Great Britain
by Bookcraft Ltd, Midsomer Norton

Contents

Tables and figure   vi
Contributors   vii
Acknowledgements   viii
Abbreviations   ix

Introduction: setting the context
Ricardo Pinto   1

1 **Housing developments in the 1980s and 1990s**
Ricardo Pinto   15

2 **Housing associations: new providers of social housing
for rent or vehicles for the privatisation of rented
accommodation?**
Judith Harrison   54

3 **Housing co-operatives: potential unfulfilled**
David Clapham and Keith Kintrea   95

4 **The origins, evolution and impact of the Estate Action
initiative**
Ricardo Pinto   121

5 **Tenants' choices: sales, transfers and trusts**
Alan Murie   154

6 **The changing role of local authority housing
departments**
Matthew Warburton   181

7 **Housing management in transition: a case study of
Hackney**
Keith Jacobs   206

Synthesis and conclusions
Ricardo Pinto   232

Index   261

Tables and figure

Tables

1.1 Housing subsidy and rent rebates in England (1993/94 prices)   27
1.2 Local authority capital expenditure in England (1993/94 prices)   29
1.3 Twentieth-century tenure patterns in England and Wales (%)   36
1.4 Phased introduction of Housing Management CCT   48
2.1 Distribution of housing associations and stock by size of association in England, 1993   57
2.2 Housing association stock by housing need, 1993 and 1989   58
2.3 Proportion of special needs funding by group   59
2.4 Housebuilding completions by sector   66
2.5 Breakdown of Housing Corporation's ADP, 1991-97   77
2.6 Housing association approvals and completions of housing for rent, 1984-93   79
2.7 Forecast of approvals and ADP funded completions, 1993-97   80
3.1 Incidence of types of co-operative in England and Wales, 1986/87   98
3.2 Tenants' satisfaction with housing management in community ownership schemes in 1986/87 and 1989   114
3.3 Effectiveness of different landlords   115
4.1 An evaluation of Estate Action schemes   134
4.2 Synthesis of impact of Estate Action   137
5.1 Right to Buy and other sales to sitting tenants by local authorities and new towns in Great Britain, 1979-92   157
5.2 Large scale voluntary transfers by local authorities in England, 1988-92   167

Figure

4.1 Estate Action agents and policy context   128

Contributors

David Clapham, Professor of Housing; and Director of the Centre for Housing Management and Development, University of Wales, Cardiff.

Judith Harrison, Operations Manager (Project Support), Housing Corporation; and Visiting Lecturer, University of Westminster.

Keith Jacobs, Senior Lecturer in Housing, University of Westminster.

Keith Kintrea, Lecturer in Housing, Centre for Housing Research and Urban Studies, University of Glasgow.

Alan Murie, Professor of Urban and Regional Studies, University of Birmingham.

Ricardo Pinto, Research Officer, London School of Economics and Political Science (when the project started); and formerly Principal Research Officer, London Borough of Hackney.

Matthew Warburton, Under Secretary for Housing and Public Works, Association of Metropolitan Authorities.

Acknowledgements

Even with the best will in the world, editing an academic book is a gamble. Those new to the game have no idea of the length of time that is likely to be required, how much effort is involved or indeed, how rewarding it will turn out to be. I would like to thank the publishers for their tolerance and all the contributors for their trust that the project would come to fruition, especially those who were so patient or were forced to meet tight deadlines. The book may be delayed, but it would never have been published without your support.

Keith Jacobs, Keith Kintrea, Alan Murie, Hal Pawson and Matthew Warburton made valuable comments on various chapters for which I am indebted. Naturally, I accept full responsibility for any remaining deficiencies in the book. In addition, some of the statistics in chapter 1 were provided by Judith Harrison; and Brian Moore and David Sands from the DoE. Lastly Sarah Johnson proof-read the final version with characteristic efficiency.

Gisela Menke deserves the greatest vote of thanks for proof-reading my contributions; never ceasing to point out just how different the British housing system is, compared to those of our Continental neighbours; but most of all for her support during the progress of this project.

The Geography Department at the LSE generously allowed me to continue using their computer and library facilities, for which I am most grateful.

The opinions expressed in this collection of chapters are those of the authors alone and do not reflect the views of any local authority, governmental or quasi-governmental organisation.

Abbreviations

ADP	Annual Development Programme
AMA	Association of Metropolitan Authorities
BCA	Basic Credit Approval
BES	Business Expansion Scheme
CCT	Compulsory Competitive Tendering
CEI	Comprehensive Estates Initiative
CHAC	Central Housing Advisory Committee
DIYSO	Do It Yourself Shared Ownership
DLO	Direct Labour Office
DoE	Department of Environment
DSO	Direct Service Organisation
EA	Estate Action
EA HIP	Estate Action Housing Investment Programme
EMB	Estate Management Board
GLC	Greater London Council
HA	Housing Association
HAG	Housing Association Grant
HAT	Housing Action Trust
HDG	Hostel Deficit Grant
HIPs	Housing Investment Programmes
HMCCT	Housing Management Compulsory Competitive Tendering
HMP	Housing Market Package
HNI	Housing Needs Index
HOTCHA	Home Ownership for Tenants of Charitable Housing Associations
HRA	Housing Revenue Account
HSAG	Housing Services Advisory Group
IT	Information Technology
LAs	Local Authorities
LCC	London County Council
LSVTs	Large Scale Voluntary Transfers
NFHA	National Federation of Housing Associations
NFHC	National Federation of Housing Co-operatives
NHS	National Health Service
PEP	Priority Estates Project
PSBR	Public Sector Borrowing Requirement
RDG	Revenue Deficit Grant
RFC	Rate Fund Contribution
ROs	(Department of Environment) Regional Offices

RSI	Rough Sleepers' Initiative
RTM	Right to Manage
SCA	Supplementary Credit Approval
SRB	Single Regeneration Budget
TA	Tenants' Association
TC	Tenants' Choice
TEC	Training and Enterprise Council
TIS	Tenants' Incentive Scheme
TMCs	Tenant Management Co-operatives
TMOs	Tenant Management Organisations
UHRU	Urban Housing Renewal Unit (Estate Action's former name)

For Peter

Introduction:
setting the context

Ricardo Pinto

Introduction

The British housing system is undergoing a period of major turbulence and change. The predictable post-war swings of policy emphasis and financial support from owner occupation to council housing and vice versa, have been swept away by the developments which were introduced in the 1980s. Owner occupation as a tenure has experienced major and rapid growth and to a large degree, this has been at the expense of the council housing tenure. Indeed, further developments such as the growth of housing associations, tenant management organisations and trusts threaten the future existence of what was once one of the two pillars of the British housing system.

These developments amount to changes which have been so fast and far-reaching as to be difficult to fully imagine at the beginning of the 1980s. Furthermore, it can be argued that although these changes are at their most advanced form in the housing area, they merely represent the tip of the iceberg. Local government as a whole has experienced a volume of central government legislation which has revolutionised the way services as diverse as social services and education are delivered. Add to this other government policies such as the opting out provisions for NHS hospitals, and the developments in the early 1990s amount to a major restructuring of the welfare state.

It is generally acknowledged that the concept of provision of state-subsidised council housing has been eroded the most, such that it has increasingly been criticised by central government, academics, the media, the general public and even residents themselves. This collection of essays aims to chart the significant changes which have taken place in the management and ownership of social housing,

within the context of the wider changes going on in the British
housing system as a whole. Central government policies towards
council housing take pride of place in this analysis, together with the
fast-expanding housing associations and tenant management organisations. Council housing is at the heart of the system driving the
changes in ownership of housing. Equally important in this book, are
the management developments which are taking place in the social
housing system through a variety of decentralisation initiatives
where, for example, the Estate Action initiative and the role of
housing associations and co-operatives have figured prominently.
The themes of social housing management and ownership are inter-
twined and inter-dependent. This issue is explored further below,
prior to a summary of the main phases of government policy from
1979 to the present day.

Before doing so, however, it is important to note that this book
does not conform to the traditional organisation of housing policy
literature. The chapters do not cover all the housing tenures since the
emphasis is on the development of social housing and its management. Whilst the book deals with council housing in various chapters
(see chapters 4, 6 and 7); housing associations (chapter 2) and
housing co-operatives (chapter 3), it does not specifically deal with
other traditional aspects such as owner occupation, private renting or
the role of building societies. These have recently been covered
elsewhere (see Birchall, 1992; Malpass and Means, 1993). More
relevant is the exclusion of chapters specifically on the impact of
neighbourhood decentralisation and the Priority Estates Project.
Although commissioned for this book, it did not prove possible to
include these contributions. A number of chapters make reference to
the influence of decentralisation in local authorities (see chapters 6
and 7 in particular), and readers are referred to the detailed analyses
of the evolution and impact of neighbourhood decentralisation
(Seabrook, 1984; Hambleton and Hoggett, 1987; Mainwaring,
1988; Cole et al., 1991; and Cole, 1993); and the aims and
achievements of the Priority Estates Project (Power, 1984; 1987;
1988).

Rather, the remaining chapters deal with a number of issues
which are not normally to be found in recent housing literature,
such as the Estate Action initiative (chapter 4) which is acknowledged to have had a significant impact on housing management. A
key theme of recent housing policy has been the increasing number

of 'exit' opportunities such as the Right to Buy, Large Scale Voluntary Transfers, Tenants' Choice and Housing Action Trusts. Chapter 5 evaluates the impact of these policies within the context of extending choices and opportunities available to council tenants. The general impact on local housing authorities and their responses to the critique of housing management are explored in the subsequent chapter which concludes with a discussion of local housing authorities' response to the latest developments with respect to the Right to Manage and Compulsory Competitive Tendering in housing management (chapter 6). The specific impact on local authorities is analysed by means of a case study of the London Borough of Hackney where 60 per cent of the housing stock is either council housing or housing association in nature, and where the management problems are very significant indeed (chapter 7). Together, the contributions in this collection of essays present important analyses of the key trends which will shape the future role, provision, management and ownership of social housing in Britain.

Management and ownership

The key housing policy which has characterised four consecutive Conservative administrations is the determination to promote home ownership. To this can be added the related aim of reducing subsidies to, and the sale or transfer of council housing stock to other owners and landlords, especially into owner occupation. It is this simplistic combination of imperatives which has largely set in train a momentum to the British housing system which gathered pace in the 1980s, dominates the 1990s and is likely to continue through to the next century.

The ideological and political considerations were clearly of significance to the twin policies discussed above (see Forrest and Murie, 1988), however, concerns over economic management were also of primary importance (see Cooper, 1985; Malpass, 1990). With the deteriorating economic conditions and the tightening effects of monetary policy, the Thatcherite governments were particularly anxious to control what was one of the biggest public expenditure items, namely council housing. Housing subsidies, particularly capital expenditure, were greatly cut back as a result, leading to a situation where English and Welsh local authorities completed just

over 3,000 dwellings in 1992. Rent levels were affected as the
government sought to encourage local authorities to charge 'affordable' rents, thus neglecting some of the key strengths of the council
housing tenure such as the historic cost and rent pooling systems.
These developments were just the starting point.

The Right to Buy policy alone constitutes the Conservative governments' single most important and successful privatisation policy,
representing 43 per cent of all revenues raised from asset sales
(Murie, chapter 5). In practical terms, this resulted in the sale of
approximately 1.7 million council properties and, because of the
related policy of restricting provision of new council housing,
directly contributed to the residualisation and polarisation of the
council housing sector (Forrest and Murie, 1983; Willmott and
Murie, 1988; Malpass, 1990). The sale of these council properties
alone accounted for about half of the transfer in ownership to owner
occupation since 1979.

The success of the Right to Buy policy cannot be attributed to the
economic advantages of the discounts offered to sitting tenants and
mortgage tax relief alone. By the beginning of the 1980s there was
already evidence of growing tenant dissatisfaction with council
housing, which was most clearly expressed with respect to unpopular council housing estates (Andrews, 1979; Burbidge et al., 1981,
Vols 1 to 3; and CES, 1984). This criticism was not entirely due to
physical factors such as design; economic aspects such as the
increasing rents and lack of investment; or social issues such as
vandalism. Although there is little direct evidence that Right to Buy
purchasers were strongly influenced by management considerations,
the *housing management style* then evident was often deeply paternalistic
and unresponsive to tenant needs. The quality and organisation of
housing management was variable and the tenants were generally
peripheral to the management of their houses and homes.

The fact that the very people who lived in council housing were
critical of the way local housing authorities managed their stock was
important to the development of Conservative housing policies.
From the start, council housing managers were portrayed by Ministers as being insensitive, discriminatory, inefficient, remote and
bureaucratic. Despite the fact that a review of available evidence on
housing tenure preferences (Forrest and Murie, 1990) indicates a
situation where 'households with direct experience of both tenures
have positive views of both home ownership and council housing'

(p. 629) and that 'the picture is not one of [council tenants] desperately seeking to exit or to own' (p. 633), the constant political criticism of perceived local authority inefficiency came to symbolise all that was wrong with council housing and encourage tenants to become owner occupiers. Poor housing management became a key justification for the steady marginalisation of the council housing tenure and in due course, the development of both new management styles within council housing as well as alternative social housing providers in place of local authorities.

Criticism of various aspects of council housing management came from the Right, Left and everything in between (see Merrett, 1979; Coleman, 1985; Henney, 1985; Audit Commission, 1986a; 1986b; Power, 1987; Minford et al., 1987; Clapham, 1989; Saunders, 1990; NFHA, 1986; 1991). However, a key point to note is that the absolute and on-going political condemnation of council housing management practices by Ministers, and thus its use as the pretext for orchestrating the end of this tenure option, does not rest on a sound and consistent basis of fact. Whilst acknowledging the many weaknesses and failures and indeed the advantages of other management agents, council housing management could never be expected to overcome the wider social and economic trends to which it was susceptible but which were beyond its control.

Moreover, a major DoE-sponsored research project undertaken by the Centre For Housing Research (1989) demonstrated that effective housing management is not related in a clear and consistent manner to different types of management form, management expenditure or even the context within which the housing management function takes place. These important findings emphasised the point that the quality of housing management varies a great deal and that it is possible to find local authorities whose management practices compared favourably with the best run housing associations, as well as poor and bureaucratic council landlords. A key conclusion of this report was that contrary to the alarmist discussion at the time, there was no identifiable crisis in council housing management (1989, p. 104). This analysis has recently been extended from 1984/85 to the present time by Bines et al. (1993), who point to a situation where good management practices such as rent arrears recovery and management decentralisation have spread much further then noted by the Centre for Housing Research. Both these reports are analysed in greater detail elsewhere in this book.

Thus it is important to note firstly, that the political criticism of council housing management predated any comparative analysis of the performance of different management types and secondly, that the continuing criticism of council housing management has not been in any way moderated by the success of DoE-funded projects such as Priority Estates Project and Estate Action or by the findings of DoE-commissioned research work discussed above. In addition, virtually no mention is made by government of the major strides made by local authorities in the 1980s and early 1990s in decentralising their management structures, involving tenants and generally improving the quality of their management style. These are amongst the key themes analysed in several of the chapters in this book, but next we discuss the main discernible phases of government housing policy as a means of setting the context for the discussion to follow in this collection of papers.

Phases in housing policy

Management and ownership are thus key themes in recent housing policy and the connection is developed in the discussion below. The developments since 1979 can be characterised as falling into several phases which highlight these twin themes and the growing boldness of central government's housing policy.

The early phase up to the mid-1980s was dominated by efforts to control public spending (the Public Sector Borrowing Requirement or PSBR), the burden of which fell on cuts to council housing capital and revenue subsidies. Whilst this contributed to a steep rise in housing rents, the effect of revenue cuts on overall housing expenditure was moderated by the rise in Housing Benefits, resulting in the restructuring of the nature of such subsidies. It was in the area of capital allocations that the pressure was most severe (see chapter 1) and as a result, council house building came to a virtual halt and local authorities began to redirect their increasingly limited capital allocations to the refurbishment and maintenance of their existing housing stock. These policies had the effect of making council housing even less attractive and criticism of ineffective housing management more potent, relative to owner occupation and other forms of landlordism.

Criticism of housing management was a continuing feature

leading up to the next phase of housing policy. The Conservative government came to acknowledge reluctantly that encouraging owner occupation at the expense of council housing in itself did not constitute a housing policy, let alone result in a balanced housing system. Attention began to turn to two issues. Firstly, the need to revive the private rented sector due to the growing demand for this form of housing (see Whitehead and Kleinman, 1986; Crook, 1992). This arose from a range of trends such as the increasing incidence of family separation and divorce, need for mobility for labour market reasons, different life-stages requiring alternative forms of housing, rising local authority rents, mortgage arrears, house repossessions and such like. Secondly, the government started to go beyond reprimanding local authorities for being inefficient and ineffective landlords and started funding two initiatives which were significant to the process of extending decentralised management practices within the council housing sector. Local authorities were already making efforts to improve their management performance (see chapters 6 and 7), however, the Priority Estates Project and the Estate Action initiative were influential in helping local authorities to extend their experiments with decentralised management styles. Both emphasised the need for tenant involvement in the management process as well as different models of management such as housing associations, housing co-operatives and concierges. Estate Action also began to tout new forms of housing solution such as the disposal of the stock to housing associations, tenant management organisations, private developers and trusts (see chapter 4).

This intermediate stage can be seen as one in which the Thatcherite government began to experiment with several of the themes which were to dominate the next phase, not least a range of options allowing the transfer of council housing stock to other sectors. Had the government been so convinced of the intrinsic inability of council landlords to provide a satisfactory management service, it would have enabled tenants to decide for themselves whether they would choose to transfer from, as well as to, council housing, but this was not an option. Housing management and ownership remained intertwined. Council housing continued to be criticised by Ministers as an ineffective form of social housing provision, even as policies were developed to further residualise and emasculate it. By contrast, owner occupation continued to be acclaimed as the tenure of choice and individual freedom even though mortgage tax relief subsidies together with house-price inflation were sufficient incentives to encourage the rapid growth of this housing option.

In the run up to the third phase, the government began to acknowledge more explicitly that not everyone could afford, or even wish, to become a home owner. This led in 1987 to the official concession that there would continue to be a need for an element of social housing in the future. However, despite growing evidence of much improved council housing management practices and general tenant satisfaction with the housing service (see various chapters), the government continued to judge that this tenure remained beyond reform. The future provision of social housing was to be handed over to the relatively small housing association (reflected in the increase in housing association investment 1988-92) and co-operative movements. Local authorities would be divested of their management responsibility via the introduction of a variety of options for tenants to exercise their newly acquired rights to transfer out of council housing. This daring political move had to be presented in such a way as to be acceptable, not least to council tenants. Criticism of council housing management was utilised once again:

In order to legitimise this strategy, it was essential for the government to gloss over those aspects of council housing dependent, at least in part, on central government action, such as the overall level of investment, the use of receipts from council house sales, or the comparative balance of housing tenure subsidies. Instead, attention turned to the failure of local authorities to carry out their responsibilities as landlords – especially in their management and maintenance functions. The failure of council housing, in short, was down to the inadequacies of local authorities.

(Cole and Furbey, 1993, p. 213)

This highlights once more the inter-dependent relationship between management type and ownership form as well as the general direction of the relationship between central and local government. The 1987 Housing Policy Review was superseded by two significant pieces of legislation which set in play by far the most radical developments to the housing system: the 1988 Housing Act and the 1989 Housing and Local Government Act. The reduction in overall housing funds and the evolution of the Housing Investment Programme system (see chapter 1) together with the above two Acts not only ensured the end of the role of councils as providers of new social housing but also sought to bring about the end of their landlord role. The thrust of the legislation made clear the government's view that in future, local authorities were to be restricted to a co-ordinating or enabling role. The enabling function remains poorly articulated several years on. Some commentators see some substance to the new role (see Bramley, 1993), though others maintain that what is actually happening is the disabling of council housing (see Malpass, 1992).

In addition, the government also signalled its intention to go beyond the partial efforts to arrest the long-term decline of the private rented sector. This was to be achieved principally through deregulation and altering tenants' security. All new private lettings became either 'assured tenancies' or 'assured shorthold tenancies' and landlords' grounds for repossession were strengthened. The Business Expansion Scheme (BES) was also extended until the end of 1993 as a means of kick-starting investment in the private sector.

The commitment to home ownership was underlined through the intention of setting up further initiatives to privatise council housing via the 'Rents to Mortgages' scheme and in the case of housing associations, via support for 'Shared Ownership' housing. However, it was in the other policies that the government's housing vision was most clearly revealed and the continuing emphasis on the relationship between management and ownership highlighted.

As discussed earlier, the role of housing associations would be extended, not least because they were perceived to be better landlords as well as being independent of local political influence. Related to this, albeit with little financial or other backing other than 'section 16' grants under the 1986 Housing and Building Control Act, the government recognised and encouraged the role played by housing co-operatives or tenant management organisations in generating greater tenant involvement in the management and control of housing.

The official handing over of the baton of social housing provision to other landlords alone would have been sufficient to bring about a gradual end to the local authority landlord function, but the government sought to go beyond this and to do so at a greatly accelerated pace. Using the familiar argument of the unreformable nature of council housing management, policies were introduced which provided tenants with a range of options to 'exit' or transfer from council housing to other options involving different landlord or ownership forms. The remaining 4 million council properties were clearly not going to be transferred sufficiently quickly via the Right to Buy or the Rents to Mortgages initiatives. Stronger measures were required if the government's aims were to be achieved. The council housing sector had already proven itself highly vulnerable to the volume of initiatives which had been placed on the statute book since 1980, so the government must have felt fairly certain that there would not be too much criticism, not least from the clients of the council housing service.

The government took it upon itself to designate Housing Action Trusts for council estates which were deemed to be so poorly run or maintained by local authorities, as to require central government intervention. The argument used was that local authorities could not be trusted to administer the large amounts of investment which the government now admits were necessary for the 'Hatted' estates. The Trusts would seek a variety of means to privatise or diversify the tenure in such estates and then hand them over to other landlords. More significantly, having introduced the options for local authorities to voluntarily transfer their entire housing stock to alternative landlords via the 1986 Housing and Planning Act, the 1988 Housing Act took this policy to its natural conclusion. Council tenants were given the option of themselves deciding whether they wished to remain within the council housing system or to transfer to some other form of management or ownership via the Tenants' Choice proposals.

Clearly this set of transfer options offered a good deal of scope for further reduction of the remaining council properties and the transformation of the sector. These developments and the need to critically evaluate their impact sets the context for much of the discussion to follow. Before doing so, the most recent developments need to be highlighted as a number of the housing certainties which characterised the Thatcherite governments have been eroded since the point when John Major took over leadership of the Conservative party.

The Conservatives' faith in home ownership began to falter after a decade of continuous support. The deliberate ratcheting up of interest rates (to 15 per cent in early 1990) in order to deal with the rising level of inflation, had the side-effect of generating intense financial pressures for owner occupiers, especially those who had purchased their housing at the peak of the house price boom in 1988 and/or those who had taken up mortgage offers which were just about affordable. Mortgage arrears and repossessions reached record levels, resulting in even further increases in homelessness. Furthermore, the house-price inflation bubble burst under the joint effect of high interest rates, increasing numbers of empty properties and a recession that stubbornly refused to sprout the then Chancellor's long-awaited 'green shoots' of recovery.

House prices plummeted and phrases such as 'mortgage rescue schemes' and 'negative equity' entered the common language and with their arrival ended the popular myth that investment in bricks and mortar would always show a financial return. Consumer confidence is slowly returning to the private property market but Ministerial claims of the inherent advantages of home ownership remain subdued. In addition, the gradual reduction in interest rates to a point where mortgage offers are highly competitive has prompted the Major government to bow to academic debate and more significantly, general criticism of the public deficit has reduced the fiscal subsidies to home ownership by making two consecutive 5 per cent cuts in mortgage tax relief.

The social and economic policies developed in the time since the demise of Margaret Thatcher have undergone a change in tone and emphasis which is even evident in the housing scene. Apart from breaching twice the hitherto sacred principle of the need to maintain mortgage tax relief, extra resources have been found for homeless initiatives (already underway following the 1989 Homelessness Review) and a capital receipts 'holiday' enabling local authorities to invest 100 per cent (as opposed to the normal 25 per cent) of their capital receipts from dwelling sales for the whole of 1993. Notwithstanding these developments, increasing home ownership remains a key theme. Significantly, the policies which drive the process of demunicipalisation of council housing have actually been added to and intensified in important ways.

These have been achieved firstly, through the new financial regime introduced by the 1989 Local Government and Housing Act which has intensified the already fragile central–local government relations with respect to social housing. Although Bines et al. (1993, para. 13.27) point to evidence that the introduction of ring fencing for the Housing Revenue Account was welcomed by housing officers, the Act has also contributed to even greater rent level increases in the council housing tenure and even fewer capital receipts with which to maintain or improve council housing (see

Malpass and Warburton, 1993). Such developments further under-mine the capacity of local authorities to maintain and manage, let alone provide an enabling housing function. They do, however, have the political attraction of further stimulating tenant dissatisfaction with their existing management arrangements and perhaps seek the attentions of other landlord/ownership forms. We shall discuss in more detail these important developments in the next chapter, and subsequent contributions will highlight the point that the negative financial effects of this Act extend to housing associations.

Secondly, yet another means is being implemented by central government to ensure the erosion of the council housing sector as one of the main pillars of the British housing scene, this time by the privatisation of council housing management itself. In the govern-ment's view encouraging local authorities to seek tenders for hous-ing management contracts will lead to improved standards of management and lower costs in the long run. This belief assumes that there will be an adequate supply of private management companies. There are professional concerns about issues such as standards, accountability and costs, but housing management Com-pulsory Competitive Tendering and the Right to Manage policy represent the pinnacle of a range of measures which are quite capable of bringing about an end to council housing provision and management.

Conclusion

The 1980s was a decade when the housing debate was very much about housing management and ownership. The growth in home ownership, the criticism of council housing management, the rebirth of the housing association movement, the increasing rights awarded to tenants and the steady demise of council housing are all compo-nents which were set in play during the 1980s. These changes in emphases were re-calibrated in 1987 and have gathered pace in the 1990s. With the election of a fourth Conservative administration in 1992, we can expect a degree of continuity to the main components of housing policy, certainly in the field of social housing. There is little doubt that the momentum of those developments will continue to affect the structure of the British housing system until the beginning of the next century. The above synopsis of recent developments sets the context for the essays to follow and the first chapter develops this framework from a legislative and policy perspective.

References

Andrews, C. L. (1979) *Tenant and Town Hall*, London, HMSO.

Audit Commission (1986a) *Managing the Crisis of Council Housing*, London, HMSO.

Audit Commission (1986b) *The Management of London's Authorities: Preventing the Breakdown of Services*, London, HMSO.

Bines, W., Kemp, P., Pleace, N. and Radley, C. (1993) *Managing Social Housing: A Study of Landlord Performance*, London, HMSO.

Birchall, J. (ed.) (1992) *Housing Policy in the 1990s*, London, Routledge.

Bramley, G. (1993) 'The Enabling Role for Local Housing Authorities: A Preliminary Evaluation' in Malpass, P. and Means, R. (1993).

Burbidge, M., Curtis, A., Kirby, K., and Wilson, S. (1981) *An Investigation of Difficult to Let Housing: Vol. 1 General Findings; Vol. 2 Case Studies of Post-War Estates; Vol. 3 Case Studies of Pre-War Estates*, London, HMSO.

CES (Centre for Environmental Studies) (1984) *Outer Estates in Britain: Interim Report – Comparison of 4 Outer Estates*, Paper 23, London, CES.

Centre for Housing Research (1989) *The Nature and Effectiveness of Housing Management in England: A Report to the Department of the Environment*, London, HMSO.

Clapham, D. (1989) *Goodbye Council Housing*, The Fabian Series, London, Hutchinson.

Cole, I. (1993) 'The Decentralization of Housing Services' in Malpass, P. and Means, R. (1993).

Cole, I. and Furbey, R. (1993) *The Eclipse of Council Housing: Housing and the Welfare State*, London, Routledge.

Cole, I., Windle, K. and Arnold, P. (1991) 'Decentralized Housing Services – Back to the Future' in Donnison, D. and Maclennan, D. (eds) *The Housing Service of the Future*, Harlow, Longman.

Coleman, A. (1985) *Utopia on Trial: Vision and Reality in Planned Housing*, London, Hilary Shipman.

Cooper, S. (1985) *Public Housing and Private Property*, London, Gower.

Crook, A. D. H. (1992) 'Private Rented Housing and the Impact of Deregulation' in Birchall, J. (1992).

Forrest, R. and Murie, A. (1983) 'Residualisation and Council Housing: Aspects of Changing Social Relations of Housing and Tenure', *Journal of Social Policy*, Vol. 12, pp. 453-468.

Forrest, R. and Murie, A. (1988) *Selling the Welfare State: The Privatisation of Public Housing*, London, Routledge.

Forrest, R. and Murie, A. (1990) 'A Dissatisfied State? Consumer Preferences and Council Housing in Britain', *Urban Studies*, Vol. 27, No. 5, pp. 617-635.

Hambleton, R. and Hoggett, P. (1987) *The Politics of Decentralisation: Theory and Practice of a Radical Local Government Initiative*, Working Paper 46, Bristol University, SAUS.

Henney, A. (1985) *Trusts the Tenant: Devolving Municipal Housing*, No. 68, London, Centre for Policy Studies.

Mainwaring, R. (1988) *The Walsall Experience: A Study of the Decentralisation of Walsall's Housing Experience*, London, HMSO.

Malpass, P. (1990) *Reshaping Housing Policy: Subsidies, Rents and Residualisation*, London, Routledge.

Malpass, P. (1992) 'Housing Policy and the Disabling of Local Authorities' in Birchall, J. (1992).

Malpass, P. and Means, R. (eds) (1993) Implementing Housing Policy, Buckingham, Open University Press.

Malpass, P. and Warburton, M. (1993) 'The New Financial Regime for Local Housing Authorities' in Malpass, P. and Means, R. (1993).

Merrett, S. (1979) State Housing in Britain, London, Routledge & Kegan Paul.

Minford, P., Peel, M. and Ashton, P. (1987) The Housing Morass: Regulation, Immobility and Unemployment, Hobart Paperback 25, London, Institute of Economic Affairs.

National Federation of Housing Associations (1986) Inquiry into British Housing, Chaired by HRH The Duke of Edinburgh, London, NFHA.

National Federation of Housing Associations (1991) Inquiry into British Housing: Second Report, York, Chaired by HRH The Duke of Edinburgh, Joseph Rowntree Foundation.

Power, A. (1984) Local Housing Management: A Priority Estates Project Survey, London, HMSO.

Power, A. (1987) Property Before People: The Management of Twentieth Century Council Housing, London, Allen & Unwin.

Power, A. (1988) Council Housing: Conflict, Change and Decision Making, Welfare State Discussion Paper No. 27, STICERD, London, LSE.

Saunders, P. (1990) A Nation of Home Owners, London, Unwin Hyman.

Seabrook, J. (1984) The Idea of Neighbourhood: What Local Politics Should Be About, London, Pluto Press.

Whitehead, C. M. E. and Kleinman, M. P. (1986) Private Rented Housing in the 1980s and 1990s, Department of Land Economy No. 17, Cambridge, Granta Editions / University of Cambridge.

Willmott, P. and Murie, A. (1988) Polarisation and Social Housing: The British and French Experience, London, Policy Studies Institute.

1

Housing developments in the 1980s and 1990s

Ricardo Pinto

Introduction

The British housing system is in a state of flux. As the introduction to the book indicated, the 1980s witnessed a number of changes to the management and the ownership of the housing stock, the majority of which emanate from, or relate to, a particular tenure: council housing. As a consequence of the salience of this sector of social housing, much of the discussion to follow traces the reasons behind the developments which have affected it to the point where the complete demunicipalisation of local authority housing is a possibility.

The 1977 Housing Policy Review (DoE, 1977) which was commissioned by a Labour government took the view that the major housing problems in Britain had been overcome and that owner occupation was the natural and normal tenure, thus bringing to an end the ambivalent struggle for supremacy that had been waged for decades between owner occupation and council housing (see Merrett, 1979). This coincided with a prolonged period of recession and a succession of Conservative governments which accepted and systematically extended the logic of the review's conclusions. The result has been a profound redefinition of the role of council housing which has reverberated throughout the housing system, and resulted in certain 'themes' to housing policy in Britain:

- criticism of local authorities' inability to manage effectively;
- growth of owner occupation, largely at the expense of council housing;
- expansion of housing associations and TMOs, the future social landlords;
- demise of council housing due to a range of 'exit' routes such as voluntary transfers;

- growth of various decentralised, tenant-led management initiatives;
- privatisation of council housing management, though this is by no means certain yet.

This profound re-orientation in housing policy did not happen over night, nor was there a predetermined Conservative housing 'master plan'. Recent housing literature has highlighted the point that housing policy does not necessarily develop in a simple linear fashion and that the process of implementing policies designed in the Department of Environment (DoE) may result in outcomes which were not necessarily anticipated (see Malpass and Means, 1993). The primary purpose of this chapter is to set the context for the discussion which follows in subsequent chapters. It seeks to unravel how the above 'themes' came to be firmly set in place during the 1980s, how they have been reinforced over time and why they are likely to continue to dominate housing developments in the 1990s and beyond.

Rejecting council housing: economic imperatives

Between the early 1900s and the late 1970s, the council housing sector in Britain steadily grew reaching 32 per cent of the total housing stock. This expansion was largely due to a broad post-World War II consensus regarding the necessity of a welfare state in general, and the value of council housing in particular. However, council housing, the provision of subsidised accommodation by local authorities, underwent a rapid transition in the 1980s. Once regarded as a major social achievement providing decent homes for people, it quickly came to acquire a completely different aura. As elaborated on below, this was partly of its own making but it was sharply accentuated by a set of government-led policies in the early 1980s which can be characterised as emphasising the following:

- the desirability and superiority of owner occupation;
- steep reductions in local housing authorities' capital resources;
- enforced rent increases due to a new council subsidy system; and
- criticisms of local authorities as housing developers and managers.

It is important to emphasise that, notwithstanding the commitment of the Conservatives to owner occupation, the driving force behind the reforms which took place in council housing (as well as other spheres of local government) stemmed from an economic view that the level of public sector expenditure was one of Britain's key problems (HM Treasury, 1979). With worsening economic conditions and the steady impact of monetary controls, public housing expenditure came under close scrutiny and eventually became a prime target for cuts. This started with the Labour government in 1975/76 but accelerated after 1979 with the election of the first Conservative administration. The Thatcher governments were particularly keen to reduce housing expenditure, one of the biggest local government expenditure items, in order to bring inflation under control and meet their political commitment to 'roll back the frontiers of the state', leading to a free market society and economy:

The monetarist approach was therefore to rely on the private sector for economic growth through the control of the monetary supply, interest rates and the Public Sector Borrowing Requirement. Government expenditure plans reflected this philosophy and substantial reductions were made in the planned expenditure on housing in the belief that private investment would make good the losses and allow housing requirements to be met.

(Cooper, 1985, p. 11)

At the same time the main political parties had come to accept owner occupation as the 'natural' form of tenure, which matched the Conservatives' policies towards privatisation and the creation of a 'property owning democracy'. The stage was set for a re-assessment of the role of council housing at a time when its desirability, crystallised most clearly in its style of management, was seriously questioned. In such a context it was inevitable that council housing would experience an unprecedented period of turbulence. We have alluded above to the Conservative governments' desire to increase owner occupation as well as the overriding commitment to reduce public housing expenditure. The main rationale used by the Conservative government for the rejection of council housing, apart from the Housing Policy Review's conclusion that housing shortages were a thing of the past (DoE, 1977), was the consistent argument by Ministers that council housing was large scale, bureaucratic, insensitive – in short, that it was badly managed.

There is little doubt that the traditional style of council housing management has had its problems. The economic policies of the government combined with criticism of the traditional housing management style provided the justification for the variety of developments which were to profoundly affect the housing scene. The perceived failings of councils as landlords, especially in relation to management and maintenance, provided a powerful driving force for the various developments that took place in the 1980s.

Housing management: a much maligned issue

When discussing the failures of council housing in providing an effective form of management which was in tune with tenants' wishes, it is important to recognise the fact that economic, social and ideological trends helped shape the way successive governments influenced the way local authorities provided, managed and maintained their housing stock. Housing management can only ever be a component contributing to the success or failure of any type of landlord; nevertheless, the discussion below notes that there were a number of factors which local authorities were able to influence but did not cope well with. In order to grasp the reasons behind these developments it is helpful to adopt an historical perspective which considers the evolution of local authority housing departments; the development of a backlog in repairs and maintenance of council stock; the main problems besetting council housing management; and a set of other influences which have meant that local authority housing managers were never fully in control of the developments which took place. Each of these is covered below.

Organisation and evolution of housing departments

It was argued in the early 1980s that unlike other local services such as education and social services, council housing was in the unique position of having a very limited political and legal framework governing the way local authorities carried out their duties as landlords (Macey, 1982). The various Housing Acts place responsibilities upon local housing authorities, but the lack of a basic frame of operation such as requiring them to convene a committee to run its housing stock, appoint housing managers and carry out inspections to ensure that procedures are adequate and adhered to, contributed to making it difficult for local authorities to operate as good landlords.

This argument was extended by Power's analysis of the origins of the housing service and the evolution of the post-war housing departments, on which the remainder of this section is based (1987a, chapter 4). This work contends that the housing management function was neglected because local housing authorities were principally concerned with housing construction and finance, rather than maintenance or running the housing stock and that this is supported by an analysis of the origin and evolution of council housing departments.

The argument is that even in the early post-war period, a number of reports by the Central Housing Advisory Committee (CHAC, 1945; 1953; 1955) were already pointing out that the housing function was fragmented and divided between various professional departments. Moreover, the reports indicated that the emphasis was on slum clearance and rehousing, rather than the management function which was generally remote and badly organised.

Power shows that the mid-1950s led to even greater council housing activity due to the policies of mass slum clearance and new construction. In the process, waiting lists rose substantially with the effect that the allocation function steadily took precedence over local management issues such as rent collection and the landlord–tenant interface became more limited. These trends were to lead to the management problems which we are now familiar with, such as rent arrears, inadequate repairs and cleaning; however, it was the developments in the 1960s which were really to intensify the problems faced by the housing management role, a point made by Cullingworth (1966). Power points to three major developments: the swing away from 'green field' sites to inner city slum clearance and replacement; the fact that those who were rehoused began to come from the poorer sections of the working class; and that they were rehoused in new, high-rise and high-density blocks of flats (see also Dunleavy, 1981).

By this point many of the problems which helped to generate a difficult management situation were already in place even though, ironically, a distinct housing management department was beginning to emerge which was increasingly unifying the management functions under one structure. Power notes the further irony that the local government reorganisation of 1974 was the final development which rendered the emergent housing departments almost unworkable. The housing departments expanded by an average of ten-fold in

terms of size of housing stock, thus increasing remoteness from
tenants and resulting in cumbersome procedures and unwieldy
management structures (1987a).
The HSAG report recommending a 'Comprehensive Housing
Service' (1978) came far too late in the day. It merely confirmed the
point that it was only in the late 1970s and early 1980s that serious
thought began to be given by the housing policy community to the
housing management role and organisational style. This analysis was
persuasive in highlighting the haphazard evolution of council housing management structures and a number of the reasons which
resulted in the plethora of housing management problems which are
highlighted subsequently in this section.

The changing nature and condition of the stock

A further factor played a significant part in the blanket Ministerial
condemnation of council housing which has been evident since the
1980s. Councils were often preoccupied with meeting housing need
by producing sufficient housing units and/or had political commitments to ensure that rents remained low. This meant that they often
underestimated the importance of other considerations such as
maintenance of the stock:

> The maintenance of council houses affects not only the quality of life for the
> families living in them, but also the value of the public assets involved. Yet,
> there has been a history of neglect of maintenance of many of the 4.8
> million council houses in England and Wales.
>
> (Audit Commission, 1986a, p. 1)

Although this criticism was forceful coming from the local government watch-dog, it actually dated back to the late 1970s. The
National Consumer Council noted that the disrepair problem had
been exacerbated because local authorities have traditionally had a
repair rather than a *maintenance* policy and inefficiency in local authority operations had resulted in deterioration of the stock (1979). The
consequence was that some local authorities were struggling with
the basic problem of trying to keep their stock in a wind and
water-tight condition (not least in the system-built and high-rise
stock), let alone ensuring that it met the needs and aspirations of
tenants.
     Local authorities are only too aware that repairs remain the
biggest single source of tenant complaints and dissatisfaction. Since

the mid-1980s councils have been strongly encouraged by both the DoE and the Audit Commission to invest more in programmed maintenance but although this is reflected in the patterns of capital expenditure, it remains difficult to finance this from rents and housing authorities have not always had the central or local political backing to invest what was required to maintain the stock properly. Whilst acknowledging local authority policy failure in this area, factors largely beyond their control have helped accelerate the process of decay and decline. For example, one of the by-products of the Right to Buy legislation is that predominantly the best properties, usually houses with gardens in good locations, have been sold with the consequence that the council housing sector is increasingly left with the less popular properties. This is what has led to the argument that this sector is becoming increasingly residualised and polarised (see Forrest and Murie, 1983; Willmott and Murie, 1988). These difficulties are exacerbated firstly, by the fact that the construction defects of a good deal of the system-built local authority properties of the 1960s and 1970s continue to come to the fore, and secondly, by the ageing of some of the stock, particularly what was built between the wars and is in urgent need of renovation.

This situation has perversely coincided with an unprecedented squeeze by central government on investment in public housing (addressed in more detail below). The reduction in capital spending has meant that repair and modernisation programmes had to be cut back precisely when awareness of the problem peaked. There has also been pressure on Housing Revenue Accounts as a result of the reduction in central government subsidy and the politicisation of the Rate Fund Contributions. This has helped force up rents dramatically which has corresponded with rising levels of arrears, thus preventing the necessary repairs from being carried out by many councils. The combined effects of the council house sales policy, the legacy of an ageing and often structurally unsound stock and central government restrictions on capital expenditure, are helping to exacerbate the housing management problems. The AMA's studies (1983; 1984; 1985) of defects in council housing concluded that the capital cost of reversing the drastic slide in the maintenance of property would total £19 billion:

- £5bn on special repairs to 500,000 non-traditional houses built 1945-55;

- £5bn on 1 million system-built dwellings including tower blocks built in the 1960s and 1970s;
- £8bn on 450,000 pre-war traditionally built units, now at the end of their 60 year life; and
- £1bn on urgent repairs of post-war traditionally built council houses.

The National Federation of Housing Association's influential 'Inquiry into British Housing' also concluded that it was necessary to deal with the urgent maintenance problems and recommended the immediate release by central government of council house sale funds for local authority capital expenditure in order to make resources 'available at once' to deal with the most urgent repairs and alterations needed (NFHA, 1985). 'Faith in the City' commissioned by the Archbishop of Canterbury concluded: 'We can see no alternative to, and recommend an expanded housing programme of new building and improvement financed by public expenditure' (1985).

These reports consistently argued that a proportion of council housing had been allowed to fall into a disgraceful condition, that this was not entirely due to local authority negligence and advocated rapid change in order to arrest the downward spiral. There was not much reaction from central government, other than encouraging local authorities to redirect their resources to refurbishment and using the findings to stress the ineffectiveness of council landlords but this evidence did act as a stimulus for innovation and change in housing management practices so as to stabilize and even improve the situation by generating greater efficiency.

The management problems confronting council housing

The previous discussion summarised some of the reasons why local housing departments came to be regarded as bureaucratic and inefficient landlords trying to come to terms with a large and growing backlog of housing disrepair. This section analyses the main reasons for the criticism of council housing management by referring to one of the most comprehensive studies of those problems (Housing Research Group, 1981). It identified the housing management problems as being the following:

- General concerns: variations in the cost of management and maintenance; levels of rent arrears; anti-social behaviour; problem estates; and social and tenure polarisation.

• *Difficulties in getting basic work done:* the cost of keeping down rent arrears; delays and difficulties of re-letting empty council properties; over-stretched and unreliable repairs service; difficulties maintaining communal areas; increasingly bureaucratic housing management; and the increasing but uncertain social role of local housing management.

• *Contradictions within the housing management role:* large scale housing management versus the ability to respond to individual circumstances; allocation to those in need versus minimising management problems; easier to manage versus cheaper to build; higher expectations but assumed ineffectiveness; and organisational simplicity versus integration.

• *Operational problems in housing management:* uncertainty for staff and tenants alike about what to achieve and expect; lack of definition about certain types of housing work; difficulties in supervision; ineffective use of staff; difficulties for staff and tenants in contacting each other; overloading of many housing staff; inappropriate use of staff; lack of routine checking of work done; lack of regular feed-up of information from local to head office; and lack of co-ordination between housing and other departments and agencies.

• *Weaknesses underlying the practical difficulties faced by authorities and tenants:* ambiguities in the definition of the obligations of councils and tenants and how they should 'normally' operate; lack of standards for monitoring activities and services; confusion over the responsibility for 'unavoidable' social problems; and the lack of control over the quality of services provided by other departments (HRG, 1981, pp. 148-155; and chapter 8).

The culmination of all these factors was first officially identified in the most unpopular estates in terms of poor design, discriminatory allocation procedures, incompetent management, serious lack of demand, high turnover of tenants and general neglect of the worst estates (Burbidge et al., 1981, Vols 1-3). This set of DoE reports concluded that the structure of housing departments was inflexible, remote from tenants and too fragmented to cope with the pressures of a then rapidly expanding stock. It confirmed the existence of major housing problems and the seriousness of the state of council housing in a number of urban authorities. It also pointed out that these difficulties also afflicted estates in smaller and relatively trouble-free local authorities, which suggested that additional factors were affecting the popularity and the manageability of certain estates (see also CES, 1984) such as poverty, isolation and stigma. The result is that there existed almost everywhere in Britain some form of unpopular and neglected council housing which ends up being 'hard-to-let', 'dump' or 'low demand' estates. As highlighted above, management is only one component of a wider set of problems but the constant political criticism of council housing management as a whole means that there was, throughout the 1980s, a sense of mounting concern which was intensified by the loss of confidence which resulted from such developments as the Right to Buy legislation, the cuts in council housing subsidy and the encouragement of alternative housing agents. All these issues can be regarded as stimuli which were to create an atmosphere conducive to change. An increasing number of councils began to experiment with a variety of methods in order to improve their management practices so as to deliver a better service to their tenants. Many councils have responded to the changed housing context and have restructured their traditional management style, organisation and administration (see chapter 6). There has been much debate on the merits of decentralisation along neighbourhood office lines as pioneered in Walsall and Islington (Seabrook, 1984; Hambleton and Hoggett, 1987; Cole, 1993); housing co-operatives as in Islington and Glasgow (see Clapham et al., 1987; Clapham, 1989; and Birchall, 1988); housing trusts as in Liverpool and Greenwich; and housing associations, among other alternative management arrangements.

Political influence and weak professionalism

The previous discussion highlighted some of the reasons for the erosion of support for council housing as a means of delivering management services to an increasingly demanding tenant. The fact that housing officers were not fully in charge of the management process was an additional reason why council housing failed to command the level of public support normally accorded to other components of the welfare state such as education and health (see Cole and Furbey, 1993). Part of the reason for this, of course, is that although the latter two services are near universal, council housing never accommodated more than about a third of the population. Although local authorities employed specialist housing managers, local politicians have always been more apt to influence the way the service was delivered, such as the allocation and rent policies, than in the other service areas. This was partly because of the relative absence of central government regulations, but more significantly because it constitutes a service that everyone can relate to. Compounded by the fragmented nature of the service, this meant that housing managers have rarely been in control of the service to the same extent as other local government professionals.

Turning to the salience of the issue of professionalism, housing managers proved unable to command the level of influence and prestige normally evident in other welfare state agents or other local government functions such as architects and finance (see Houlihan, 1988; Laffin, 1985). It is only in recent years that evidence has emerged of the professionalisation of this service under the influence of the Institute of Housing, but even this has occurred within the context of continuing government critique of their landlord practices, the fact that not all local authorities actually have a central housing department and that the staff are poorly qualified and trained (Audit Commission, 1986b; Bines et al., 1993).

Given this background, it was not entirely surprising that the council housing management function failed to command user support by virtue of being careful and considerate landlords. The combined influence of central government economic and social policies; interference by local councillors; fragmentation of management functions; and lack of professional direction and control meant that a number of councils did not develop appropriate management practices. These developments were to lead the government directly to the conclusion that council housing was an unsuitable option for rented accommodation provision and management. As discussed earlier, this must be seen within the government's wider ideological and economic imperatives.

The housing policy community in the 1980s came to be dominated by questions which challenged many of the basic assumptions underlying the last 70 years, including the very necessity for council housing. The following sections analyse the factors which have brought to a head the revolution in the housing system in the last decade starting with an analysis of the economic imperatives and concluding with the key policies.

Housing finance: capital, revenue and reform

The previous section discussed how the management problems arose in the council housing tenure and the way they manifest themselves. This section seeks to illustrate the salience of some of the financial elements which have contributed to the current developments in management and ownership of the housing system. Whilst the rest of this chapter analyses the ways in which central government has influenced council housing since 1980, it is important to bear in mind that these developments represent the extension of trends established under the previous Labour government or even before that (see Malpass, 1990). The difference is that since the mid 1980s the emphasis has became consistently more extreme. Readers are referred to Hills (1991), and Malpass et al. (1993) for more detailed accounts of the financial mechanisms implemented by recent governments and their progressive impact on social housing.

The Housing Revenue Account (HRA)

Given the Thatcherite commitment to reduce the burden of public expenditure, it was inevitable that major changes would occur to the council housing finance system. A subsidy system was introduced in Part VI of the Housing Act, 1980, based on the principle of deficit financing. This meant that the amount of subsidy received by local authorities depended upon an evaluation of their annual expenditure on servicing debt and management and maintenance (reckonable expenditure); and the amount which local authorities were expected to raise from rent and rate fund contributions (reckonable income) towards meeting the costs. Local authorities had to balance their books with regard to housing expenditure and any shortfalls were to be borne by income from increased rents and/or rates. Combined with the fact that the Secretary of State was given much greater discretionary powers to determine subsidy levels, this was used to systematically reduce the general exchequer subsidies, thus undermining the main mechanism behind the creation of council housing (Hughes, 1987, pp. 14-15).

By reducing the level of subsidies the financial system resulted in dramatically increased rent levels throughout the council housing sector. It has been argued that the government's objective was to undermine the historic cost financing system by using the new subsidy system to push up rents to a level nearer to current market

Table 1.1 Housing subsidy and rent rebates in England (1993/94 prices)

Year	Local authority rent rebates (£m)	HRA subsidy rebate element (£m)	Housing HRA Subsidy (£m)
1979/80	1,371		3,149
1980/81	1,559		2,970
1981/82	2,216		1,725
1982/83	2,902		952
1983/84	2,818		476
1984/85	2,892		553
1985/86	2,915		627
1986/87	2,940		791
1987/88	2,856		666
1988/89	2,850		618
1989/90	2,894		718
1990/91	2,855	2,626	1,546
1991/92	3,074	2,772	1,235
1992/93	3,565	3,054	1,036
1993/94	3,970	3,248	877
1994/95	4,135	3,271	800

Source: Statistics supplied by DoE.

value and that this was borne out by the fact that what was taking place was not a reduction in subsidy but a restructuring of the nature of subsidies (see Loughlin, 1986). Thus although housing subsidies fell fairly consistently between 1980 and 1990 and has since resumed its downward path, Table 1.1 demonstrates that this was offset by the growth of income-related rent assistance claimed by council tenants. It is worth noting, however, that because of the rapid increase in rents, the level of council tenant rent arrears increased markedly (Audit Commission, 1984). Combined with the availability of generous discounts, this created a powerful incentive for the better-off council tenants to exercise their Right to Buy, thus reinforcing the transformation of the public rented sector into a residual or targeted welfare sector (see Malpass, 1990).

The capital account

Although they had to obtain approval for each individual scheme, until the late 1970s local authorities were largely free to set the size of their own capital programmes on housing expenditure, while central government exercised indirect influence via the operation of the subsidy system. However, increasing pressure on public expenditure, high inflation and the elimination of an absolute housing shortage resulted in a perceived need to rationalise public housing investment. The result was an attempt to introduce cash limits to control public expenditure through a system of annual local authority bids and central government allocation which was started under the 1974 Housing Act and culminated in the 1977 Green Paper, 'Housing Policy: A Consultative Document', which proposed the creation of the Housing Investment Programmes (HIPs). HIPs was sold as a:

new form of housing plan, based on a comprehensive assessment of the local housing situation. The main element will be a reasoned capital budget covering the local authority's own capital spending plans – related to its broad housing strategy – for the coming 4 years. On the basis of these plans the government will make capital spending allocations to each authority. Once the allocations are settled, authorities will be free to go ahead with the minimum of intervention by central government.

(DoE, 1977, para. 9.06)

HIPs was initially intended as a replacement for individual scheme approval in order to give housing authorities more discretion within an overall ceiling on borrowing, however, there was another aspect to the system which was to assume increasing importance, namely 'the unprecedented degree of control which central government could henceforth exercise over local authority housing provision' (Aughton, 1986, p. 5), although this was undoubtedly also the intention of the Labour government that introduced it. The HIPs system, supplemented by the 1980 Local Government, Planning and Land Act, came steadily to be used as a tool through which central government could more easily control a steadily diminishing aggregate council housing capital allocation.

Since the introduction of HIPs housing capital expenditure has declined dramatically in real terms, with the result that local authority investment in housing construction has collapsed since 1980 (see Table 1.2). This is the direct result of the fundamental changes to the housing finance system, the changing subsidy system and the capital controls introduced. The traditional council housing finance system had been established on the assumption that there was a housing shortage and that local authorities had an important role to play in overcoming it. Since 1980, a system of public housing finance has been set-up based on a rather different set of assumptions. Table 1.2 shows that there has been a switch in the balance of capital expenditure away from new build towards the rehabilitation of existing public and private stock in the local authority sector and it is the Housing Corporation that has been directed towards new build (see chapter 2). Central government has encouraged local authorities to provide grants for the renovation of private housing; authorities have no longer been required to conform to detailed controls such as the Parker-Morris space and heating standards and housing cost yardsticks (Merrett, 1979); and more importantly, since 1990 the DoE's power to penalise any local authorities which did not accept the new role envisaged by the central government has grown as a result of the discretionary allocation of HIPs resources.

All these diverse strands were part of a housing strategy which enabled central government to maintain tight control over capital expenditure and pursue a strategy which maintained the ideology of promoting owner occupation. The fact that the impact of such policies had begun to be felt even before the 1980s indicates that such a trend did not originate from the Conservative government but, as an analysis of the capital expenditure illustrates, has undoubtedly been greatly accelerated.

Table 1.2 Local authority capital expenditure in England (1993/94 prices)

Year	New house building (£m)	Renovation (£m)	Total direct investment (£m)	Total gross capital exp. (£m)
1979/80	2,617	1,778	4,909	7,244
1980/81	2,005	1,391	3,780	5,669
1981/82	1,363	1,175	2,842	4,985
1982/83	1,212	1,702	3,234	5,719
1983/84	1,153	1,940	3,437	6,035
1984/85	1,174	2,060	3,588	5,633
1985/86	882	2,004	3,280	4,608
1986/87	678	2,252	3,379	4,469
1987/88	642	2,450	3,563	4,600
1988/89	761	2,508	3,794	4,749
1989/90	869	3,637	5,182	6,312
1990/91	510	1,962	2,770	3,606
1991/92	276	1,590	2,172	3,021
1992/93	120	1,534	1,807	2,712

Source: Statistics supplied by DoE.

The last decade has witnessed substantial changes to the HIPs system, cuts, moratoriums, encouragements to spend, new restrictions on the use of capital receipts and so on, all of which have resulted in substantial disruption of authorities' strategies and investment programmes (see Gay, 1985). A further development is that the HIPs allocations have become progressively less important in housing capital investment patterns relative to other sources of investment funds such as capital receipts and Estate Action. Major distortions have become apparent as a result. For example, the capital receipts generated in the shires and the south (bar London) have been very great, thus increasing their share of usable resources relative to the authorities in the northern regions, the metropolitan districts and inner London (Malpass and Murie, 1990). To the extent that capital receipts prop-up the local authority housing investment programme, the fact that they have tailed off in the 1990s is a major threat. In the short run, the effect of government reductions in allocations has not been too severe because of the accumulated backlog of receipts and the temporary Treasury relaxation of rules enabling local authorities to use 100 per cent of capital receipts in 1993. In the long term substantial additional new money will be needed, especially if the private housing market fails to revive faster.

The main point to note is the extent to which the nature and role of the HIPs system has metamorphosed to reflect shifts in central government policies and priorities, not least the requirement of major reductions in the levels of council housing capital expenditure. Developments outside the HIPs system have further eroded it. Less and less borrowing permission is allocated via HIPs. The remainder of borrowing approval is determined in relation to capital receipts or held back and allocated by the DoE through some other route such as Estate Action HIP (see Pinto, 1993), nevertheless, it should be noted that the HIPs system still allows local authorities much more freedom to determine their own priorities than the funds available through Estate Action, City Challenge and other recently developed targeting mechanisms.

Synopsis of recent financial legislation

It is clear from the above discussion that the housing finance system was far from ideal. Although the government conceded the need for a fundamental review of the financial regime, this was neither because of a desire to alleviate the squeeze on capital and revenue subsidies nor to deal with the perverse financial effects. Rather it was because the 1980 system proved insufficiently flexible for central government to control local government housing expenditure. The 1989 Local Government and Housing Act sought to change this.

The capital side: Basic and Supplementary Credit Approvals

There were four main difficulties with the capital system. Firstly, although the government succeeded in its subsidy cutting aims, it failed to bring about local capital expenditure to a level which was consistent with public expenditure plans as a whole. There was much over/underspending because of difficulties in predicting the growth of capital receipts and authorities' propensity to spend those receipts. Secondly, the 1980 system resulted in a situation where the highest level of capital receipts were accumulated in areas with lower levels of housing need and vice versa. Thirdly, it did not prevent authorities from undertaking capital expenditure outside the framework of legislation because authorities proved adept at exploiting loopholes in order to maintain levels of capital spending above those desired by the government, thus distorting its expenditure plans. Fourthly, the frequent changes in primary and secondary legislation no longer provided a stable framework within which long-term capital programmes could be efficiently managed (see Malpass, 1993a, pp. 18-19; Malpass and Murie, 1990).

Under the new arrangements local authorities receive Basic Credit Approvals (BCAs) plus Supplementary Credit Approvals (SCAs) which set the maximum resources which authorities can obtain through conventional methods such as borrowing but the government is now able to take account of capital receipts in deciding individual allocations, thus aiding the targeting of resources. Authorities are now required to set aside against debt 75 per cent of receipts from disposal of HRA assets and 50 per cent of most other receipts. There are no restrictions on how the remaining portion is invested. It was expected that:

In general, the impact of the new capital controls will vary from place to place, but it is clear that the intention is to give central government much tighter control over local authority expenditure. The application of capital receipts to the redemption of debt will severely constrain capital programmes in many areas, but it will also have the effect of reducing debt charges falling on the housing revenue account. On the other hand, the elimination of the cascade effect will place considerable pressure on rents to support continued expenditure on maintaining and refurbishing existing council stock.

(Malpass, 1990, p. 171)

The revenue side: ring-fencing the housing account

In principle, the objective here was to make the whole system simpler, fairer and more effective (DoE, 1988, pp. 5-6). The new regime incorporates three changes: a redefinition of the HRA deficit and thus what counts as subsidy; an attempt to differentiate increases in rents and management and maintenance costs; and the creation of a 'ring-fence' around the HRA. It is the last component which has drawn the greatest comment. It represents an attempt to establish a tightly defined HRA so that authorities are no longer able to make Rate Fund Contributions (RFCs) from their surplus HRAs, which used to represent a significant amount of general assistance. There is thus a redefinition which collapses housing subsidy, rate support grant and rent rebate subsidy into one HRA subsidy to be paid to authorities. By widening the definition of what counts as the deficit on the HRA all authorities which maintain HRAs (even those with no deficit) are brought back into the grip of the subsidy system, with the effect of re-introducing a strong element of central leverage on rent increases. Indeed, in the first two years of operation of the new regime, council rents in London authorities increased by about 50 per cent, whilst the average increase for England as a whole was 30 per cent. Another dramatic though expected development, was further reductions in capital spending, helping to produce subsidy savings for central government (Malpass and Warburton, 1993).

All these developments have clearly been led by a desire to reduce capital and revenue subsidies to council housing; increase the level of rents to reflect the costs of management and maintenance, though with the side-effect of generating a greater incentive for existing council tenants to exercise their Right to Buy or to opt out of council housing; speed up of the residualisation of the council housing stock and the polarisation of council tenants (see Forrest and Murie, 1990); and generally restrict the scope of local authority housing activity. Further loss of autonomy results from two main issues: the ring-fenced HRA means that authorities cannot use the council tax to support the housing service and neither can they transfer HRA surpluses into the general fund; and secondly, they have lost access to their accumulated capital receipts. In addition, one of the government's stated objectives was to improve the performance of local authorities in managing and maintaining their housing stock but it appears that:

The effect of the new capital control system, restricting the use of capital receipts to 25 per cent and a much reduced total of receipts in the housing slump, is that there has been a massive reduction in repair and maintenance spending on the council stock. The scale of the reduction is as much as 57 per cent in London, and averages 23 per cent overall.

(Malpass *et al.*, 1993, p. 43)

The initial results of research assessing the effects of the new financial regime for council housing depict a lamentable situation, despite recent evidence that ring-fencing has also had positive side-effects (see Bines *et al.*, 1993). Capital investment has been further constrained and rents have been hiked upwards, but there has also been an unintended consequence in that there is now even less expenditure on repairs and maintenance thus adding to the growing problems of this form of housing relative to the plethora of other forms of landlordism or ownership preferred by government.

A new housing era: developments in social housing policy

Previous sections emphasised the economic and managerial rationale which has resulted in a situation where government no longer considers local housing authorities to be satisfactory landlords. This section charts the policy developments which have resulted in the various 'themes' to housing policy which were highlighted in the introduction to this chapter. Reference is made to three phases of Conservative government housing policy which reveal the inter-twined nature of the housing management and ownership themes.

This section will illustrate that in the first phase, the original route chosen by central government was to promote the Right to Buy where tenants were given the option of buying council properties at discount, thereby rapidly increasing the levels of home ownership. In the intermediary phase, the government began to recognise the inadequacy of a housing policy solely concerned with owner occupation and tried to stimulate the growth of alternative landlords other than local authorities, such as housing associations and tenant

management organisations. Part of the discussion relates to the role
played by Estate Action and Priority Estates Project in generating
enthusiasm for estate based management; as well as alluding to the
major innovations which took place across the country under the
banner of decentralisation (see Cole et al., 1991). Having queried the
value of having a council housing sector at all, a range of options for
transfer such as Large Scale Voluntary Transfers and housing management Compulsory Competitive Tendering have been placed on the
statute book with the primary intention of enabling large portions of
housing stock to 'exit' the council housing tenure. Taken as a whole,
this panoply of measures could potentially spell an end to council
housing and represent the main factors which will influence the
tenurial changes to the British housing system in the future.

The initial phase: displacing council housing

The first Thatcherite administration sought to achieve little beyond
the sale of council houses and support for owner occupation. This
section explores these developments and the various attempts to
revive the private rented sector.

Council house sales

The Conservative government was committed to increasing owner
occupation and went to great lengths to ensure that the council
house sales succeeded (see chapter 5 for a fuller discussion). The
political motive relates to the importance of this policy for the
Conservatives' electoral strategy, since promotion of home ownership and council house sales have proved popular in encouraging
traditional Labour voters to switch their allegiance to the Conservative party. The economic argument was equally potent given its link
with the rationale of monetarist policy seeking to reduce the size of
the public sector and the burden of public expenditure. The effect
has been that council housing has borne the brunt of public
expenditure cuts as discussed in the previous section. The discounts
have acted as a major inducement for residents to opt out of the
council housing system. The attractive financial terms combined
with rising council rents generated by the deficit finance system,
proved highly tempting. The ideological argument relating to this
tenure form was also significant, namely that a house of your own is
inherently better and encourages independence and thrift, while a
large council housing sector with the necessary subsidies are both a

drain on the nation's resources and an unacceptable extension of state control (Short, 1982, p. 64). Whilst this view seriously ignored the extent of public subsidy to owner occupation via mortgage tax relief, it was not surprising that the sale of council housing took on such a significance within the Conservative party, not least because this seemed to be the most advantageous way of maintaining and extending home ownership.

Though the sale of council housing was not by any means a new phenomenon (see Holmans, 1987, pp. 204-206), the impetus given to sales by the provisions of the 1980 Housing Act proved to be among the most successful reforms introduced under this legislation. Secure tenants of three years' standing acquired the option of buying the freehold of their house or the long lease of their flat on extremely favourable terms. Although the purchase price was based on market value, the tenant was entitled to a discount on such a value of 33 per cent plus 1 per cent for each year by which the tenant's period as a secure tenant exceeded three years.

This package of incentives proved very attractive and in the years 1980 to 1983 close to 500,000 dwellings, representing about 10 per cent of the public housing stock, were sold under the scheme. This resulted not only in a relative decline but also to an absolute reduction in public sector dwelling numbers and accentuated the processes of residualisation and polarisation which were already underway. Sales peaked in 1982 and in order to maintain the impetus, additional incentives were provided in the 1984 Housing and Building Control Act in the form of a relaxation of residential qualifications and an increase in the maximum discount. A second peak in sales was attained in 1988. The number of council properties sold under this legislation now approaches the 2m mark and has contributed to a significant portion of the increase in home ownership since the 1980s. Table 1.3 highlights the changes in housing tenure since the early part of this century. There is little doubt that the Right to Buy has been spectacularly successful (see chapter 5), but the government has no intention of slackening the pace of transfers of individual social housing units to owner occupation, as indicated by the 'Rents to Mortgage' and 'Shared Ownership' schemes.

Nevertheless the image of the impact of the Right to Buy policy is no longer as rosy as in the 1980s. This is partly because, as indicated in the Introduction to the book, the home ownership bubble has burst, but also because many leaseholders are critical of the govern-

Table 1.3 Twentieth-century tenure patterns in England and Wales (%)

Year	Owner occupied	Local authority	Private landlords	Housing association
1914	10.1	0.9	89.0	
1938	32.0	11.0	57.0	
1951	29.0	18.0	53.0	
1961	44.0	24.0	32.0	
1971	53.0	28.0	19.0	
1981	59.0	28.0	11.0	2.0
1991	69.0	20.0	8.0	3.0
1991 (UK)	67.7	21.8	7.4	3.1

Source: DoE Annual Report, 1993.

ment's failure to enable them to resell their flats or to help them avoid the heavy capital costs associated with refurbishment of their blocks by the freeholders (local authorities). It is also important to note that as the government tries to push home ownership as far down the line as possible, it is inevitably those on lower incomes who are taking up the option. The rapidly increasing number of mortgage arrears and home possessions in recent years has demonstrated clearly that home ownership is not a housing panacea, especially where those on low incomes or insecure jobs are concerned. According to Ford, in 1993 one in twelve mortgage holders were at least 12 months behind with mortgage payments and approximately 60,500 properties were repossessed (1993). It is perhaps this that has prompted the government to recognise that there will continue to be a need for some sort of 'safety net' to support those who cannot afford to buy (see DoE, 1989; Glennerster, 1990).

Stimulating the private rented sector and rent control

Private rented housing in Britain has experienced a steep decline since the early 1900s when it accounted for 90 per cent of the total housing stock, to the present day where the figure is closer to 8 per cent (see Table 1.3). Although it has become a marginal tenure, and despite the stock's poor physical condition which tends to be older and lacking in amenities in comparison to both council and owner occupied housing, the sector occupies a crucial position in the housing market. It is highly diverse and caters for the very wealthy, pensioners and

migrants among others, and its importance lies in that it offers
immediate access to housing (NFHA, 1985; Best *et al.*, 1992).

The salience of a thriving private rented sector and its implications
for labour mobility explain why successive governments have attempted to revive it, albeit with little success. Right-wing groups
such as the Institute of Economic Affairs argue that the housing
market has been in a tangle for generations due to the state
intervention policies which were introduced:

> with the best intentions but have led to the worst of outcomes. We find
> ourselves with too little housing accommodation of the right kind in the
> right places. Moreover, there is a cost not only in terms of hardship, but in
> terms of a less efficient economy, a less mobile labour force, and higher
> unemployment.
>
> (Minford *et al.*, 1987, p. xi)

Minford *et al.* blame the Rent Acts, the subsidies to council rents, the
subsidy to owner occupiers through mortgage tax relief and the
system of planning restrictions on land for housing, for aggravating
the situation (1987). Numerous measures have been taken in an
attempt to deregulate and revitalise the private rented sector. The
1980 Housing Act introduced two new tenancies – 'shorthold'
tenancy, meaning a fair rent but limited security of tenure (1-3
years) and 'assured' tenancy meaning security of tenure, but market
rent. The overall aim of the Act was to stop the decline of the private
rented sector by allowing higher rents, a shorter period between rent
increases and a reduction in the security of tenure afforded to the
tenants (Short, 1982, p. 66), but in contrast to the Right to Buy, the
initial measures designed to stimulate the private rented sector had a
negligible impact.

Yet there remains a need for a sector which provides immediate
access to accommodation without the need for registration, substantial deposits or the intention to remain in the district, as in the case
of owner occupation and council housing. This reduction of tenure
options has been roundly criticised. The NFHA makes a strong case
for two groups who are in particular need of this form of tenure,
namely those who cannot afford to buy (such as those who are
unemployed, too old for mortgages, single parents and on low or
irregular income) and who equally would not be able to afford to
pay high rents without assistance via income support or subsidy to
reduce rents; and those for whom owner occupation is inappropriate

including students, those new to an area or temporarily there and current owner occupiers unable to cope with the full costs and responsibilities of ownership due to age, incapacity, debt or poverty. This category includes the majority of the population at some point in their lives (NFHA, 1985, pp. 24-26) and the argument has become even more potent in the 1990s (NFHA, 1991).

The government has indicated that it will continue to attempt to generate a vigorous private rented sector, to relax rent controls for tenants and to establish the 'Right to Rent' but considerable doubts remain as to how significant rent regulation and security of tenure are, compared to the difference in financial assistance to the owner occupied sector. Mortgage tax relief cost approximately £7bn and capital gains tax exemption on principal residences a further £2bn in 1988/89. Tax relief has now depreciated to £4bn (1992/93) due to the combined effects of the reduction in MIRAS and lower interest rates, nevertheless, it was not surprising that landlords with vacant possession preferred to sell their properties in order to maximise their investment. Moreover, private landlordism in Britain does not attract tax breaks such as depreciation allowances, tax relief on rental income and on capital gains (Ginsberg, 1989).

In recognition of the above points the 1988 Finance Act extended the Business Expansion Scheme (BES) to housing investment with the intention of offering tax breaks to people with the resources and willingness to put them on risky start-up ventures. Research suggests that as many as 10,000 dwellings were produced as a result of the BES, two-thirds of them newly built (Crook et al., 1991) and that it has been a factor in slowing down the decline of the private rented sector. The more significant factor has been deregulation. The 1988 Housing Act has led to the creation of about 480,000 new tenancies, only a small percentage of which was generated by BES as discussed above (see Coleman, 1992). This deceleration of the rate of decline can be attributed to the housing market slump which has resulted in large numbers of home owners unwilling or unable to sell, with the side-effect that many have tended to rented out their homes until such a time as the property market recovers. This would suggest that the trend represents a temporary reprieve for the private renting sector and has led to the conclusion that:

deregulation and weakening tenants' security did not adequately serve to close the gap between what tenants could afford to pay in rents and what landlords needed to charge in order to get a competitive rate of return. While subsides were provided, the BES was seen only as a kick-start to attract investment and not as a continuing support for private renting [BES ended in 1993]. Apart from the costs which such subsidies would mean if kept in place for a substantial period, the provision of subsidies would be an acknowledgement that the market, left to itself, was not capable of providing affordable and acceptable housing to rent.

(Kemp, 1993, p. 71)

There would appear to be three main reasons why private renting is set to continue to decline as a housing option in Britain. The provision of tax relief for owner occupation is a key factor behind the relative unattractiveness of the private rented sector to investors, yet is unlikely to be abolished in the near future, given the primacy of owner occupation to the government's housing policy. Second, the experience of BES indicates that the revival of the private rented sector is dependent on various financial incentives which are in conflict with the professed aim of containing public expenditure due to the current public sector deficit. Third, the government is dependent on private investors to implement their policies for this tenure, yet these investors are not sufficiently persuaded of the attractiveness of this tenure in relation to the alternatives. This means that despite the temporary reprieve, housing in this tenure is likely to continue drifting into owner occupation when the housing market recovers.

The intermediate phase: alternative agents

Housing commentators tend to characterise the mid-1980s as the 'implementation' or 'drift' phase in Conservative housing policy. Perhaps it would be more accurate to describe it as the 'experimentation' phase, the period when two themes came to the forefront and which were to drive much of the subsequent policy in the post-housing policy review phase: an awareness of the importance of renting as a tenure, and hence a new orientation towards housing associations and co-operatives and the creation of the Estate Action initiative, which together were to establish many of the concepts employed in the third and more radical phase.

Housing associations

The evolution of the housing association movement is the subject of an extremely detailed analysis in chapter 2. This section merely provides a brief sketch of recent developments in this area. Suffice to say that the government has come to accept the need for an intermediate form of tenure and now sees associations as the main vehicle for the future construction and management of social housing, even taking over former council property:

> Our new policies put housing associations on centre-stage. We see them as the major providers of new subsidised housing for rent and as possible alternative landlords for dissatisfied council tenants.
>
> (David Trippier, Minister at the DoE, reported in Voluntary Housing, Feb. 1989)

The government's confidence in the value of this tenure as a potential alternative to council housing is so great that it has even taken the step of re-classifying associations as belonging to the 'independent' rented sector, despite the degree of public subsidy necessary to make them viable. In such a climate, associations have expanded at such a rate that they were already building more homes in 1987/8 than the council housing sector (the figures for 1992/93 were respectively 33,000 and 2,000 units). Nevertheless the housing association movement remains a small tenure both in terms of number of properties (714,000 versus 4m in the council sector) and the overwhelming majority of the 2,200-odd associations are very small, owning under 100 units (Housing Corporation Factsheet, 1993).

Associations are non-profit making organisations and have traditionally housed those in need but the government was clearly attracted by their specialist nature and the absence of party politics. They were, therefore, increasingly commended as models for housing management, being small, locally based and well-suited to the climate of housing opinion, although some of the larger housing associations already had a larger housing stock in the 1980s than many District Councils. As 'unpopular' council estates became more widespread, so practitioners became more interested in models of intensive and localised management structures as well as increased tenant participation. Housing associations were increasingly lauded by government as good models of housing management, although the influential report by the Centre for Housing Research questions this assumption, stating that: 'Good management performance and low costs were not the preserve of a single organisational type, and similarly for poor performance and high costs' (1989, para. 9.4).

This illustrates the problem faced by government. While it has come to rely upon this tenure to push forward with its policies, housing associations are not necessarily the most appropriate vehicle for its housing objectives. The 1988 Housing Act restructured association finance with the effect that since April 1989 the level of grant has been fixed at the start of projects and the schemes have been funded by a mixture of public and private finance. The ratio of public subsidy varies according to region and type of development, but averaged initially at 75 per cent and is now down to 62 per cent. A question mark still hangs over whether associations will be able to raise sufficient resources from financial institutions to meet the requirements of the planned expansion of this sector and the implications for the rent levels and affordability in this sector are charted in chapter 2.

Housing associations only account for 3 per cent of the housing stock (see Table 1.3) so the sector's main route for rapid expansion is via the combined effects of the new planned capital investment, Large Scale Voluntary Transfers and Housing Management CCT (see below), although the latter would involve only a change in management rather than ownership. But leaving aside the Treasury's concern over the public expenditure implications of stock transfers (see chapters 2 and 5), housing associations have reacted cautiously to these transfer routes. In any case, there were immediately arguments in some corners that they should not be the only choice of alternative landlord: 'In putting so much emphasis on housing associations, the Government may be refloating Local Authority housing under a new flag of convenience but on the old sea of public money' (Coleman, 1988, pp. 40-41).

Chapter 2 analyses the various pressures which have operated on this tenure as a result of the government's expectations and the new financial regime introduced in 1988. In the meanwhile local authorities will continue to be constrained from providing much new housing for general needs and the government has instead sought to encourage them to turn their reduced capital investment programmes to their existing stock and to the improvement of their management and tenant involvement practices via the PEP and EA initiatives.

Priority Estates Project (PEP) and Estate Action (EA)

The DoE funded PEP to work with tenants and local authorities in an attempt to develop a model of integrated estate based housing management for the most unpopular council housing estates. PEP sought to bring about organisational changes to the traditional centralised local authority housing structure. This model for estate improvement developed over time and culminated in a three volume guide to local housing management (Power, 1987b) which recommended the following ten ingredients:

- estate based office;
- local repairs team;
- control of local lettings;
- control of local rents and arrears;
- tenant involvement;
- small scale capital works;
- residents involved with caretaking, cleaning etc.;
- local staff with decentralised powers;
- identifiable project manager; and
- locally controlled management and maintenance budget.

A survey was conducted of 20 local estate management schemes which argued that such decentralisation initiative could indeed transform housing estates (Power, 1984), but it is worth noting that although this initiative was claimed by central government, only three of these estates were PEP projects. The rest had been initiated by local authorities themselves, underlining the point that local authorities were reacting to the growing evidence of problems in the most problematic parts of their housing stock. In addition, recent studies on various aspects of PEP and estate based management although generally supportive of such initiatives, have also highlighted some caveats. For example, the recent study of its potential for reducing crime argued that:

the PEP model does have a potential for reducing crime. However, on the estates studied during this research, all of the successes were only partial – they occurred in either one or other of the experimental estates, or only for particular areas or groups of residents on the estates. Two obstacles to the wider effectiveness of the PEP model on the estates studied were: firstly, the 'quality' of implementation; and secondly, the instability of the residential communities arising from population turnover, social heterogeneity and the 'subterranean culture' within estate communities.

(Foster and Hope, 1993, p. x)

Other studies have looked into the cost-effectiveness of the PEP estates and found that as expected, both running and capital expenditure were higher on such estates but that they were generally more cost-effective in securing high tenant satisfaction (CAPITA, 1993). The most significant of these recent studies has evaluated the impact of estate based management as follows:

- it does tend to improve the standards of the housing service and the quality of life for tenants;
- decentralisation did improve most aspects of the housing service, especially short term repairs, raised tenant satisfaction and was associated with reduced levels of property damage and nuisance;
- working with tenants was time consuming but vital to community building and informal social control;
- the housing management function must be enlarged to include the task of mobilising support to sustain the 'at risk' individuals and the social fabric of at risk estates;
- it highlighted the inter-agency, inter-disciplinary nature of the housing management function; and
- 'In short, estate based management is a necessary but not a sufficient condition for combatting housing and social decay on deprived housing estates.'

(Glennerster and Turner, 1993, p. xi)

The last point is particularly noteworthy in emphasising the fact that organisational changes can only do so much to improve the social and economic environment faced by tenants on the most problematic housing estates.

The experience of PEP was particularly significant to the creation and orientation of Estate Action and chapter 4 presents one of the first attempts to addresses origins, evolution and impact of this particular DoE initiative. Estate Action was the government's second major venture in trying to stimulate changes in council housing management, tenant practices as well as ownership forms, and as such, played a key role in helping formulate the government's next phase of policy. The initiative was an important experiment with respect to transfers of council housing stock to new organisations such as trusts, Estate Management Boards and private sector landlords; the selection of estates designated as HATs; and generally acted as a significant spur to improved management via the funding to estate based management, concierge schemes, neighbourhood offices, co-operatives and such like.

The experience of Estate Action (and PEP) is important in

illustrating the revolution that was occurring in the way local authorities themselves were improving their management practices and redefining the role of the tenant in the management of their stock. Rapid growth in decentralisation initiatives was one way of counteracting government criticism of council housing. A number of other local authorities were also developing even more wide-ranging and imaginative schemes (see also chapter 6), as the literature on neighbourhood decentralisation demonstrates (see Cole et al., 1991; Cole, 1993). The Centre for Housing Research (1989) and more recently Bines et al. (1993) have both pointed to the extent to which local authorities have decentralised their housing management functions.

The radical phase: demunicipalisation?

The government felt a need to carry out a fundamental review of housing policy in 1987 for four main reasons: first, there were clear examples of housing policies which were no longer working, such as the local authority capital finance system, where the government had lost control over a significant amount of capital spending and/or leverage over council rents. Second, the very success of some policies such as the Right to Buy required new developments, causing the government to look for ways of reducing the council housing stock even faster. Third, the government's recognition of the importance of a rented sector, together with its apparent hostility to council housing caused a further rethink on the need to revitalise the private rented sector; as well as a clearer posture towards housing associations and co-operatives. Lastly, this coincided with the emergence of a new approach to the provision of public services where the state became increasingly a purchaser, rather than a provider of services (Malpass, 1993b, pp. 34-35).

The most significant phase of Conservative housing policy was signalled by the White Paper (DoE, 1987b) which proposed markedly different solutions for the council housing problems and was followed up with two major Acts of Parliament. The 1988 Housing Act introduced powerful new mechanisms such as Tenants' Choice and Housing Action Trusts; further deregulation of the private rented sector; and a new financial system for housing associations and co-operatives. The 1989 Local Government and Housing Act which introduced a new financial regime for local authorities was discussed earlier in the section on housing finance. Together with the remodelled

Large Scale Voluntary Transfer option, these developments represented major threats to the future of the council housing tenure, however, even these transfer options are arguably not as significant as the potential impact of the Right to Manage and housing management CCT, which have recently entered the statute book. These major policies and their significance with respect to developments in housing management and ownership are briefly introduced in the remainder of this chapter.

Tenants' Choice (TC)

Introduced in Part IV of the 1988 Housing Act, this piece of legislation extends the rights and choices given to council tenants in 1980 through the Tenants' Charter and the Right to Buy. Potentially the most powerful instrument available under the Act, council tenants individually (in houses) or collectively (in flats) can choose to transfer their existing homes to another landlord. Independent landlords must be approved by the Housing Corporation as 'appropriate' (viable and competent) social landlords before they may take over council housing stock. The choice is determined via a voting system whereby non-voters are assumed to be in favour of transfer, possibly because the government anticipated lack of interest from council tenants.

The government's immediate aims via Tenants' Choice are to give more options to council tenants who either do not wish to or cannot exercise their Right to Buy and to expose council housing to competition which might result in a better standard of services. For their part, local authorities are primarily opposed to the policy because of their desire to retain their housing stock. They fear that the government introduced 'ring-fencing' as a way of forcing up rents and to encourage tenants to opt out of council control either by exercising their Right to Buy or through Tenants' Choice. Chapter 5 analyses these developments in detail, however, suffice to say at this point that the procedures designed to facilitate Tenants' Choice were found to be extremely cumbersome and this option appears to have been de-emphasised by the government.

Housing Action Trusts (HATs)

Sections 65-92 of the 1988 Housing Act contain strong powers enabling Trusts appointed by the government to take over large patches of the 'worst' council housing; repair and modernise the stock; improve the living conditions and general environment of the area; secure diversity of tenure; and transfer the stock to alternative private landlords in due course.

An analogy can be drawn to Urban Development Corporations in that the HATs will take over estates for five years without any obligations and accountabilities to the local populace. This is justified by the government by maintaining that relieving housing authorities of their most difficult housing stock will enable them to concentrate their efforts and resources on the remaining stock. Chapter 5 unravels the reasons why HATs have come to be perceived as one of the government's clearest failures in relation to housing policy. Plans for all six estates originally earmarked for HATs have either been dropped by the government or rejected by the tenants with the result that this policy has undergone an unexpected change in nature. Concessions such as those relating to the balloting of tenants and the possible return of HAT stock and tenants to their 'parent' local authorities, greatly blunted the aims of this piece of legislation. So much so in fact, that a number of local authorities that were originally hostile to HATs, such as Tower Hamlets, subsequently queued up to designate their own HAT estates. This is a reflection of both the dilution of the government's original proposals and the ideological softening of a number of Labour-controlled local authorities.

Large Scale Voluntary Transfers (LSVT)

This policy was first unveiled under the 1986 Housing and Planning Act and the 1988 Housing Act elaborated on how councils could of their own volition dispose of some or all of their housing stock. Under LSVT no requirement is made of local authorities to consult the tenants affected, other than offering alternative accommodation, although the Secretary of State must be satisfied that the tenants support the developments. A crucial difficulty remains that when LSVT goes ahead, tenants who vote 'No' or abstain will also be obliged to transfer to the new landlord. Despite these concerns, a number of authorities have so far transferred their entire stock to newly-created housing associations because of the financial advantages and its potential as a mechanism for both retaining and even expanding the supply of rented social housing. These two issues may yet persuade other local authorities that so little scope exists for the proper management and maintenance of the council housing under their own control that LSVT may be the only means of providing a decent landlord service for their tenants.

Chapter 5 addresses the point that although its impact was not fully anticipated by central government, LSVT has the potential of being much more significant than HATs and Tenants' Choice but it is worth noting that because of the Treasury-inspired concerns about the public spending implications, the government now appears to be signalling a U-turn in policy. By restricting the number of LSVTs per year, it is clearly beginning to constrain the potential of this policy yet central government is far from satisfied about the range of options which now exist for stock to 'exit' the council housing tenure.

Housing Management Compulsory Competitive Tendering (HMCCT)

In June 1992 the government published a consultation paper 'Competing for Quality in Housing', which gave notice of its intention to extend the Compulsory Competitive Tendering (CCT) procedure to housing management. This legislation requires local authorities to set standards for housing services in consultation with tenants and then seek private sector tenders for housing management contracts. The rationale for introducing HMCCT was set out as follows: 'The government considers that its proposals will ... provide a means by which the poorest performing authorities can raise their standards of management so that tenants receive a better service in future' (DoE, 1992a, para. 2.5), and the hope is that HMCCT will stimulate efficiency and lead to reductions in management costs in the long run.

The HMCCT process was further refined by the follow-up report (DoE, 1993) which stressed the importance of providing a comprehensive housing service to tenants and proposed that the following housing management tasks be elements of the 'defined activity' under CCT:

- rent and service charge collection;
- allocating properties and arranging lettings;
- enforcement of tenancy agreements;
- management of vacant properties;
- management of repairs and maintenance; and
- management of caretaking and cleaning.

(DoE, 1993, para. 27)

Although sometimes difficult to separate, functions such as housing benefit administration, processing of Right to Buy and homelessness

Table 1.4 Phased introduction of Housing Management CCT

Band	Units	% of stock	Date
1	Less than 15,000 units	Whole stock	April 1996
2	Less than 15,000 units	Whole stock	April 1997
3	15,000–30,000 units	First 60%	April 1996; rest 1997
4	15,000–30,000 units	First 60%	April 1997; rest 1998
5	More than 30,000 units	First 40%	April 1996; rest in 2 years

Source: DoE, 1993, para. 38.

determinations will not be subject to housing management CCT. Local authorities have been placed in five 'bands' which determine the speed with which they are required to introduce HMCCT (see Table 1.4), they must all do so within three years. Moreover as this will clearly be a major undertaking two factors will be taken into account: the size of the housing stock and an authority's ability to achieve readiness. The latter refers to the extent to which authorities have decentralised their housing management, the number of management functions performed at an area/estate level, purchased suitable Information Technology (IT) systems and developed appropriate tenant consultation arrangements. A further consideration for the phased introduction of CCT is that there might otherwise 'be a strong risk of overloading the market' (DoE, 1993, para. 33).

The guidance was at pains to point out that housing authorities' strategic or enabling role will not be subject to HMCCT and the government has gone out of its way to ensure that the HMCCT policy is as flexible as possible. The form, model, period and size of contract packages are to be decided in relation to local circumstances and, as long as it does not deter competition, authorities are simply directed to consider the scale which will make housing management most effective and accessible to tenants. It is quite clear that Ministers hope that the legislation will lead to:

- further decentralisation of management;
- bring management closer and make it more accessible to tenants; and
- 'reduce the preponderance of large and monolithic housing managers'.

Chapters 6 and 7 explore a range of issues such as how local authorities have responded to the government critique of housing management and their initial attitude to CCT for housing management. Finally, it is worth noting that although the HMCCT legislation is of major significance for the council management service in December 1992, the government unveiled yet another proposal, the Right to Manage.

Tenant involvement and the Right to Manage

The government has made the Right to Manage option available to council tenants because it:

reflects two broad and interlocking aims of the Government's housing policy: to increase the effectiveness of local authority housing management, and to improve the quality of life on council estates. Effective housing management needs to be responsive and flexible, and able to take account of local needs and priorities ... Local services are best monitored by those who receive the services directly. The Government is therefore committed to further diversification of housing management, and to an increasing role for tenants in deciding the level of service they want, selecting the organisation which is best able to deliver that service within the resources available, and monitoring its performance.

(DoE, 1992b, p. 5).

The Right to Manage appears to have developed from the experience of LSVT, although delegation of housing stock to Tenant Management Organisations (TMOs) such as housing co-operatives (see chapter 3), also appears to have impressed government sufficiently for it to now require councils to 'support tenants in the process of empowerment which can lead to tenants themselves managing their own estates' (DoE, 1992b, p. 6). Moreover, the government also appears to have learned from the evolution of the HATs, not least the need for tenants' needs and priorities to be fully taken into account and is all the more reason why the Right to Manage is likely to prove a potent issue for the council housing sector. TMO estates run by tenants will fall outside the scope of HMCCT and the stock will remain in local authority ownership.

Conclusions

The overall direction of the developments in housing policy suggests that a government which when elected had few housing policies other than the determination to reduce capital and revenue subsidies to council housing and increase owner occupation via sale of council property, has increasingly aspired to replace council housing completely.

Under this vision for the British housing system, the existing council housing stock will in due course be financed, managed and owned by a variety of landlords, other than local authorities, including private investors, trusts of various sorts, housing associations, building societies, housing co-operatives among other forms of landlord. These developments came about in various phases and were underpinned firstly, by a complete faith that local authority landlords were so bureaucratic and unconcerned about the housing service as to be beyond reform and secondly, that home ownership should be encouraged at all costs. The discussion has highlighted that the evidence for the first tenet is far from conclusive and that the second is hardly a panacea for a balanced housing system.

Following on from this, the above analysis indicated that the government's housing policy aims have not always been reflected in the policy outcomes. The policy objectives can be unclear or contradictory but even where this is not the case, the legislative and the implementation processes can often lead to unexpected outcomes (see Malpass and Means, 1993). Thus although the government's recent housing aim may have been to bring about the demise of council housing, this chapter highlighted the point that this does not appear to be proceeding entirely to plan. Council housing may have been buffeted by a storm of criticism, much of which was well-directed, but despite the impact of a steady stream of legislation, it still makes up 20 per cent of the housing stock and is unlikely to disappear according to government's schedule. This analysis of the general direction of housing policy since the 1980s serves to prime the subsequent discussions about the impacts that these developments in housing ownership and management will have in the 1990s and beyond.

References

AMA (Association of Metropolitan Authorities) (1983) Defects in Housing 1: Non-traditional Dwellings of the 1940s and 1950s, London, AMA.
AMA (1984) Defects in Housing 2: Industrialised and System-built Dwellings in the 1960s and 1970s, London, AMA.

AMA (1985) Defects in Housing 3: Repair and Modernisation of Traditionally Built Dwellings, London, AMA.

Andrews, C. L. (1979) Tenant and Town Hall, London, HMSO.

Archbishop of Canterbury's Commission on Urban Priority Areas (1985) Faith in the City: A Call for Action by Church and Nation, London, Central Board of Finance of the Church of England.

Audit Commission for Local Authorities in England and Wales (1984) Bringing Council Tenants' Arrears Under Control, London, HMSO.

Audit Commission (1986a) Improving Council Housing Maintenance, London, HMSO.

Audit Commission (1986b) The Management of London's Authorities: Preventing the Breakdown of Services, London, HMSO.

Audit Commission (1986c) Managing the Crisis in Council Housing, London, HMSO.

Aughton, H. (1986) Housing Finance: A Basic Guide, 2nd edn, London, Shelter.

Best, R., Kemp, P., Coleman, D., Merrett, S. and Crook, T. (1992) The Future of Private Renting: Consensus and Action, Joseph Rowntree Foundation, York.

Bines, W., Kemp, P., Pleace, N. and Radley, C. (1993) Managing Social Housing: A Study of Landlord Performance, London, HMSO.

Birchall, J. (1988) Building Communities the Co-operative Way, London, Routledge & Kegan Paul.

Birchall, J. (ed.) (1993) Housing Policy in the 1990s, London, Routledge.

Burbidge, M., Curtis, A., Kirby, K., and Wilson, S. (1981) An Investigation of Difficult to Let Housing: Vol. 1: General Findings; Vol. 2: Case Studies of Post-War Estates; Vol. 3: Case Studies of Pre-War Estates, London, HMSO.

CAPITA Management Consultancy (1993) Priority Estates Project Cost-Effectiveness Study: Summary of Findings, London, HMSO.

CES (Centre for Environmental Studies) (1984) Outer Estates in Britain: Interim Report – Comparison of 4 Outer Estates, Paper 23, London, CES.

CHAC (Housing Management Sub-Committee of the Central Housing Advisory Committee of the Ministry of Housing and Local Government) (1945) Management of Municipal Housing Estates: Second Report, London, HMSO.

CHAC (1953) Councils and their Houses: Eighth Report, London, HMSO.

CHAC (1955) Unsatisfactory Tenants: Sixth Report, London, HMSO.

Centre for Housing Research (1989) The Nature and Effectiveness of Housing Management in England: A Report to the Department of the Environment, London, HMSO.

Clapham, D. (1989) Goodbye Council Housing?, The Fabian Series, London, Hutchinson.

Clapham, D., Kemp, P. and Kintrea, K. (1987) 'Co-operative Ownership of Former Council Housing', Policy and Politics, Vol. 15(4), pp. 207-220.

Cole, I. (1993) 'The Decentralization of Housing Services' in Malpass, P. and Means, R. (1993).

Cole, I. and Furbey (1993) The Eclipse of Council Housing: Housing and the Welfare State, London, Routledge.

Cole, I. Windle, K. and Arnold, P. (1991) 'Decentralized Housing Services – Back to the Future' in Donnison, D. and Maclennan, D. (eds) The Housing Service of the Future, Harlow, Longman.

Coleman, D. A. (1988) Housing Policy: Unfinished Business, London, Bow Publications.

Coleman, D. A. (1992) 'Private Rented Housing: The Next Steps' in Best, R., Kemp, P., Coleman, D., Merrett, S. and Crook, T. (1992) The Future of Private Renting: Consensus and Action, Joseph Rowntree Foundation, York.

Cooper, S. (1985) Public Housing and Private Property, London, Gower.

Crook, A. D. H. (1993) 'Private Rented Housing and the Impact of Deregulation' in Birchall, J. (1993).

Crook, A. D. H., Kemp, P., Anderson, I. and Bowman, S. (1991) Tax Incentives and the Revival of Private Renting, York, Cloister Press.

Cullingworth, J. B. (1966) Housing and Local Government, London, Allen & Unwin.

DoE (1977) Housing Policy: A Consultative Document, London, HMSO.
DoE (1987a) The PEP Guide to Local Housing Management Vols. 1 to 3, London, HMSO.
DoE (1987b) Housing: The Government's Proposals, Cmnd 214, London, HMSO.
DoE (1988) New Financial Regime for Local Housing Authorities: A Consultation Paper, London, HMSO.
DoE (1989) The Government's Review of the Homelessness Legislation, London, HMSO.
DoE (1992a) Competing for Quality in Housing, London, HMSO.
DoE (1992b) Tenant Involvement and the Right to Manage, London, HMSO.
DoE (1993) Compulsory Competitive Tendering of Housing Management, London, HMSO.
Duncan, S. and Kirby, K. (1983) Preventing Rent Arrears, London, HMSO.
Dunleavy, P. (1981) The Politics of Mass Housing in Britain, 1945-75, Oxford, Clarendon Press.
Ford, J. (1993) 'Debt Casts a Long Shadow', Roof, July–August, Vol. 18, No. 4, pp. 18-19.
Forrest, R. and Murie, A. (1983) 'Residualisation and Council Housing: Aspects of Changing Social Relations of Housing and Tenure', Journal of Social Policy, 12, pp. 453-468.
Forrest, R. and Murie, A. (1990) Residualisation and Council Housing: A Statistical Update, School of Advanced Urban Studies, Working Paper No. 91.
Foster, J. and Hope, T. (1993) Housing, Community and Crime: The Impact of the Priority Estates Project, Home Office Research Study No. 131, London, HMSO.
Gay, O. (1985) Housing Investment Programmes and Capital Receipts, Background Paper No. 162, London, House of Commons Library Research Division.
Ginsberg, N. (1989) 'The Housing Act, 1988 and its Policy Context: A Critical Commentary', Critical Social Policy, Issue 25, Vol. 9(1), pp. 56-81.
Glennerster, H. (1990) 'A Decentralised Housing Service: What Does it Mean?' in Bennett R. J. (ed.) Decentralisation, Local Government and Markets: Towards a Post-welfare Agenda?, Oxford, University Press, pp. 207-220.
Glennerster, H. and Turner, T. (1993) Estate Based Housing Management: An Evaluation, London, HMSO.
Hambleton, R. and Hoggett, P. (eds.) (1984) Decentralisation and Democracy: Localising Public Services, Occasional Paper 28, Bristol University, SAUS.
Hambleton, R. and Hoggett, P. (1987) The Politics of Decentralisation: Theory and Practice of a Radical Local Government Initiative, Working Paper 46, Bristol University, SAUS.
Hills, J. (1991) Unravelling Housing Finance, Oxford, Clarendon Press.
HM Treasury (1979) The Government's Expenditure Plans 1984-85 to 1986-87, Cmnd 7746, London, HMSO.
Holmans, A. (1987) Housing Policy in Britain, London, Croom Helm.
Houlihan, B. (1988) Housing Policy and Central–Local Government Relations, Aldershot, Gower.
HRG (Housing Research Group) (1981) Could Local Authorities Be Better Landlords?, London, City University.
HSAG (Housing Services Advisory Group) (1978) Organising a Comprehensive Housing Service, London, HMSO.
Hughes, D. J. (1987) Public Sector Housing Law, 2nd edn, London, Butterworths.
Kemp, P. (1993) 'Rebuilding the Private Rented Sector?' in Malpass, P. and Means, R. (1993)
Laffin, M. (1985) Professionalism and Policy in Central–Local Government Relations, Farnborough, Gower Press.
Loughlin, M. (1986) Local Government in Modern States, London, Sweet & Maxwell.
Macey, J. (1982) Housing Management, London, The Estates Gazette.
Malpass, P. (1990) Reshaping Housing Policy: Subsidies, Rents and Residualisation, London, Routledge.
Malpass, P. (1993a) 'Housing Policy and the Disabling of Local Authorities' in Birchall, J. (1993).
Malpass, P. (1993b) 'Housing Policy and the Housing System Since 1979' in Malpass, P. and Means, R. (1993).
Malpass, P. and Means, R. (eds.) (1993) Implementing Housing Policy, Buckingham, Open University Press.

Malpass, P. and Murie, A. (1990) Housing Policy and Practice, 3rd edn, Basingstoke, Macmillan.
Malpass, P. and Warburton, M. (1993) 'The New Financial Regime for Local Housing Authorities' in Malpass, P. and Means, R. (1993).
Malpass, P., Warburton, M. Bramley, G. and Smart, G. (1993) Housing Policy in Action: The New Financial Regime for Council Housing, Bristol University, SAUS.
Merrett, S. (1979) State Housing in Britain, London, Routledge & Kegan Paul.
Minford, P., Peel, M. and Ashton, P. (1987) The Housing Morass: Regulation, Immobility and Unemployment, Hobart Paperback 25, London, Institute of Economic Affairs.
National Consumer Council (1979) Soonest Mended: A Review of Repair, Maintenance and Improvement of Council Housing, London, NCC.
National Federation of Housing Associations (1985) Inquiry into British Housing, Chaired by HRH The Duke of Edinburgh – (1) The Evidence, London, NFHA.
National Federation of Housing Associations (1986) Inquiry into British Housing, Chaired by HRH The Duke of Edinburgh, London, NFHA.
National Federation of Housing Associations (1991) Inquiry into British Housing: Second Report, York, Chaired by HRH The Duke of Edinburgh, Joseph Rowntree Foundation.
Pinto, R. R. (1990) 'An Evaluation of the Estate Action Initiative: Aims Versus Achievements', Housing Review, Vol. 39(2), pp. 45-48.
Pinto, R. R. (1991) 'Centre/Local Interaction in Renovating Run-down Estates: The View of Local Housing Authorities on the Estate Action Initiative', Local Government Studies, January–February, Vol. 17(1), pp. 45-62.
Pinto, R. R. (1993) The Estate Action Initiative: Council Housing Renewal, Management and Effectiveness, Aldershot, Avebury.
Power, A. (1984) Local Housing Management: A Priority Estates Project Survey, London, HMSO.
Power, A. (1987a) Property before People: The Management of Twentieth Century Council Housing, London, Allen & Unwin.
Power, A. (1987b) PEP Guide to Local Housing Management, Vols. 1, 2 and 3, London, HMSO.
Power, A. (1988) Council Housing: Conflict, Change and Decision Making, Welfare State Discussion Paper No. 27, STICERD, London, LSE.
Seabrook, J. (1984) The Idea of Neighbourhood: What Local Politics Should Be About, London, Pluto Press.
Short, J. R. (1982) Housing in Britain – The Post-War Experience, London, Methuen.
Whitehead, C. M. E. and Kleinman, M. P. (1986) Private Rented Housing in the 1980s and 1990s, Department of Land Economy No. 17, Cambridge, Granta Editions / University of Cambridge.
Willmott, P. and Murie, A. (1988) Polarisation and Social Housing: The British and French Experience, London, Policy Studies Institute.

2

Housing associations: new providers of social housing for rent, or vehicles for the privatisation of rented accommodation?*

Judith Harrison

Introduction

Since the implementation of the Housing Act 1988 housing associations have assumed their present 'centre stage' position in terms of new social housing provision. As the recipients of both considerable government grants for the development of new housing and of properties formerly owned by local authorities, their importance in terms of ownership and the future management of housing is now significantly greater than at any other time in their history. The potential new roles for housing associations resulting from present housing policies raises diverse possibilities for their future. Is it likely that they will eventually replace local authorities as the predominant owners and managers of social housing, or are they being used temporarily by government as vehicles for the eventual privatisation of all rented accommodation?

This chapter looks at the historical aspects of the development of housing associations. Some of these aspects have again become a feature of housing associations today. Housing associations have been used in the past by different governments to implement different policies at different times, they have been considered as either quasi-private or quasi-public organisations, depending on the emphasis of these policies. With the exception of their role in assisting local authorities to discharge their statutory responsibilities towards the homeless, the majority of housing associations are now

---

* The views expressed in this chapter are entirely personal, and do not necessarily reflect the views and policies of the Housing Corporation.

being pushed by present policies towards the private end of the public/private spectrum. The chapter therefore concludes by raising possible scenarios for housing associations in the future.

The present policy for housing associations also needs to be viewed within the context of the successive Conservative governments' overall policy of market regulation in areas which previously formed part of the welfare state. In housing, this policy has been formulated in terms of encouraging owner occupation, deregulating rents and reviving the private rented sector. These aims were encapsulated in the Housing Act 1988, one of the major pieces of housing legislation of this century. The implications of the 1988 Act for housing associations are examined in greater detail below, after some consideration is given to the nature of housing associations, who they house, and the main pieces of legislation which have affected their development.

What sorts of organisations are housing associations?

'Housing Association' is a generic term used to describe the various agencies which together form the voluntary housing movement. The movement is described as 'voluntary' because housing associations are managed by committees whose members are unpaid volunteers. In addition, some housing associations also engage volunteers to perform certain functions within the organisation.

The Housing Associations Act 1985 defines a housing association as a society, company or body of trustees which is established for the purpose of providing, constructing, improving, managing, facilitating or encouraging the construction or improvement of housing accommodation; and which does not trade for profit, or whose constitution or rules prohibit the issue of capital with interest or dividend exceeding such rate as may be determined by the Treasury, whether with or without distinction between share and loan capital. Some associations do make a profit, but surpluses must be used for housing purposes and cannot be distributed to their members.

The term 'housing association' can cover different sized organisations set up at different times, in different ways and to meet different needs, with different policies and different management styles, but which all have the above definition in common. Housing associations are each unique organisations and, whilst many share common features, they are not necessarily homogeneous entities. The changes brought about by the Housing Act 1988 will, therefore, have affected different housing associations in different ways.

In order to receive public subsidy in the form of grants, housing associations must be registered with the Housing Corporation, a non-departmental public body or quango, which channels funds to, and monitors the activities of, registered housing associations and co-operatives in England. Housing associations in Scotland and Wales are funded and monitored by similar quangos: Scottish Homes and Tai Cymru respectively. The Housing Corporation, in addition to registering housing associations as suitable organisations to receive funds and to allocating those funds to them, is also responsible for monitoring the organisation and performance of associations.

The Housing Corporation's overall aim is to support the social housing sector in England by working with housing associations and others to provide good homes for those in housing need. According to the Tenants Guarantee (Housing Corporation, 1991, p. 3) 'the essential purpose of registered housing associations is to provide accommodation for those who are inadequately housed or homeless, and for whom suitable housing is not available at prices within their means, or at all, elsewhere in the local market'.

Units owned by registered housing associations

In spite of their present importance in policy terms, housing associations only owned 3 per cent of the stock of dwellings in England in 1991 (see chapter 1). A survey of stock owned by registered housing associations in England for the year ending 31 March 1993 (Housing Associations in 1993, Housing Corporation, 1994) shows that there were 2,165 housing associations (excluding co-ownership societies) registered with the Housing Corporation in 1993. As can be seen in Table 2.1, the majority of these associations is small. The average stock of dwellings owned by registered associations is 330. It is, however, worth noting that 60 per cent only owned twenty-five homes or less, that over four-fifths of the stock was in the hands of 8 per cent of the associations with over 1,000 homes, which is of comparable size to many local authorities. The largest twelve associations owned a quarter of the total stock.

The total stock of self-contained property for rent is 714,300

Table 2.1 Distribution of housing associations and stock by size of association in England, 1993.

Size of association (homes)	No. of HAs	%	Av. stock owned	%	Stock owned (000s)
0	438	20			
1-5	276	13	3	0	0.8
6-25	583	27	13	1	7.7
26-100	459	21	52	3	23.7
101-250	131	6	151	3	19.7
251-1,000	117	5	562	9	5.6
1,001-2,500	93	4	1,520	20	141.7
2,501-10,000	56	3	4,901	39	274.4
Over 10,000	12	1	15,063	25	180.7
Total	2,165	100	330	100	714.3

Source: Housing Associations in 1993 (Table 2.2), Housing Corporation, 1994.

units. This figure has increased by 37.5 per cent in the five years since 1989, when the total housing association stock for rent stood at 519,600 units. Nearly half of these units were bedsits or one bedroom dwellings. In addition to these self-contained dwellings for rent, registered associations owned 65,900 hostel bedspaces in 1993.

Tenants of housing associations

A breakdown of housing association stock owned, by housing need for which it is used is shown in Table 2.2. General needs housing is a term applied to accommodation provided for tenants who do not require any special housing management support. The term 'special needs' is applied to the accommodation requirements of people who are deemed to have particular needs that are either not being met through ordinary housing or for whom general needs housing is inappropriate in some way (Cope, 1990, p. 221). The Housing Corporation defines special needs housing as that required by tenants who have a need for intensive and supportive housing management.

Special needs housing can be structurally different from other housing or the same; it can be self-contained or shared. It can be for people who are statutorily homeless, who also have a special need or for people who simply have a specific need for supportive housing.

Table 2.2 Housing association stock by housing need, 1993 and 1989

| | 1993 | | 1989 | |
	Stock owned (000)	%	Stock owned (000)	%
Tenants				
General needs	526.5	73.7	370.8	71.4
Elderly	176.0	24.6	144.3	27.7
Wheelchair	8.8	1.2	4.5	0.8
Special needs	3.0	0.4	N/A	
Total	714.3	100.0	519.6	100.0
Hostels				
Elderly	1.0	18.9		
Special needs	4.3	81.1		
Total	5.3	100.0	N/A	N/A
Bedspaces				
Elderly	12.1	18.4	10.9	23.3
Special needs	53.8	81.6	35.8	76.7
Total	65.9	100.0	46.7	100.0

Source: derived from Housing Associations in 1993 (Tables 3.1 and 4.1), Housing Corporation, 1994. Housing Associations in 1989 (Table 6.7), Housing Corporation, 1990.

It can require particular expertise in terms of both development and management of the special needs housing. Both these functions can either be carried out by specialist housing associations, or the special needs properties can be owned and developed by a generic housing association and subsequently managed by a voluntary agency under terms set out in a management agreement. The housing special needs groups funded by the Housing Corporation in recent years is shown in Table 2.3.

The proportion of the Housing Corporation's rental programme which is allocated to the funding of special needs housing has decreased significantly over the five years shown in Table 2.3. The issue to be addressed now within the context of Care in the Community is to what extent is the development of new housing for people with special housing needs necessary, and to what extent can existing housing resources be used together with appropriate care and support services instead of special new provision.

Table 2.3 Proportion of special needs funding by group

Group	1989/90	1990/91	1991/92	1992/93	1993/94 (estimate)
	%	%	%	%	%
People with:					
alcohol related problems	1.5	1.3	1.1	1.9	2.4
drug related problems	2.1	0.1	0.3	0.5	0.6
mental health problems	13.4	13.9	13.8	16.9	13.6
learning difficulties	14.8	11.2	11.8	12.3	14.9
physical disabilities	16.6	20.6	21.2	18.4	20.9
AIDS/HIV	0	6.6	3.8	4.6	3.0
Frail elderly	31.9	26.2	20.5	14.7	17.5
Ex-offenders	3.5	0	3.0	2.9	1.7
Refugees	2.0	6.1	7.6	6.7	6.8
Vulnerable mothers and babies	4.9	2.9	3.3	7.7	4.5
Women's aid	1.6	3.0	3.0	2.2	4.4
Young people at risk	7.7	8.1	10.7	11.3	9.7
Total	100	100	100	100	100
Total special needs funding	£133m	£58m	£175m	£165m	£130m
% of rental programme	18.0%	11.3%	13.0%	11.0%	10.4%

Source: Housing Corporation Annual Allocation Statements.

Management of registered housing associations

The governing body of most housing associations is the Committee of Management. The Committee comprises between seven and fifteen unpaid volunteers who are elected by the members of the association. Up to five additional Committee members can be co-opted to provide particular skills or representation to the Committee, but they do not have voting rights. An NFHA survey into housing association membership carried out in 1985 (Cope 1990, p. 45) found that:

• there were 130,000 shareholding members throughout the housing association movement;
• two-thirds of associations had less than fifty members;
• only four associations had more than 1,000 members; and
• elections were only necessary, because nominations for the Man-

agement Committee exceeded the number of vacancies, in 7 per cent of associations.

Cope (1990, p. 44) notes that the management of a housing association stems from the policies and decisions taken by the committee of management. The committee is legally responsible for the activities of the association, and it is therefore essential that it exerts full control to ensure that the association is both effective and accountable to tenants and the local community.

The roles of the committee are therefore those of promoter of the association, policy maker, monitor of progress and performance, custodian of funds, landlord and employer. The committee can set up sub-committees to share the workload that it undertakes. Sub-committees can be structured according to function, for example, finance, development, management; or they can reflect the organisational structure and geographical spread of the association.

The details of housing management functions of housing associations are to a large extent similar to those of local authorities although, in most cases, carried out on a much smaller scale. Like local authorities, these functions can either be carried out from a central location or from decentralised offices, by members of staff who are either generic of specialists, or by a combination of these options, for example, some generic staff in decentralised offices, and certain functions carried out in a central office by specialists.

Historical development and the changing role of housing associations

Housing associations have performed different functions within the context of overall housing provision, depending on the different factors and policies operating at the time. The housing association movement can trace its roots back to the almshouses of the twelfth century. Their charitable basis was again a reason for further development in the nineteenth century when many of the housing trusts were set up as a result of endowments from rich benefactors such as George Peabody, Edward Cecil Guinness and Samuel Lewis. These philanthropists responded to the housing needs of the working classes living in the appalling conditions of the new expanding towns of the Industrial Revolution. At the same time organisations which became known as 'philanthropy at five per cent' were set up to provide both labourers with housing and their investors with a limited return. This initiative was intended to demonstrate that private capital could solve the housing problems without the need to resort to the possibility of direct state intervention.

Both these types of organisation, however, failed to provide housing for the very poor because rents were set at levels to either maintain standards by avoiding overcrowding in the case of the trusts, or to provide a 5 per cent return on investment in the case of the philanthropic organisations. The basis of early housing association development was therefore that private investment had a role to play in financing the development of housing for rent, albeit that the rents on the accommodation produced were too high for those on low incomes. In addition to these early problems of affordability, the quantity of housing produced by the associations was relatively small in relation to housing need at the time. These two issues are again very much alive for the housing association movement today.

By 1919 it had become clear that housing subsidised by the state would be necessary to house those who could not afford accommodation provided by housing trusts and who still lived in overcrowded private rented accommodation. Government intervention in social issues had arrived on the political agenda. The period between 1919 and 1960 was one of general consensus on the significant role of public sector housing. The emphasis of Labour government policy during this period was the provision of housing for rent through the creation of new homes owned by the local state, or the municipalisation of existing homes. There was therefore no significant role for housing associations, although traditional philanthropic housing trusts were able to receive subsidies through local authorities to continue housing the poor.

In the 1960s and 1970s, however, conditions again favoured the development of housing associations. The Housing Act 1957 introduced by the Conservative government had deregulated rents in the private sector which resulted in a period of tenant harassment and high rents known as 'Rachmanism' after the infamous landlord. At the same time, the popularity of many local authorities as landlords had declined because of the effects of large scale slum clearance programmes – the breakup of communities and the development of inhospitable high rise dwellings. The problems arising from these effects were aggravated by the insensitive and bureaucratic management style of many local authorities (see chapter 1). These developments in the public sector reduced the popularity that it had previously enjoyed as an alternative to the private rented sector. Housing associations were consequently used by governments to alleviate the problems being experienced in both sectors. In addition, external factors contributed to housing problems at this time. The 1960s also saw the 'rediscovery' of poverty, the deterioration in the inner cities and a growing recognition of the consequent homelessness. Shelter, the housing charity which emerged in the late 1960s, assessed the need for provision in a number of cities, of homes for those on low incomes. They sought to promote housing associations, often with church connections. These could secure loans from local authorities to upgrade unfit houses and bring them back into use as secure rented accommodation for the homeless and those on low incomes. The development of housing associations during the 1960s and 1970s was encouraged by the following legislation.

Housing Act 1961

This Act introduced by a Conservative government, made £25m available for the provision of loans to non-profit making housing associations to provide new housing for letting at cost rents. This fund was introduced to compensate for the decline of private renting and to reduce the pressure for local authority acquisition of privately rented accommodation. The Act established a dual system of association provision: traditional housing trusts were to continue to receive subsidies from local authorities to house the poor, whereas the new cost rent housing societies were to house middle income earners. These societies operated on a commercial basis, except for the fact that they were non-profit making. They charged economic rents and did not allocate accommodation according to need.

Housing Act 1964

This Act, also introduced by a Conservative government, created the Housing Corporation to work with housing societies, building societies and government to provide loans for cost rent and co-ownership schemes. This form of voluntary provision, the provision of housing at cost through trust ownership, became known as the 'third arm in housing'. (Morton, 1989, p. 8). From 1964, an increasingly large share of state support for housing associations was channelled through the Housing Corporation, rather than via local authorities. In subsequent years, however, cost renting was eclipsed by co-ownership because the rising costs during the development period of the rented schemes, for which subsidy was not available, resulted in unacceptably high rents. In addition, it became difficult to continue the support for this form of housing provision when more acute housing need was being experienced elsewhere, as noted above, in the increase in homelessness.

Housing Finance Act 1972

Under this Act 'fair rents', which had been set up by the Rent Act 1965 for the private sector, were extended to the voluntary sector. Within this rental structure housing associations had no responsibility for rent setting. Rent allowances were introduced for housing association tenants in line with local authority rent rebates.

The Housing Corporation was authorised to make loans to associations to provide rented housing, which would attract a revenue deficit subsidy from the government. Housing associations were thus becoming empowered as alternative providers of subsidised housing for rent. They were, however, still generally regarded as non-government housing providers at this stage, developing housing for the most part by means of loans rather than subsidies. During this period the development of co-ownership projects declined for similar reasons as the demise of cost renting: steep rises in land prices, construction costs and interest rates.

Housing association activities still remained distant from those of local authorities, albeit that they became key players in the urban renewal programmes of the 1960s and 1970s. Rogerson (1988, p.7) notes that association activity was concentrated in areas of urban stress where little other investment was taking place. It provided a catalyst for the shift in government urban policy in the late 1960s and early 1970s from comprehensive redevelopment to retention and rehabilitation.

Housing Act 1974

This Act introduced the system of deficit funding – Housing Association Grant (HAG) – which provided the basis of the enormous subsequent growth in the role and output of housing associations which were registered with the Housing Corporation. The Corporation was also given powers to require compliance with procedures, the submission of accounts in a particular format, powers to restrict the disposal of land, to investigate suspected mismanagement, malpractice or misdemeanour, and to replace committee members or to transfer property (Malpass and Murie, 1987, p. 157).

The Housing Act 1974 was introduced by a Labour government, albeit on the basis outlined by the previous Conservative administration. The Act presented a marked contrast to the Labour party's previously antagonistic attitude to housing associations during the period of their own municipalisation policies in the early 1960s. Back and Hamnett (1985, p. 402) note that this change was due to the Labour party's hopes that housing associations would:

- exert public influence, however imperfectly and unaccountably, over the improvement of privately rented stock;
- help to rehouse poor tenants occupying privately rented property;
- and so help to achieve social ownership of privately rented stock.

Housing associations were thus seen by the Labour party as an acceptable extension of the public housing sector. Whereas the unsubsidised cost rent schemes of the 1960s had been introduced by Conservative governments which had regarded housing associations only as alternative private sector landlords, prior to the introduction of HAG in 1974.

The HAG deficit funding, introduced by the 1974 Act, covered on average 85 per cent of development costs on general needs housing schemes. The rest of the development costs were financed by a mortgage, which could be viewed as a precursor to the system of private finance introduced by the Housing Act 1988. The 1974 Act also introduced a system of two discretionary revenue grants, one on an association's Property Revenue Account known as Revenue Deficit Grant (RDG), and the other to cover revenue deficits on hostels known as Hostel Deficit Grant (HDG).

Following the 1974 Act there was a period of rapid expansion of housing association activity. The Housing Corporation's programme moved from co-ownership to subsidised rental with an increasing emphasis on rehabilitation. Housing provided by housing associations, at this time and up until the Housing Act 1988, was generally complementary to local authority housing in terms of the types of development undertaken – usually small scale new build and rehabilitation as opposed to the large scale new build developments undertaken by local authorities. It was also complementary in terms of people housed – single people, couples and those with special housing needs as opposed to families with general housing needs.

In the period of housing association development up to the 1980s, key reasons for the support from governments had been, on the part of the Conservatives in 1961, to redress the decline of the private rented sector and reduce the growing power of local authorities. The Labour party, on the other hand, had used housing associations to extend the boundaries of the public sector. This difference in ideology of the two main political parties remains consistent with their policies towards housing associations in present times.

The 1980s

The Conservative government, which has been in power since 1979, has been consistently committed to considerable reductions in public expenditure and to finding market solutions to social problems. In housing terms this has been expressed in a reduced role of the state in the provision of housing, based on the belief that, because there is a national crude surplus of stock, the provision of housing falls outside the boundaries of the welfare state. This has led to overall reductions in public subsidy for social housing and the expectation that private investment will step into the funding vacuum so created. Incentives have been made available to increase owner occupation, for example, Right To Buy and Low Cost Home Ownership.

The reduction in total public sector subsidy since the late 1970s is illustrated by the reduction in housebuilding completions shown in Table 2.4 below. This table also highlights the relative protection afforded to housing associations during this period, as opposed to the considerable reductions suffered by local authorities well in advance of the Housing Act 1988. The main legislation in the 1980s affecting housing associations in outlined in the following paragraphs.

Housing Act 1980

This Act introduced the Right to Buy for tenants of non-charitable housing associations, extended the powers of housing associations to carry out low-cost home ownership schemes known as shared ownership, improvement for sale schemes and leasehold schemes for

Table 2.4 Housebuilding completions by sector

	1976	1981	1986	1991
Housing associations	14,618	17,363	11,055	17,603
Local authorities and new towns	124,512	58,413	20,575	8,569
Sub-total	139,130	75,776	31,630	26,172
Private enterprise	138,477	104,001	155,557	132,291

Source: Social Trends 23, 1993 (Table 8.5, p. 115) Central Statistical Office.

the elderly; and set up a secure form of tenancy for public sector tenants, including housing association tenants, with additional rights known as 'the tenants charter'.

Housing and Building Control Act 1984

Under this Act the ability to promote home ownership was extended to all housing associations by creating a new discretionary form of 'Home Ownership for Tenants of Charitable Housing Associations' (HOTCHA) through a system of discounts which could be used by tenants to purchase dwellings in the private sector. The 1980 and 1984 Acts give an indication of the government's diverse attitude to housing associations. They appear to have been viewed, on the one hand, in this context in the same light as local authorities, and therefore subject to similar measures to decrease the sector and promote home ownership through the Right to Buy and HOTCHA. The government also had, in housing associations, organisations which could, on the other hand, be used to expand home ownership through a variety of measures beyond the scope and intent of most local authorities.

Housing Act 1988

The role set out for housing associations in the Housing Act 1988 clearly confirms the government's view that they can be used to effect major social changes – as initiators, in becoming the main providers of new social housing for rent, and as catalysts, in reducing the virtual monopolistic role of local authorities in this area. The Act represents a distinct move away from the former consensus of the previous 40 years, during which local authorities were seen as the main providers of social housing for rent. The new role for local authorities was to become strategic enablers and planners, rather than providers. Measures designed to encourage a more active private rented sector were also introduced by the Act. In addition, the transfer of already developed local authority property to housing associations or private landlords was made possible through Tenants' Choice (see chapter 5) and the provisions for Housing Action Trusts (HATs).

Other reasons for the introduction of the Act were to provide greater incentives for efficiency, and to spread the amount of funding available for future housing development by attracting private finance to be mixed with HAG. This new financial framework established by the Act has resulted in increased competition for HAG amongst housing associations, which has in turn had repercussions on other aspects of social housing: the location of new developments, the types of development, contracting arrangements and construction standards. The result has been an increase in the amount of social housing provided and a reduction in the amount of grant needed per unit, a phenomenon known as 'HAG stretch'. However, the main effect of this new financial regime on the consumers of social housing has been an increase in rents charged, as a result of the combination of reduced grants and the need to service larger private loans.

Since the 1988 Act, the development of new social housing has been almost exclusively undertaken by housing associations. They have at the same time taken on aspects of private sector organisations such as competition and moves towards cost renting, thus reversing the trend of the previous two decades in which they were largely seen as extensions of the public sector in the provision of social housing.

The result of the Act for housing associations has been a major cultural change, which has affected their internal organisation and their roles as providers and managers of social housing. One of the effects of the Act has been the introduction of a quasi-market system (Le Grand, 1990) into social housing provision which is consistent with the government's aim of breaking state monopolies and of privatising services previously provided by the welfare state. Housing associations have adopted a business, rather than a voluntary, ethos in order to survive in the new 'market' for social housing.

Aspects of both the public and private sectors are now merged in housing associations, resulting in organisations which compete with one another, whilst still, in some ways, seeking to maintain a social conscience as well as responding to their new realities as a cohesive movement. This 'split personality' feature of the housing association movement has presented housing associations individually, and the movement collectively, with different challenges and different potential solutions. These developments have highlighted the tensions which already existed within the housing association movement and amongst housing associations. These tensions and contradictions in terms of the diversity of objectives, different priorities in meeting housing need and of different management styles have been brought into sharp relief in the new role for housing associations created by the Act. The responses of individual housing associations to these changes has been equally varied (Harrison, 1992).

Another consequence of the Act has been the emergence of the 'purchaser/provider' split of functions within the social housing world, in parallel with similar developments in health and social services. Local authorities could now be said to be the purchasers, through the Housing Benefit system, of accommodation provided for the statutory homeless by housing associations.

The main features of the Housing Act 1988 and their effects are summarised under the following headings:

New financial arrangements incorporating the combined features of predetermined fixed HAG, reduced HAG mixed with private finance, and the end of RDG and of HAG for major repairs for new schemes

Under these new financial arrangements, costs eligible for grant funding on housing association schemes are estimated, and the amount of HAG is determined, at the start of the scheme. The proportion of eligible scheme costs for which HAG can be paid is fixed at the level announced annually by the DoE. The remaining costs are covered by private borrowing, and the cost of this borrowing determines, together with management and maintenance costs and a contribution towards future major repairs, the level of rents to be charged.

This is the reverse of the 1974 Act system whereby HAG was calculated and paid at the end of the scheme development period on the basis of actual development costs, rather than on costs estimated before development takes place. The level of grant was calculated individually on each scheme, rather than being fixed at a predetermined level. The grant calculation was based on the 'fair rent' registered by the Rent Officer; and the size of the mortgage which this rent could service, after allowing for management and maintenance costs. Any eligible development costs which were not covered by the mortgage were then covered by the grant. Under this old system, subsidy was therefore driven by rents with grant levels as the variable in the calculation. Now, subsidy is determined by fixed grants, and rents are the variable output of the calculation.

The national average amount of HAG per scheme within the 1988 Act framework was initially reduced from 85 per cent to 75 per cent (except in the cases of special needs schemes and major repairs on pre-1988 Act schemes where the grant rate has remained at 100 per cent). The national average grant rate of 75 per cent stayed at that level for the first three years following the implementation of the Act, but was reduced to 71 per cent in 1992/93 and 67 per cent in 1993/94. The government's decision to further reduce the grant rates to an average of 62 per cent for 1994/95 was made in spite of the Parliamentary Select Committee's recommendation that grant levels be maintained at the rate of 67 per cent. The government's intention is that the average grant rate should be further reduced to 55 per cent by 1995/96.

Since the 1988 Act cost overruns during the development period which result in project costs exceeding certain limits are no longer eligible for HAG. In addition, HAG is no longer available to fund either major repairs or RDG on schemes developed under 1988 Act procedures. Associations are expected to bear additional development costs, make provision for future major repairs and cover the revenue costs of the scheme, including the interest on the private loan, through the rents.

These measures, as well as reducing the government subsidy to housing associations, are designed to make housing associations operate on a basis which is more comparable with private than with public organisations. The effect is to reduce some of the previous advantages which housing associations have had in competing with private developers and landlords for the provision of social housing. Nevertheless, private organisations still remain at a disadvantage in comparison with housing associations in that they do not currently have access to HAG.

Housing associations do not, however, have the single focus of private organisations. Since the 1988 Act they have become organisations split between their links with the private sector through their use of private finance, their ability to take on development and financial risks, and their need to assume a business ethos, on the one hand; and on the other hand, the push to take on the role of the public sector in terms of being the producers of new social housing for rent and therefore the main source of housing for the statutory homeless. In addition to this, for some associations there are the conflicts involved in trying to continue providing housing for their traditional tenant groups.

The introduction of assured tenancies, needed to complement the new financial arrangements, for new housing association tenancies

Rents on housing association accommodation developed since the implementation of the 1988 Act are expected to cover all capital, future repairs and revenue costs. The effect has been a dramatic increase in housing association rents for new developments since the abolition of the 'fair rent' system and its replacement by assured tenancies. The introduction of assured tenancies from January 1989 was an essential corollary to the mixed funding regime and fixed grant rates established in the Housing Act 1988. A crucial aspect of these tenancies is that rents are set by negotiation between the landlord and tenant. Housing associations now need this flexibility in order to assure private lenders of the security of their investment, and to be able to react to changes in grant rates. This 'rental flexibility' is a market characteristic of the basis on which associations now operate.

The abolition of 'fair rents' on new housing association developments has resulted in some housing associations operating a dual rent system for their tenants; fair rents for tenancies let before January 1989, and assured or unregulated rents for new tenancies let after January 1989. Other housing associations have managed to avoid this by pooling rents. Many of the larger housing associations have been able to offset some of the development costs, which would otherwise result in high rents, by drawing on their reserves. It is, however, unlikely that this is an option which will be available to them indefinitely, especially given the actual and forecast reduction in grant rates unless acquisition and building costs remain correspondingly low. The NFHA (Research Report 16, 1992) shows that:

- since 1988 average rents for new tenancies have increased at three times the rate they would have done under the 'fair rent' regime;

- since January 1989 average rents for new tenancies have increased two and a half times faster than the rate of general inflation;
- there has been a widening of the overall range of rents in new housing association lettings between assured rent and fair rent lettings, between smaller and larger new let units, between new lets and relets, and between regions;
- rent increases have, on average, been lower for larger associations;
- 40 per cent of associations were attempting to 'harmonise' their fair and assured rents.

The research also found that rents planned for the homes approved, but yet to be completed, in the two years studied, 1989-91, were consistently above the average 'reasonable market' rent set by the rent officer service for private tenancies in the same area. The resulting issue of affordability of housing association rents, which is examined in more detail below, has been one of the most intractable debates for the housing movement in recent years.

The transfer of development and financial risks from the state to the association

The onus is now on associations to ensure that estimated costs of development are as accurate as possible when finalising bids for funding. Any additional development costs have to be funded by cutting other costs or increasing the amount of the private loan required, and consequently increasing the resulting rents. The theory is that this system will ensure efficiency and cost effectiveness in the development process. The development risk of unforeseen costs is now borne by associations, rather than being met by HAG, as well as the new financial risks involved in raising private finance.

There is concern that the pressure to achieve value for money, measured by the Housing Corporation as unit cost, and the need to keep development costs down, to avoid cost overruns or high rents, will lead to a reduction in the physical standards of housing association developments. In terms of space standards, the NFHA (Research Report 16, 1992) notes that the average floorspace area of newly built homes in 1989/90 was about 9 per cent below the Parker Morris standard, and that average floorspace areas appear to have fallen by 10 per cent since 1987/88.

One of the effects of the increased development and financial risks for housing associations in terms of covering additional development costs is noted by the NFHA (Research Report 16, 1992) as a dramatic decline in both the number and proportion of new rehabilitation schemes – from 85 per cent of the Housing Corporation's programme in 1986 to 50 per cent in 1989, and to less than 20 per cent by 1991. The report also notes that the switch to new build schemes has been accompanied by a shift in development work out of the inner cities. The proportion of approvals in the 'Urban Programme' authorities fell from 68 per cent in 1987/88 to 43 per cent in 1990/91.

This trend is partly because of the increased competition between housing associations who consider the costs on new build, involving standard design types, easier to control. New build appears to offer more opportunities for economies of scale, and therefore reduced costs and lower rents. Such developments are more likely to take place on green field sites rather than in the inner city. This trend could, however, also be attributed to changes in local authority policies and priorities, and to the lack of a strategic framework for the development of new units through rehabilitation.

In recent years, new development has been re-established in some inner city areas through 'volume building' contracts, in which large quantities of standard design housing are negotiated between developers and consortia of housing associations to be provided on dispersed vacant sites. Wherever the new build takes place, however, there could be problems involved for housing associations in moving from their traditional development style and scale to the new styles and scales being developed as a result of the 1988 Act. Page (1993, p. 46) notes that where housing associations have produced large estates with characteristics similar to those which have caused problems for local authorities, they have tended to run into the same problems. He further notes that whereas local authority estates generally took two or three decades to reach a state of decline, housing association estates are meeting similar problems in under five years. Page presents evidence which suggests that the reasons for this are concerned with both the new estates and the populations on them.

Increased consumer choice through Housing Action Trusts and Tenants' Choice

Another way in which the 1988 Act reduced the power of local authorities as landlords was to seek to reduce their existing stock through Tenants' Choice and Housing Action Trusts (HATs). Under the Act housing associations were empowered to compete with private landlords for the transfer of local authority stock into their ownership through Tenants' Choice or into their management through HATs. In practice, since the implementation of the Act, there have been remarkably few transfers of local authority stock through either of these two routes, both of which involve considerable investments of resources in the lengthy consultation, negotiation and statutory stages (see chapter 5).

A comparatively more successful means of achieving the transfer of local authority stock has been through Large Scale Voluntary Transfers (LSVT), a process set up before the Housing Act 1988 and in which the transfer is initiated by the local authority involved. Under this scheme local authorities can transfer up to 4,000 units of stock to an existing or specially created housing association, following a ballot of tenants involved.

In all three of these means of transferring local authority stock to alternative landlords, housing associations have, to date, been the preferred option over private landlords. For as long as these means of stock transfer are available to local authorities or their tenants, it seems that they will therefore continue to contribute to the growth of the housing association sector.

Are housing associations effective as the new providers of social housing?

In the period since the implementation of the Housing Act 1988 the public profile and the internal organisation of the housing association movement has changed considerably. Any assessment of the effectiveness of housing associations has to take into account the size and diversity within the movement, the different aims and objectives, as well as the results of the split pressures on associations to perform both public sector and private sector functions. The assessment is considered below in terms of the housing needs which associations seek to satisfy, the new units produced under the post 1988 Act regime, the cost of producing the units, the outturn rents, and the management styles of associations.

Need for social housing

The growth of accommodation provided by housing associations during the twentieth century in comparison with the changes in accommodation provided by other sectors is illustrated in Table 1.1, chapter 1. The proportion of housing stock owned by housing associations in England and Wales was only significant enough to count as of the 1981 Population Census. This reflects the sizeable growth in housing association stock which took place following the introduction of HAG in 1974.

In recent years the decision on the allocation of funds for housing by the government, whether to local authorities or the Housing Corporation, is made in the context of the government's priorities of reducing public expenditure in the form of capital subsidy and of promoting home ownership, rather than on any basis of assessed need for social housing. In addition, the government's assumption is that the private sector will step into the vacuum created by the reduction in public funds for social housing. The government does not therefore expect public subsidy to necessarily cover the cost of all the demand for social housing development.

Whitehead and Kleinman (1992, p. 4) note that:

the need for additional social provision arises where households cannot gain access to, or afford acceptable standards, of private sector housing. The exact nature of that provision will depend on local conditions in the housing market and the wider economic environment. Not all such provision need involve new building. Some of these requirements can be met by subsidy to ownership or private rental on the one hand or by purchase of existing private housing by the social sector on the other.

Whitehead and Kleinman put recent estimates of additional units of social housing required in England per annum for the ten years between 1991 and 2001 onto a common basis and summarised them as follows:

1. DoE evidence to the Inquiry into British Housing, 1992:   0
   Based on a crude surplus of dwellings over households in 1981.
2. Audit Commission, 1992:   c.20,000
   This represents the difference between household growth and the expected output of dwellings in the private sector.
3. National Housing Forum, 1989
   Institute of Housing, 1990
   Audit Commission, 1992:   c.80,000
   This estimate is derived from three separate estimates using the same model, and has been harmonised to arrive at a single estimate by standardising the assumptions made. To arrive at the annual requirement for new social housing, the model takes the

net household increase and adds to it concealed households, properties which are unfit or scheduled for demolition, temporary accommodation, and a vacancy reserve and then subtracts the output of new private dwellings.

4. Bramley, 1991:   75,000–115,000
   This 'bottom up' snapshot and is calculated by taking, in local areas, the percentage of households unable to buy a dwelling, adding household formation and subtracting social sector relets to arrive at the need for additional provision locally. The local needs are added up to give regional and national needs.

5. Whitehead and Kleinman, 1992:
   (Sensitivity analysis: 53,000–141,000)   100,000
                                                                central estimate
   Kleinman and Whitehead used a 'gross flows approach' which takes gross household formation by household category, and adds the tenure propensity of each category to arrive at the demand for social housing from new households. The model also takes account of the demand from households moving from owner-occupation, private renting and in-migrants; subtracts the new social output, social relets and net private sector lettings to produce the residual demand for social housing.

The estimates produced by the various models detailed above are for social or subsidised housing, whether the subsidy is in the form of revenue or capital and whether the need is filled from new dwellings or by a more effective use of the resources already available. Since the immediate post-war period, a consensus has not been reached in housing policy terms, as to an agreed estimate of new social housing provision. Housing associations do not, therefore, have a national target for the foreseeable future of the needs which they should aim to meet in their new role as major providers of social housing. With the exception of 1992/93, (see Table 2.6) the quantity of new units of social housing produced by housing associations, however, has been relatively small compared with these estimates of need.

Units produced

The amount of the Housing Corporation's spending limit, its Annual Development Programme (ADP) is set annually by the Treasury in consultation with the Department of the Environment (DoE) as part of the government's annual expenditure round. The Housing

Corporation and the National Federation of Housing Associations (NFHA) are consulted by the DoE as to the size and content of the ADP, which also includes receipts.

While this top down process is taking place, the Corporation conducts a parallel bottom up exercise in which housing associations are invited to bid for funds for projects to be developed in the next and subsequent financial years. These bids invariably exceed the ADP limit eventually announced by the government, but nevertheless provide a guide as to the demand for development funding. During the same period, local authorities follow a similar process by submitting bids for Credit Approvals for their Housing Investment Programmes (HIPs). In recent years the DoE has moved towards merging the ADP and HIP bidding processes so as to maintain a central overview of all housing resources allocated to local authority areas.

Once the ADP is announced it is divided amongst the Housing Corporation's nine regional offices on the basis of the Housing Needs Index (HNI). Housing associations are subsequently allocated funds by the Corporation's regional offices on the basis of a combination of the following factors: the association's past performance, the value for money provided by the scheme as measured in terms of the dwelling unit cost, the priority accorded to the type of scheme in the Corporation's regional policy statement, and the priority given to the scheme by the local authority in which the scheme will be situated. The Housing Corporation's ADP is divided into:

- *schemes for rent*: new schemes, transitional schemes, housing schemes for people with special housing needs involving intensive and supportive housing management, major repairs on pre 1988 Act schemes, and Mini HAG for short life schemes; and
- *schemes for sale*: conventional (1980 Act) shared ownership sale schemes which are primarily intended for first time buyers who could not otherwise afford to buy and who thereby release the pressure on local authority or housing association accommodation for rent, Do It Yourself Shared Ownership (DIYSO) in which grants are given to tenants to arrange their own shared ownership schemes on private properties, and Tenants' Incentive Schemes (TIS) – under which grants are given to tenants to purchase properties on the open market, thereby vacating a property for rent to those who cannot consider the option of ownership.

Table 2.5 shows the breakdown by type of housing provision within the Corporation's ADP over recent years and the projected breakdown for future years.

Within the ADP between 1991 and 1994, the Housing Corporation had an annual target of capital and revenue grants to fund 3,000 new bedspaces for people with special housing needs. The capital figure for these units is included in the table above. In addition to this figure for the 3,000 units supported by Corporation revenue funding, it is estimated that the rental programme will also contain a further 1,500 units of housing for people with special needs where the level of management does not justify revenue funding. Within the above figures there is also provision for two other targeted areas of need which are not shown separately in the table but which are monitored by the Corporation: housing for the statutory homeless and rural housing.

Table 2.5 Breakdown of Housing Corporation's ADP, 1991-97

	1991/92	1992/93	1993/94	1994/95	1995/96	1996/97 (indicative)
	m	m	m	m	m	m
Housing for rent						
Rental schemes	1,394.0	1,512.0	1,414.2	1,136.2	962.2	935.1
HMP	–	591.0	–	–	–	–
HOTCHA/TIS	37.0	52.0	–	–	–	–
Major repairs	58.0	80.0	93.4	74.5	77.5	79.7
Mini HAG	7.0	10.0	12.1	19.6	19.0	18.0
Sub-total rent	1,496.0	2,245.0	1,519.7	1,230.3	1,058.7	1,032.8
% Total programme	94%	95%	83%	81%	72%	69%
Housing for sale						
Shared ownership	89.0	83.0	101.7	98.3	104.2	112.4
DIYSO	–	43.0	130.0	92.8	170.2	204.2
TIS	–	–	75.0	81.6	93.2	100.9
Sub-total sale	89.0	126.0	306.7	272.7	367.6	417.5
% total programme	6%	5%	17%	18%	25%	28%
Other expenditure	–	–	2.0	12.0	52.0	52.0
Grand total	1,585.0	2,371.0	1,828.4	1,515.0	1,478.3	1,502.3

Source: DoE Annual Report 1994, Table 3, and King in Inside Housing, Vol. 11, No. 1, January 1994.

In recent years funds have been taken out of the national ADP before it is distributed to the Housing Corporations' regions, or 'topsliced' off the ADP, to fund special government initiatives, for example, City Challenge, and the Rough Sleepers' Initiative (RSI). In the case of City Challenge, funds were allocated on the basis of local authorities chosen by the DoE. In the case of the RSI (1992 and 1993) funds were allocated to associations chosen by the Housing Corporation on the basis of their previous performance in housing development and on their ability to provide value for money, rather than as a result of a bidding process.

The tendency for large, robust associations to be selected for the development of accommodation under special initiatives, linked with the increasingly strong competition for HAG funds in the bidding process, has led to the development of partnerships and consortia of associations in an attempt to increase their strength in the selection process. This tendency mirrors to a large extent the partnerships which the government has sought to foster amongst the various housing agencies, public and private, which were previously very separate and geared only to meet the needs of one specific form of tenure. Many large scale developments are now undertaken by a partnership between a local authority, housing associations and private developers, providing a mixture of rented accommodation and social housing for sale (see chapter 7).

Many small and specialist housing associations have linked with larger associations to form development consortia in order to survive the risks of the post 1988 Act world, and to raise the necessary private finance. In some cases, more drastic action, such as a permanent merger, is required for survival. Harrison (1992, p. 21) notes that the concern of small, special needs and black and minority ethnic housing associations is that they will lose their individual identity within such arrangements; and that joint housing allocation arrangements are likely to lead to the housing of more statutory homeless people, rather than the particular groups of homeless people whose needs these associations were set up to meet. This is seen by many as a threat to the traditional diversity of the voluntary housing movement, which had been the basis of its growth before 1988.

These concerns of the small and specialist associations are in marked contrast to the reaction of many of the larger associations who are able to take on the role of housing the statutory homeless, take over the management of former local authority stock and who

Table 2.6 Housing Association approvals and completions of housing for rent, 1984-93

Year	Completions	Approvals
1983/84	20,658	16,725
1984/85	25,335	18,368
1985/86	21,329	17,099
1986/87	19,981	13,305
1987/88	18,183	16,518
1988/89	13,925	19,959
1989/90	17,728	16,198
1990/91	19,843	12,275
1991/92	25,819	38,021
1992/93	56,758	68,241

Source: Housing Corporation Annual Report 1992/93 (derived from Appendix 2).

feel confident about responding to new government initiatives. It is easier to compete within the current development and financial framework on the basis of providing general needs accommodation. Housing associations' achievement in terms of the provision of new social housing for rent in the years 1983 to 1993 is illustrated in Table 2.6.

Randolph (1993, p. 44) looks at the reasons for the low number of completions immediately after the implementation of the 1988 Act. This was principally because of unforeseen transitional difficulties experienced in changing from the pre-1988 Act procedures and funding framework to the new systems required by the 1988 Act. Nevertheless, the NFHA (Research Report 16, 1992) notes that during the years 1989/90 and 1990/91 it is estimated that the addition of private loans to HAG resulted in 4,700 more new homes than would have been produced under the pre-1988 Act framework.

In order to achieve this output housing associations have bridged the gap between the public and the private sectors by entering the business world, using their assets to borrow funds to supplement HAG. During the years 1988 to 1993 around £2.0bn of private finance has been loaned to housing associations.

The net capital for the Housing Corporation's ADP was reduced in the November 1993 budget by almost a fifth, £334m in 1994/95 and by £250m in 1995/96. This budget effectively brought to an end the 'honeymoon period' which housing associations have enjoyed in

Table 5.7 Forecast of approvals and ADP funded completions, 1993–97

	1993/94 estimate	1994/95 low	1994/95 high	1995/96 low	1995/96 high	1996/97 low	1996/97 high
Approvals							
Rent	38,900	28,500	32,900	22,400	27,200	24,100	29,500
Sale	16,200	13,900	16,500	18,500	21,900	18,800	22,200
Total	55,100	42,400	49,400	40,900	49,100	42,900	51,700
Completions							
Rent	42,800	37,600	46,000	28,700	35,100	23,800	29,200
Sale	14,800	15,000	18,000	18,000	21,200	18,200	21,400
Total	57,600	52,600	64,000	46,700	56,300	42,000	50,600

Source: King, Inside Housing, Vol. 11, No. 1, 1994.

relation to other sectors of housing and public spending since the Housing Act 1988. In spite of the reduced ADP, the Corporation remains confident that the original estimate of 150,000 completions over the three years following the budget is still possible as shown in the forecast of housing association completions and approvals up to 1996/97 given in Table 2.7.

Other changes within the Housing Corporation's development programme have been brought about as a result of government housing policy encapsulated in the November 1993 budget. One of these is a reduction from 3,000 to 2,500 in the target number of bedspaces for special needs housing which receive capital and revenue support. Another change is an increased emphasis on sale schemes which are expected to account for an increased proportion of ADP funds and unit output at the expense of funding available for rented schemes. This is illustrated in Tables 2.6 and 2.7 above. Table 2.6 shows the proportion of ADP funding for rental schemes falling from 94 per cent in 91/92 to 69 per cent in 1996/97.

Housing associations have proved themselves to be innovators in meeting housing need in recent decades. The innovation has either been generated internally within the housing association movement or has been a result of government initiatives. Examples of internally generated innovation are the supportive and semi-supportive schemes for people with special housing needs, schemes which involve the imaginative use of temporary accommodation, short life housing and housing conversions of properties with other former uses, private sector leasing, and 'Foyer' schemes, which are special residential schemes linked to training opportunities for the young single homeless. Government initiatives have largely involved housing associations in moves to promote increased home ownership, for example through shared ownership, TIS and DIYSO; or changes of tenure, for example HATs and Tenants' Choice. The government has also used housing associations as catalysts to encourage the private sector in areas of more complicated development such as the DoE's Flats Over Shops initiative.

Value for money

Value for money, if measured only in terms of grant unit costs, has increased. The average amount of HAG per unit has been stretched from £50,115 in 1989/90 to £34,078 in 1992/93, a reduction in the cost of HAG per unit of 32 per cent in four years. This has largely been achieved because of the impact of the recession on land and property prices, and building costs.

If, on the other hand, value for money were to be defined and measured using more parameters, for example, in terms of the costs to the consumer in rent levels, and to the government in Housing Benefit costs, it is less likely that the result would be similarly successful. A value for money assessment could also include some measure of the cost to the consumer, and of satisfaction gained from the product, as well as the production costs. Social housing is not a product whose value for money can be tested in the market – it is a commodity whose production is influenced by government subsidy, and whose consumers do not operate on the basis of free choices.

Rents and affordability

If the success of housing associations were to be considered in terms of providing affordable rented accommodation for those in housing need, there is some doubt as to whether associations would be deemed to have been as successful as on their development record examined above. As already noted, the price of reduced grant rates combined with commercial borrowing and HAG stretching has been the increase in housing association rents. Subsidy, formerly directed towards capital costs, was universal in that it reduced building costs and kept rents low for the benefit of all housing association tenants. The philosophy is now to target subsidy specifically at those who need it in the form of revenue assistance through Housing Benefit.

In producing properties with high rents, housing associations are faced with the following problems:

- the combination of the new levels of rents and the effects of the Housing Benefit tapers which results in people in low paid employment being caught in the 'poverty trap' of not being able to afford the new rents from their income and not being able to claim Housing Benefit either. In effect they have a choice between low paid employment with the impossibility of affording housing association accommodation, or having the accommodation but becoming unemployed in order to be able to claim Housing Benefit;
- where development costs and future rent levels have been linked to Housing Benefit levels, there is also a consequent risk that any changes in the Housing Benefit system would adversely affect the ability of some tenants to pay rents on the properties produced.

The Tenants' Guarantee (Housing Corporation, 1991) states that 'Associations are ... expected to set and maintain their rent at levels which are within the reach of those in low paid employment'. There is, however, no consensus as to what constitutes a rent level which is within the reach of, or affordable to, those in low paid employment. Research (Housing Corporation, 1992b) covering the period October 1990 to September 1991 concluded that there was no generic affordability problem. The research found that:

- at average national rents for the size of house suitable for their needs, different household types spend different proportions of their net income on rent;
- affordability (rent:income) ratios are highest for single people, with 24 per cent of them paying over 30 per cent of their income on rent;
- and much lower for families with children, 16 per cent of those with one child pay over 25 per cent of their income on rent, and none of those with three children pay over 25 per cent of their income on rent.

The Corporation research also noted that affordability patterns vary regionally, and that analyses based on mean incomes and rents can disguise the real affordability position of individual households.

The ability of housing associations to continue housing those people in priority housing need on low incomes is largely beyond the control of housing associations themselves, and depends on government decisions on the amount of capital subsidy through the level of the grant rates on new development, and on the level of the revenue subsidy available to the individual through Housing Benefit. Subsequent research (Housing Corporation, 1993b) shows the effects of poverty and unemployment traps on housing association tenants and notes that judgements about rents and affordability may need to account for the context within which housing associations work.

Conclusions from NFHA (Research Report 16, 1992), covering the period April 1989 to September 1991, have already been noted earlier in connection with rent rises associated with the 1988 Act financial regime for new developments. The NFHA research also concludes that new housing association tenants are poor by any standard of measurement. On average, in 1991, new housing association households had incomes of only 40 per cent of those of working households nationally. In addition, new housing association tenants have become poorer since 1988 when comparing their income with national earnings. Average earnings had increased by 21 per cent while household incomes for new tenants rose by only 13 per cent over the period covered by the research.

The NFHA research shows that association rent increases had risen at three times the rate of household incomes, indicating a substantial decline in affordability in the first two years of the regime. Average affordability rates for all new tenants rose steadily from 22 per cent in 1989 to 25 per cent in 1991. This research concurs with the Housing Corporation's research (1993b), showing that single adults under 25 had the highest rent:income ratios – 30 per cent in 1991. Residual incomes for tenants moving into new lets fell from £42 to £31 over the period. The proportion of new working tenants who are estimated to be eligible for housing benefit increased from 30 per cent to 45 per cent. The average weekly housing benefit paid nearly doubled from just over £4 in 1989 to just under £8 in 1991. The conclusion is that housing benefit has partially taken the strain of mixed funding and deregulated rents, but that this increased dependency on housing benefit has deepened the poverty trap (Randolph, 1993, p. 48).

It is ironic that a government committed to 'rolling back the frontiers of the state' has in fact fostered the creation of a dependency culture for housing association tenants. The NFHA (1993) notes that by 1996 typical households in this 'dependency ditch' would need 66 per cent more net income in order to escape from the ditch. This issue is, however, greater than that of financial arrangements for housing development alone, it is linked to macro economic issues such as unemployment, low pay and poverty. Without the housing benefit system or an equivalent subsidy, housing associations would be in the same position as they were at the turn of the century – providers of accommodation at rents too high for those in low paid employment.

Access to housing

The NFHA (Research Report 16, 1992) does not reveal any evidence during the two years studied of housing associations moving 'up market' in terms of the tenants who they house. It remains to be seen whether this will continue to be the case as grant rates fall further. Housing associations have, in general, therefore been successful so far in continuing to house the people who have traditionally been their tenants. There is however concern that certain groups of traditional housing association tenants, the single homeless and people with special housing needs are becoming increasingly vulnerable in terms of access to housing in the post-Housing Act 1988 world.

Single adults are not recognised as a statutory priority for housing unless they are 'vulnerable' under the homeless legislation. Harrison (1992, p. 51) highlights the cultural specificity of homelessness and notes that the homelessness of single people is treated with less priority than the homelessness of families because of the centrality and primacy of the nuclear family which underpins all welfare, including homeless, legislation.

The aim of community care is to house people who are becoming frail, or who have mental health problems or learning difficulties in their own homes for as long as possible, supported by a range of health care and social services, thus avoiding the need for residential or institutional care. More recently community care has been associated with the closure of long stay hospitals through the government's 'Care in the Community' initiative launched in 1991. Both the broad policy and the initiative have given cause for concern due to the lack of housing opportunities for those leaving institutions and the shortage of community based care and support services. Housing associations, as the main providers of new social housing, are likely to feel the pressure of increased demand for special needs housing because of the expectations raised by Care in the Community legislation.

Although this legislation was implemented on 1 April 1993, there is a lack of inter-agency planning for the implementation of the legislation and confusion persists in the voluntary housing movement as to where the responsibility now lies for funding of certain projects which are covered by the legislation. Amidst this confusion, the proportion of the Housing Corporation's ADP allocated to providing housing for people with special needs fell from 18 per cent in 1988/89 to 10.4 per cent in 1993/94, as illustrated in Table 2.3.

Research into the need for social housing noted above has not, to date, gone into the level of detail which would identify and quantify special housing needs. This has now become a necessary and overdue adjunct to the ideals embodied in the Community Care legislation. The fact that this has not already taken place is, however, consistent with the government's reliance on market mechanisms to resolve social problems. It remains to be seen whether the market can respond to the demand for social housing in general, and to special housing needs in particular.

Because the demand for all housing association accommodation for rent far exceeds the supply, allocation policies and selection procedures for new tenants must be concerned with eligibility for housing and deciding on priorities for those who are eligible. Section 106 of the Housing Act 1985 requires all associations to publicise their allocations policies including the rules which determine priority between applicants.

In the absence of a system of common waiting lists administered on behalf of all housing agencies operating within a defined geographical area, housing associations liaise with local housing authorities, social services, health authorities and voluntary agencies in order to reach a decisions on priorities. Housing associations in receipt of public funds for development are required to offer nomination rights of 50 per cent of lettings on the accommodation so provided to local authorities. In addition, Section 72 of the Housing Act 1985 requires housing associations to assist local authorities in meeting the needs of the statutory homeless, and to honour nomination agreements with local authorities.

Nomination agreements between housing associations and local authorities are often the only means whereby local authorities can house the statutory homeless. Some local authorities have sought to increase the proportion of their nomination rights with housing associations in return for disposing of land to associations for development below market value or at nil cost, or for providing HAG for new housing development.

There is a tension between local authorities, who still retain the statutory responsibility for housing priority homeless households but not the means, and housing associations who now have some of the means but not necessarily the appropriate stock or the tradition of using their dwellings almost exclusively for the statutory homeless. Before the rise in homelessness and the decrease in housing resources which has taken place over the last decade, the allocation of their dwellings was very much considered to be the internal affair of housing associations. Their provision was considered complementary to that of local authorities, and they therefore provided a safety net for those who could not obtain private or public sector accommodation. As associations now take on more of the statutory homeless there is concern that the safety net has been removed, leaving the streets as the only option for many people who they would formerly have been able to house.

Ownership, management and accountability

The only research undertaken to date which offers some comparisons between local authorities' and housing associations' effectiveness as managers of social housing (McLennan, 1989) concludes overall that housing associations are regarded as slightly more effective than local authorities, but incur higher costs. The report also concludes that local authorities, however, perform better than housing associations with respect to economy and efficiency. The myth of local authorities as remote, customer insensitive and expensive organisations with poorly trained and demoralised staff as against housing associations being effective, caring, and involved with tenants is challenged by the findings of the report. In addition, the traditional explanations in terms of local authorities operating with poor stock and among poor households are shown to apply equally to housing associations.

Page (1993) notes that the direction in which new housing association development has been pushed since the Housing Act 1988 will result in housing associations becoming the owners and managers of large estates. He further notes:

The language of associations illustrates the change: 'sensitive' solutions are a thing of the past, the challenge now is to maximise the numbers and minimise the price. Although the scale is different, the 'numbers game' which led directly to the housing disasters of the sixties is being played again, this time by housing associations instead of councils.

A snapshot of housing associations in 1993 (Housing Corporation, 1994) shows that:

- the proportion of homes vacant and available for letting fell from 2 per cent in 1981 to 0.9 per cent in 1993;
- the proportion of homes vacant but not available for letting fell from 5 per cent in 1981 to 1.5 per cent in 1993;
- in developing associations with 250 or more homes: on average 99 per cent of rent due was collected; 90 per cent of repairs were completed within target.

The effectiveness of housing associations as owners and managers of social housing is also linked to their accountability or lack of it. Housing associations are managed by Committees of members who, at best, are elected by the membership of the association. The results of the NFHA research quoted above, indicate that in the vast majority of cases the members are appointed unopposed.

The accountability of housing associations is spread across the following areas:

- Housing associations which are in receipt of public funds are registered with the Housing Corporation, which ensures that they are appropriate bodies to receive public funding, and which funds and regulates the activities of associations within the parameters set out by government. Housing associations are therefore accountable to Parliament, through the Housing Corporation, for the public funding which they receive in the form of grants, and for their performance in terms of government policies.
- The Housing Corporation is in turn regulated by the Department of the Environment, and its accounts and annual report are presented to Parliament by the Secretary of State. The members of the Housing Corporation's Board or Executive Committee are appointed by the Secretary of State.
- One of the key areas of housing association accountability has centred on the area of tenant involvement and participation. In response to criticisms of unaccountability, some associations have

sought to involve tenants more in recent years, either by increasing information to tenants, or consulting and negotiating with them, or involving them in decision making. The Tenants' Charter sets out the management targets for secure or fair rent tenants, whereas the Tenants' Guarantee sets out the guidelines for assured tenants.

The Performance Criteria for Housing Associations (Housing Corporation, 1992a) states that associations need to demonstrate accountability for their service to tenants and prospective tenants by providing them with full and clear information about their tenancy, consulting with tenants, obtaining feedback in effective and structured ways, encouraging and enabling tenants to influence the association's policy and practice, and to take part in decision making processes, conducting their affairs openly and by publicising and effectively operating a complaints procedure.

• Associations are also accountable to the institutions which lend them the private finance to develop new housing schemes. These institutions have a major interest in ensuring the financial viability of associations and the security of their investment. It is possible in the future that these organisations might wish to have a greater say as to who is housed in developments which they have funded so that they can ensure that the level of rental income is sufficient to repay their loans.

• Finally, housing associations are accountable to their staff in terms of complying with employment legislation and codes of practice. In respect of their roles as employers and landlords, associations are expected to demonstrate good practice in the promotion of equal opportunities and race equality.

Discussions on accountability usually focus on public sector organisations. Housing associations are, however, privately constituted and managed bodies and yet they receive considerable public funds and are under pressure to satisfy public housing priorities in terms of housing the statutory homeless. In comparison with local authorities, housing associations as public sector organisations are centrally controlled and can be considered democratically unaccountable at a local level. If, however, housing associations are considered as mainly private sector organisations, then the different ways in which they are accountable, as described above, far exceed the expectations of accountability in other private sector organisations. In effect, the fact that they are a mixture of both sectors, is inevitably reflected in the standards of accountability which they achieve.

Relationships with central government

The measures on which associations are judged successful or otherwise are all controlled to some extent by central government. To the extent that housing associations are dependent on central government grants, the Housing Corporation and housing associations are agents of central government in carrying out the housing policies which the government wishes to see implemented swiftly and effectively. Whether the government initiatives take the housing association movement in the direction in which it wishes to go is no longer a consideration. The NFHA puts forward strong arguments against many of the directions of present government policy, for example, on grant rates reductions, affordability and reduced funding for rental schemes, but at the end of the day the housing associations depend on government grants to survive. The government controls the purse strings, they call the tune and associations have to dance. Since the Housing Act 1988 many housing associations have proved themselves capable of speedily and willingly taking on the new role required of them.

The blueprint for government housing policy is the contents of the Housing Act 1988. The framework proposed in the Act is now set up and is working well in the government's terms. Some of the vacuums in housing policy, not addressed by the contents of the 1988 Act, have been filled by either government, Housing Corporation or housing association initiatives or innovations. These innovations have had the effect of incremental changes to policy, so subtle that they are only recognisable as policy changes in retrospect or once they become established practice. Cases in point are the annual reduction of HAG rates, the innovation of volume building to further reduce HAG per unit, and the Housing Market Package (HMP), examined below, in which associations were chosen to perform rather than being selected on the basis of competitive bids.

The experience of the HMP demonstrated that central government has, in many of the larger housing associations, organisations which are willing to respond to the challenges of government initiatives put to them. The HMP was a result of the Autumn Statement 1992 in which Housing Corporation funds were brought forward from future years to enable housing associations to purchase properties on the open market to provide accommodation for rent. The purpose of this initiative was both an attempt to solve the generic problem of empty stock in the private sector whilst demand was high in the public sector, and to 'kick start' the housing market, resulting in an upturn in the economy as a whole. A total of £577m had to be spent in four months, 81 housing associations were chosen to be involved and 18,430 vacant homes were purchased, 2,400 more than the original target. Nevertheless, the initiative was not sufficient to achieve its macro-economic objectives.

Central government's use of housing associations for this sort of initiative is far more effective than trying to use local authorities. The government has direct control over the associations through the Housing Corporation, and its plans are not therefore frustrated by potentially conflicting agendas at the local political level. In addition, the selection of housing associations increases the competition between them, and therefore in the government's terms, the efficiency of the providers.

Conclusions and issues for the future

Housing associations, throughout their development, have straddled the spectrum of public–private housing provision, at different times appearing to be either quasi-private or quasi-public organisations. The combination of the Housing Act 1988 and the present homelessness crisis has forced associations to face towards each end of this public–private spectrum at the same time. Associations now seem to be pulled in opposite directions. Their existence as private sector organisations has been emphasised with the need to compete for funding and to raise private finance, but, as the providers of new social housing, there is new pressure on them to house the statutory homeless.

The legislation which has affected housing associations during the 1980s has been marked by the government's ambivalence towards them. At times they have been subject to similar privatising legislation as local authorities, for example, Right To Buy and cash incentive schemes. Subsequently they were encouraged to take over the previous roles of local authorities, and they are now being steered towards adopting more of the characteristics of private sector organisations. These various directions are not as mutually exclusive as they might at first appear to be, but indicate a progressive use of housing associations as agents for the privatisation of socially rented accommodation.

Unlike the situation in the Health Service where trusts have had to be created in order to implement the government's policy of privatisation, the same policy direction in terms of housing has been facilitated by the fact that the trusts or associations were already set up. The government has been able to use housing associations, which were already established as credible housing providers, to implement the 1988 Act and the policies which stem from it.

Housing associations as replacements for local authorities

Local authorities' role as strategic enablers, when viewed in conjunction with provisions for Compulsory Competitive Tendering (CCT) (see chapter 6), is potentially that of purchaser of housing rental services. Some housing associations are likely to play a key part in taking over the management of local authority stock under CCT. How the associations involved then perform as housing managers will reflect on the reputation of the housing association movement as a whole. The potential growth of housing associations under CCT is in addition to their growth by other means: as developers, through LSVT and Tenants' Choice.

Some housing associations are now the same size, if not larger than, some local authorities. There is a danger, as capital grants and revenue subsidies are reduced, that housing associations will eventually encounter the same underfunding problems which have confronted many local authorities since 1979. Housing association development has changed in emphasis from rehabilitation to new build, some of this on large estates. Page (1993) notes that there are lessons for housing associations to learn from the local authority experiences, and that the development of new homes is not just about providing dwellings but also about ensuring the conditions for communities to flourish. The geographical spread of housing association property, often to a considerably greater extent than the boundaries of a local authority, would result in new dimensions to the problems previously experienced by local authorities. If this scenario were to be developed further, it is possible that housing associations will eventually be subject to measures which would diminish their power as owners and managers of social housing in the same way as local authorities have been.

Subsidies: future directions

The reductions in HAG within the framework introduced by the Housing Act 1988, although partly effected to reflect low interest rates as well as the depressed land prices and construction costs of the recession, have moved housing associations towards the provision of cost rented accommodation. The government has stated clearly that grant rates will be further reduced in the foreseeable future. It is not clear whether this is a planned policy trend to phase out subsidy in line with government policy to reduce public expenditure and so move housing associations closer to the private sector. The test would be whether the grant rates would be correspondingly increased to reflect rises in interest rates, land prices and building costs should these occur again as in the early 1970s.

The recent move towards an emphasis in the proportion of the Housing Corporation's programme allocated to schemes for sale, as noted above, is also a return to the type of housing association provision of some decades ago. This is in line with the government's policy priority of home ownership, but is in contradiction with their policy of housing associations now being the main providers of social housing for rent, especially within the context of reduced overall resources. Is it therefore possible that the policy pendulum will swing back again so that in future the role of local authorities or other similar bodies will be revived to supply affordable housing because housing associations will not able to provide enough accommodation at low enough rents, as happened in 1919?

Such a scenario does not seem likely in the present policy context. It seems more likely that the move towards cost or market rents in all sectors will either lead to a reduction in subsidy in sectors currently favoured in this way, or an increase in the availability of subsidy to all sectors. Section 28 of the Local Government Act 1988 gives local authorities discretionary powers to issue capital grants, at the same level as HAG, to investors in new or refurbished private housing for rent. This expenditure would of course count against an authority's Basic Credit Approval, and this perhaps partly accounts for the low take up of these discretionary powers. The possibility of subsidy, or HAG, direct to private investors has been raised for consideration. If this were to be implemented, the intensity of competition between housing associations for funds would be further increased.

Competition between housing associations has increased as they have adopted a business ethos. They not only compete for HAG, but also for private loans, local authority land, and in some cases for local authority stock. In embracing the opportunities of the brave new world after the 1988 Act, the challenge for associations is to take on the best of the new whilst still preserving the best of the old. The issue is to what extent associations will be able to become competitors with a social conscience retaining their traditions of housing those in housing need and promoting diversity of housing provision. Or, will such ideals become increasingly difficult and will their role therefore become the vehicles for the privatisation of rented housing and the landlords of the new cost renters?

The future for housing associations is unclear as they emerge in new roles as traders in the market in a commodity not entirely suited to free market transactions. During this evolution, control from the centre has therefore had to remain strong. Coleman (1992, p. 137) notes that for the first time consumption and provision of social housing for rent now reflects local costs, however buffered by subsidy, but that it is not really in the private sector at all because it is safely wrapped in a system of approvals, regulation and control. The question is whether this is the case because of the recognition that such housing, in view of its very nature, cannot be entirely privatised, or whether the market experiment in this field has not yet evolved to this extent and has not yet, therefore, become government policy.

References

Back, G. and Hamnett, C. (1985) State housing policy formation and the changing role of housing associations in Britain, *Policy and Politics*, vol. 13, no. 4.
Coleman, D. (1992) The 1987 housing policy: an enduring reform? in Birchall, J. (ed.) *Housing Policy in the 1990s*, Routledge, London.
Cope, H. (1990) *Housing Associations Policy and Practice*, Macmillan, London.
Harrison, J. (1992) *Housing Associations after the 1988 Housing Act*, Working Paper 108, SAUS publications, University of Bristol.
Housing Corporation (1989) *Housing Associations in 1988: analysis of HAR/10 returns*, London.
Housing Corporation (1990) *Homes for the Nineties: a plan for action*, London.
Housing Corporation (1991) *The Tenants' Guarantee*, London.
Housing Corporation (1992a) *Performance Criteria for Housing Associations*, London.
Housing Corporation (1992b) *The Affordability of Housing Association Rents*, London.
Housing Corporation (1993a) *Annual Report 1992/93*, London.
Housing Corporation (1993b) *The Affordability of Housing Association Rents – Second report*, London.
Housing Corporation (1994) *Housing associations in 1993: analysis of statistical information*, London.
King, D. (1994) How we made the most of losing £300m, *Inside Housing*, vol. 11, no. 1.

Le Grand, J. (1990) Quasi-markets and social policy, Studies in Decentralisation and Quasi-markets, Working Paper 1, SAUS publications, University of Bristol.

Maclennan, D. (1989) The Nature and Effectiveness of Housing Management in England, HMSO, London.

Malpass, P. and Murie, A. (1987) Housing Policy and Practice, Macmillan, London.

Morton, J. (1989) The First Twenty Five Years, Housing Corporation, London.

National Federation of Housing Associations Research Report 16, (1992) Housing Associations after the Act, Randolph, B. (ed.), NFHA, London.

National Federation of Housing Associations (1993) Leaping the Ditch of Dependency: reality or wishful thinking?, Background briefing note, NFHA, London.

Page, D. (1993) Building for Communities: a study of new housing association estates, Joseph Rowntree Foundation, York.

Randolph, B. (1993) The re-privatisation of housing associations in Malpass, P. and Means, R. (eds) Implementing Housing Policy, Open University Press, Buckingham.

Rogerson, J. (1988) Housing association rehabilitation in Wales and the transfer of risks: a case of conflicting objectives?, MBA Dissertation (unpublished), Glasgow University.

Whitehead, C. and Kleinman, M. (1992) A Review of Housing Needs Assessment, LSE Housing, London School of Economics and Political Science, Housing Corporation, London.

3

Housing co-operatives: potential unfulfilled

David Clapham and Keith Kintrea

Introduction

In 1974 local authorities were empowered to set up tenant management co-operatives (TMCs) in their own stock and the Housing Corporation was allowed to give Housing Association Grant (HAG) to par-value co-operatives. These moves, by the then Labour housing minister and co-operative enthusiast Reg Freeson, were the starting point of the slow and uneven growth of co-operatives as a form of 'social housing' in Britain, that is as an alternative to traditional forms of rented housing, such as council housing.

This chapter starts with a brief history of the co-operative sector in Britain and an overview of the sector today. The focus is then placed on 'public rented' co-operatives, that is those organisations which can be regarded as a form of 'social housing' because it is in this area where the major growth has occurred. In the next section the experience of developing co-operatives in the current policy environment is examined. This is followed by an evaluation of the impact of co-operatives, focusing on three main issues. Do they enhance resident control? Are they better housing managers? Do they help to build or retain communities?

The conclusion is that co-operatives seem to be an effective way of running public rented housing, but that their development is fraught with difficulties. Some of these are inherent in the co-operative concept, but others are determined by the policies of central government and local authorities. In the final section the prospects for the sector in the near future are reviewed and measures necessary for a stable and successful co-operative sector are outlined.

The co-operative sector

The history of the co-operative sector in Britain stretches back to the early nineteenth century when they mainly took the form of terminating building societies. These were generally formed by skilled workers who banded together to pool their savings and build houses which were then allocated to their members. Once all the members were housed the society terminated and members became owner-occupiers. When permanent building societies, along modern lines, began to be established from 1845 onwards the initial terminating model was little used.

There were a few examples of working class housing co-operatives providing housing for rent set up in the second half of the nineteenth century (Birchall, 1991) as well as a number of middle-class experiments to establish co-operative living as an alternative to individualised house-keeping for middle-class women. Pearson (1988) has identified 15 schemes in England initiated during the period 1875-1925 with many being associated with the Garden City Movement. Co-partnership societies founded from 1901 onwards also had strong links with Garden Cities with several of the earliest schemes being set up in Hampstead Garden Suburb and Letchworth. Co-partnership societies were organised on the basis of collective land ownership and joint management through an elected board. The progress of co-partnership schemes was boosted by government financial help through the Public Works Loan Board.

In the period just before the First World War co-operatives seemed poised to make a major contribution to British housing, drawing support from influential figures such as Raymond Unwin and Ebenezer Howard, and from the Liberal Party. However, co-operative ideas were never really dominant within the Labour movement which campaigned actively for state provision of housing through local councils. Therefore, although state subsidy was available for co-partnership societies in 1919, it was councils who became the major providers of 'social housing'. Co-operatives fell by the wayside partly because they could not meet the acute housing shortage quickly. This was because of their financial structure and the need to create a large number of small co-operative organisations. However, the major reason why they were not more widely adopted was their lack of political support (Clapham and Kintrea, 1992).

In the period between the wars no fresh ideas or major new schemes of co-operative housing being developed have been uncovered. No state support for co-operative housing was forthcoming until 1960 when co-ownership co-operatives were promoted by the Conservative government. Co-ownership was explicitly based on the successful co-operative sectors in Norway and Sweden (Clapham and Kintrea, 1987) in which members held an individual equity stake in part of their dwelling while the co-operative held a larger collective loan and provided a means of housing management. In Britain, co-ownership was essentially a means of bringing a form of home ownership to those who could not afford the real thing and its collective elements were never fully developed. Co-ownership ran into problems during the 1970s as downpayments became almost the equivalent of a deposit for house purchase and wrangles developed in many schemes about the value of residents' downpayments. After the Conservative government in 1980 encouraged co-ownership schemes to wind up and transform into individual owner-occupation most did so.

The present policy interest in co-operatives stems from 1974 when the Labour housing minister was Reg Freeson, a co-operative enthusiast. During the early 1970s a number of co-operatives had been set up, such as the Granby and Canning Co-operatives in Liverpool and the Holloway Tenant Co-operative in London. Freeson allowed the Housing Corporation to give Housing Association Grant (HAG) to par-value co-operatives and encouraged local authorities to set up tenant management co-operatives. Par-value co-operatives are a form of collective housing ownership; residents have no equity stake in the co-operative and pay rent under an occupation agreement. Tenant management co-operatives are a form of collective housing management. The co-operative has no ownership rights over the houses, but carries out management functions according to an agency agreement signed with the parent landlord. Freeson's encouragement was the start of an important expansion of the overall number and geographical coverage of co-operatives in Britain. Significantly, also it was the start of official support for types of housing co-operatives which were more of a substitute for traditional rented housing than any co-operatives which had hitherto been seen in Britain.

Despite this support, which was not withdrawn under the Conservative administrations of the 1980s, the co-operative sector has grown slowly and unevenly. The best picture of the structure of the sector in England and Wales in the 1980s comes from a survey in 1986/7 in which a total of 487 co-operatives of all types were identified (Table 3.1). Unfortunately, this has not been repeated, and more up-to-date information is not available. In addition, in March 1993 there were 46 housing co-operatives registered in Scotland with Scottish Homes (21 of them in Glasgow), most of which were 'Community Ownership' Schemes. (Community Ownership denotes the transfer of local authority housing to small resident-controlled agencies which include community-based housing associations as well as co-operatives.) In addition to those designated co-operatives there were also at least 16 other housing associations which could be described as Community Ownership schemes. There are no reliable figures for tenant management co-operatives in Scotland, though there appeared to be about 30 in 1993, again with a heavy concentration in Glasgow.

Most co-operatives are small compared with other forms of housing organisation. Seventy-five per cent of co-operatives in England and Wales have less than 50 units of accommodation (McCafferty and Riley, 1989). However, the largest co-operatives were tenant management co-operatives. In Scotland several of the Community Ownership co-operatives have over 400 properties. Therefore, the 'public rented' co-operatives in which we are mainly interested here are generally larger than co-operatives in general.

Table 3.1 Incidence of types of co-operative in England and Wales, 1986/87

		Nos.	%
Par-value, except short-life		166	34
Short-life		71	15
Co-ownership		132	27
Tenant management in property owned by:		101	21
local authority	41		
housing association	33		
par-value, other	27		
Secondary co-ops		17	3
Total		487	100

Source: McCafferty and Riley (1989).

There is a substantial geographical concentration of co-operatives. For example, 80 per cent of all tenant management co-operatives in England and Wales are in London, while par-value co-operatives are disproportionately found in Merseyside and the North West of England. In Scotland, the majority of co-operatives of both kinds are in Glasgow.

A number of points emerge from this brief review of the co-operative sector. First, co-operative housing in Britain has a long history but it has failed to emerge as a major sector as it has, for example, in Sweden and Norway (Clapham, Kintrea, Millar and Munro, 1985). The major reason for this is the equivocal political support it has achieved. Although co-operatives have drawn support from across the political spectrum, they have not been a major plank in the housing programme of any of the main political parties. In particular the Labour movement has not fostered co-operative housing in the way that it did in Norway and Sweden.

As a result, the progress of co-operative housing has been slow and halting and has been concentrated in particular localities such as London, Liverpool and Glasgow where political coalitions and housing market conditions have been favourable. For example, in the 1970s in London many co-ops grew out of the needs of squatters being recognised. 'Short-life co-ops' were established in older inner-city property which was brought up to a basic physical standard pending clearance or major rehabilitation. In Glasgow a pragmatic Labour local authority supported co-operatives as a way of getting rented housing stock in the city improved while averting tenant discontent in a policy which was consistent with its objectives of decentralisation and tenant involvement. A Conservative-controlled Scottish Office supported the creation of co-operatives as a way of reducing local authority involvement in housing and promoting tenure diversification when it was clear that the Right-to-Buy was making only slow progress in reducing the large concentrations of council housing in central Scotland. Tenants supported the idea primarily as a means of getting their houses improved, although some at least were also motivated by a desire to gain more control over their housing situation (Clapham, Kemp and Kintrea, 1987).

In Liverpool, the rise of co-operatives was associated with a minority Liberal administration which held power in the late 1970s and early 1980s. Co-operatives were promoted as an alternative vehicle for the renewal of nineteenth century inner-city housing and run-down council estates (Ospina, 1987; Walker, 1991). Therefore, co-operatives have grown in particular locations and specific market niches (e.g. short-life housing, renewal of public housing in Glasgow and Liverpool) where support has been available. Particular kinds of co-operative have been adopted to meet individual circumstances, for example equity-sharing co-operatives to provide a stepping-stone to owner-occupation, par-value co-operatives to renew older housing and tenant management co-operatives to manage difficult-to-let housing estates. As a result the sector is very diverse with the different kinds of co-operatives varying substantially in who they house, the stock they own or manage and in their organisational form. However, it is clear that the least successful variant has been co-operatives which also have the greatest individualist element. They have been viewed by households and policy-makers alike as an inferior form of home ownership and have been dogged by complex and uncertain financial arrangements which seem to offer little benefit to households. It is as an alternative to traditional public rented housing in the form of par-value and tenant management co-operatives that the sector has grown in the last decade and it is on these forms of co-operative that we now concentrate.

Developing co-operatives today

At first glance the current policy environment would seem to be favourable to the growth of co-operatives. The desire of the Conservative government to break up council housing and to increase residents' responsibility for their housing and the commitment of all the major political parties to decentralise housing management and develop tenant involvement seem to indicate that co-operative forms of housing ownership would be favoured. However, co-operatives are only one form of alternative housing management of several that might be promoted and there are many difficulties in setting up new co-operatives in the current legal and institutional framework. In turn, this raises doubts about the political desire to support co-operatives as chances to reform this framework have been missed.

There are some disadvantages inherent in co-operatives when compared to other forms of 'social housing'. As mentioned earlier, the co-operative sector in Britain is characterised by small, nominally independent organisations. On the whole, existing co-operatives are unwilling to expand greatly on the grounds that they will become too large to retain active involvement and contact with their membership. This means that expansion of the co-operative sector relies on new organisations continually being created. The development of a co-operative is a process which can be lengthy and complex, involving questions of short and long term finance, organisational structures, and training and support for residents. It is widely agreed that co-operatives take greater time and effort to establish than other forms of housing management, and that they require substantial help with initial development and training (DoE, 1989). Therefore, it is much more difficult to create a co-operative out of local authority housing, especially if the local authority is hostile, than for the properties to be transferred to an existing housing association. Similarly, it is easier for a local authority to transfer voluntarily all or a large part of its stock to an existing housing association or one created specially for the purpose, rather than to create a large number of small co-operatives. This means that co-operatives have not been well placed to expand by means of large scale voluntary transfers and Tenants' Choice.

The major recent opportunity for additional support for co-operatives surrounded the appointment in 1988 of a review body by the Department of the Environment to examine the existing arrangements for promoting and supporting co-operatives in England and Wales. The review was set up by the then housing minister William Waldegrave in response to concern from the co-operative movement. In particular, there was considerable concern about the position of 'secondary co-operatives' which existed to provide services to primary co-operatives, that is the bodies that own or manage co-operative housing. Secondary co-operatives perceived themselves as being in a precarious position and under threat from the Housing Corporation, a body which they mistrusted profoundly.

A major difficulty recognised by co-operative activists was that co-operatives were not subject to clear government policy, nor was there separate legislation which defined co-operatives and their powers. Instead, co-operatives had to be promoted on the back of policies that favoured housing associations and tenant participation generally, within a legal framework which was derived from several different sources, and embodied many areas of uncertainty. The

National Federation of Housing Co-operatives (NFHC) put forward proposals to create a new legislative framework for co-operatives and proposed that control of par-value co-operatives should be moved away from the Housing Corporation to a new national co-operative agency with extensive powers to support, promote and regulate them. However, the review team (made up largely of government and Housing Corporation officials) dismissed these radical suggestions. In its report *Tenants in the Lead* (DoE, 1989) the review team saw co-operatives as one of many forms of tenant involvement, none of which should be singled out for what they saw as special attention. Nevertheless, they recognised problems with the existing arrangements for the promotion of co-operatives and put forward proposals for a revised system.

The review was concerned to increase the number of promotional bodies in order to give prospective co-operative groups more choice and to widen the existing geographical coverage. In addition, it was noted that many existing groups of tenants were dependent on support from their local authority. Some local councils, such as the London Borough of Islington, actively supported co-operatives but most provided no help at all. Therefore, the review suggested a new and expanded form of financial support for new co-operatives in England which, wherever possible, was to be paid directly to potential co-operative groups rather than to the promotional agencies. The groups could then purchase the help they required in order to form a co-operative.

Financial support directly from the DoE has been made available in the form of 'Section 16' funding. In the early 1990s this has been used primarily to support tenant management co-operatives, however, it has also been made available to tenants wanting to form estate management boards (EMBs). These are said to be easier to establish than co-operatives and more suited to larger estates (Bell, Bevington and Crossley, 1990). EMBs also allow local authorities to retain a greater role than in a tenant management co-operative as the council still carries out housing management tasks. Many estates where estate management boards and tenant management co-operatives have been established have attracted capital funding from the DoE's Estate Action budget. Estate Action allows councils to spend money on physical improvements provided that tenants are involved. Spending on the promotion and development of new estate management boards and tenant management co-operatives under the Section

16 regime rose from £0.9 million in 1988/89 to £5.2 million in 1992/93. The DoE reported in mid-1993 that 64 development programmes had been completed, 50 of which were tenant management co-operatives. In addition, a further 46 organisations were at the development stage, and 98 tenants' groups were involved in feasibility studies (DoE, 1993).

The formation of par-value co-operatives in England is much more problematic, largely reflecting both the restrictions on Section 16 finance and the policies and practices of the Housing Corporation. Although some Section 16 funding can be used to explore the setting up of an organisation to take over the ownership, as well as the management of a housing estate, in practice this has happened rarely. In any case the largest tranche of Section 16 funding is specifically intended to develop tenant management co-operatives and estate management boards. Similar schemes of revenue funding have been established by the Housing Corporation for existing housing association tenants and for unregistered groups. However, the establishment of par-value co-operatives in England is dependent on the Housing Corporation's willingness to register new co-operatives and to provide capital finance and all the signs are that the Housing Corporation does not support the growth of co-operatives.

Following *Tenants in the Lead* (DoE, 1988) housing co-operatives were conflated within the Corporation with tenant participation more generally and clear policy was lacking. After a three-year wait since its first public draft the *Housing Co-operative Strategy* (Housing Corporation, 1993) was published. The chief element of this was to pass the burden of identifying a role for co-operatives and setting targets for capital spending to each of its nine regions. Prior to this, changes to registration criteria for new housing associations served to disadvantage co-operatives. The Corporation requires the management committees of new housing associations to be 'capable of continuing proper stewardship of social rented housing' (Housing Corporation 1991, p. 6). This means that registration usually depends on a demonstration of experience and knowledge by committee members. For residents' groups wishing to set up a co-operative this is made more difficult than for the professionals who typically make up the committee of associations created out of large scale voluntary transfer.

The development of new ownership co-operatives in England from any source is hindered also by the present weaknesses in the network of development and support agencies. In particular, secondary co-operatives, which have played a key role since the 1970s in promoting new par-value co-operatives, have been fraught with financial and managerial problems (Ospina, 1987). They have tended to be small, operating within one city or region, and their geographical spread throughout Britain has been very uneven. There is no doubt that the lack of a comprehensive network of appropriate service agencies has been a major factor in the slow and uneven growth of co-operative housing in England over the last 20 years (Duncan, 1991).

Secondary co-operatives have also suffered from a disjointed and poorly resourced funding system. In general, promotional work with new co-operatives in the early and mid-1980s was under-funded, and development work was ragged, resulting in an uneven flow of income from development allowances. The main income of secondaries was earned through the direct provision of services to primary co-operatives and many secondaries were forced to cross-subsidise their activities by charging existing co-operatives high fees for housing development and management services in order to cover abortive and under-funded promotional and feasibility work. This resulted in poor value-for-money for existing primary co-operatives and an insecure financial position for many secondaries.

The Housing Corporation has attempted to deal with the weakness of support agencies in a number of ways. Existing secondaries are being encouraged to develop a property base, either by merging with, or taking over an existing housing association or by taking over properties owned by the primary co-operatives. The objective is to secure the finances of secondary co-operatives by obtaining an asset base and a regular and secure income from rent. However, while some secondaries have changed and are surviving many others have gone out of business.

The channelling of start-up funds (such as Section 16) through tenants' groups is intended to create a more contractual and business-like arrangement between primary groups and secondaries, thus ending the old practice of cross-subsidisation. The new arrangement is also intended to widen the range of agencies providing support with some housing associations, private consultancies, the Priority Estates Project and the Tenant Participation Advisory Service being encouraged to promote and develop co-operatives. To some extent, this policy has been successful and the number of agencies approved to deliver training under Section 16 has risen from 18 in 1989 to 30 in 1993. However co-operative groups representing ownership co-operatives continue to complain about the lack of support agencies sensitive to their needs (Confederation of Co-operative Housing, 1993), and the geographical coverage of agencies in Britain remains very uneven, with an over-concentration in the London area.

The establishment of new par-value co-operatives has also been hampered in England by the new financial regime introduced for housing associations by the government in 1989. For a full account of this see chapter 2. The main features of the changes were reductions in the average level of Housing Association Grant (HAG) for capital works and the requirement that associations raise a proportion of capital costs in the form of loans from private sector financial institutions. The procedure for setting rents was also changed with loan repayments and expenditure on management and maintenance having to be met wholly from rents. Thus, associations must bear the risk of rental payments being insufficient to balance expenditure.

This financial regime is not to the advantage of co-operatives for several reasons, many relating to their size. First, most co-operatives are small and relatively young. Therefore, they have few assets to back up private borrowing. Second, their small size means that co-operatives have only a very restricted capacity to meet unexpected costs out of rental income. Third, small co-operatives are unable to benefit from economies of scale in management and maintenance compared to large associations. Fourth, co-operatives may have a problem in convincing private financial institutions that they have the expertise to carry out development at an acceptable level of financial risk.

Co-operatives have attempted to cope with the new financial regime in a number of ways. Some have concluded development agreements with larger housing associations, essentially asking them to carry out new housing development on behalf of the co-operative. In this way, co-operatives can tap into private funding. An alternative approach is for co-operatives to enter into a consortium with one or more other associations in order to share expertise and risk.

In England in the early 1990s, the new financial regime and the policies of the Housing Corporation have resulted in a substantial fall in the formation of new co-operatives. In 1988/89 18 new par-value co-operatives were registered; by 1991/92 this had fallen to three. In 1989/90 when the old regime was still operating HAG-funding for co-operatives stood at £48.5m, equivalent to almost 16 per cent of the Corporation's spending on rental housing. Three years later in 1991/92, HAG funding for co-ops was just over 2 per cent of the expenditure programme (229 houses). Recent years have seen a small expansion in the number of units, but little increase in co-operatives' share of the programme. The most recent outturn figures indicate an expenditure of £27.2m in 1992/93 on nearly 600 units, representing under 2 per cent of the programme, while projections for 1993/94 indicate the Corporation will spend £32.6m, representing 2.7 per cent of the rental programme.

The difficulties of setting up a co-operative out of local authority housing is unlikely to be eased substantially by the introduction of the Right to Manage. From April 1994 groups of tenants have been given for the first time the right to set up a tenant management organisation (TMO) (see Scott et al., 1994). The term TMO embraces both TMCs and EMBs, and is now the DoE's preferred description of tenant-led organisation for housing management in local authority estates. The term TMO itself could be taken as an indication of the withdrawal of support for the idea of co-operatives by government. However, since April 1994 new TMOs have not been permitted to rely on local authority staff to deliver housing services; instead they must be independent organisations which make their own arrangements for staffing. On one hand, this strengthens the potential control of tenants; but on the other the requirement to take over staffing makes the establishment of a TMO a more formidable task than setting up an estate management board.

The Right to Manage means that providing that they conform to certain constitutional requirements, tenants groups can serve a Right to Manage notice on their local authority. This triggers a study examining the feasibility of a TMO. If this results in a positive vote by tenants, a TMO development programme can start. The development programme is designed to train the tenants' group in the skills and knowledge needed to run a TMO. Provided a majority of tenants agree and the tenants' group can show that it is competent the local authority must enter into a management agreement with the tenants and a TMO can be established.

In principle, then, tenants can now set up a TMO against the wishes of their landlord. But the creation of a TMO without the backing of the landlord is likely to be an extremely problematic undertaking for any group of tenants. It is difficult enough to develop the confidence, skills and knowledge necessary to run a TMO even with the full support of the landlord and without having to overcome the many difficulties which a hostile landlord could place in its way. Therefore, it is unlikely that the Right to Manage will provide much more of a stimulus to the creation of co-operatives when local authorities are unwilling to support them. However, because TMOs are exempt from CCT it may be that an increasing number of local authorities find them a palatable alternative.

Obstacles to establishing co-operatives can be overcome with appropriate political support, as the experience in Scotland shows. In contrast to England, in Scotland the major growth in the 1980s and 1990s has been in par-value co-operatives created through the Community Ownership programme. The programme grew out of attempts by Glasgow District Council to use funding earmarked for spending on private sector housing on upgrading its own stock. It devised the strategy of forming par-value co-operatives to tap into this finance whilst achieving the Council's objectives of decentralising housing management and involving tenants in running their own housing. Although the original financial motivation has disappeared and central government has insisted that Community Ownership co-operatives should be registered with Scottish Homes and financed through HAG, the programme has grown and has been actively promoted by local authorities and Scottish Homes throughout Scotland.

Scottish Homes does not share the distrust exhibited by the Housing Corporation in England about creating par-value co-operatives directly from council housing. Also, Scottish Homes has adopted a less ambitious and more flexible approach to private finance than its English counterpart. Thus, the average level of HAG in Community Ownership schemes has been 92 per cent, which is very high in relative terms (More, 1991).

The higher priority given to the creation of ownership co-operatives in Scotland compared to England reflects different housing and political circumstances. In Scotland, Right to Buy sales have not succeeded in rapidly depleting the council sector and large scale voluntary transfers of local authority housing have made no impact so far. Tenants' Choice has been a complete non-starter and the legislation to create Housing Action Trusts does not apply in

Scotland. In consequence, central government has seen Community Ownership as a way of breaking up council housing, even if it is relatively expensive to the public purse and does not result directly in increased owner-occupation. Local authorities in the central belt of Scotland are mainly Labour-controlled, and see Community Ownership primarily as a way of gaining access to capital finance, although there is some limited commitment to the idea of co-operative housing. Tenants have adopted a similar view, being mainly attracted to Community Ownership by the prospect of having their houses improved, although the idea of exerting control over their own housing through a co-operative is attractive to some tenants, particular once they have viewed the achievements of other Community Ownership co-operatives. There is, therefore, a coalition of interests supporting Community Ownership in Scotland, although it is unlikely that it would exist if any of the other mechanisms for the dismemberment of council housing had been more successful.

In conclusion, the co-operative sector has experienced some growth in the last few years as the fortunes of council housing have declined. Nevertheless, progress has been slow, partly because of the inherent difficulties in creating co-operatives and partly because of a lack of political support, especially in England. Whereas in Scotland there has been a rapid increase in par-value co-operatives formed from council housing, in England growth has been slower and concentrated on tenant management co-operatives.

The achievements of co-operatives

The case for co-operatives is often made on ideological grounds (for example, Ward, 1974; 1985; 1990). However, if co-operatives are to flourish and grow in the current policy climate where they are in competition with other forms of 'social housing', co-operatives need to show to policymakers and to tenants that they can be effective. Here, three aspects of co-operatives are briefly examined. Do they enhance resident control? Are they better housing managers? Do they help to build or retain communities? (For a fuller review of these issues see Clapham and Kintrea, 1992.)

Do they enhance resident control?

It is easy to make the simplistic assumption that co-operatives equate with resident control, as though co-operatives exist in a political, economic and legal vacuum, and are able to act as their residents choose. In reality co-operatives are heavily constrained, in the case of tenant management co-operatives mainly by the supporting local authority or housing association, and in the case of ownership co-operatives by the Housing Corporation or its equivalents.

A tenant management co-operative is bound by the agency agreement signed with the landlord, which lays down the respective powers and obligations of the parties. The attitudes of landlords (and of tenants' groups) may vary considerably and so may the autonomy of tenant management co-operatives. For example, a landlord may insist that the co-operative adopt a particular allocation policy or use its own building workers for repairs.

Co-operatives registered with the central government quangos such as the Housing Corporation, are subject to a number of controls which cover the criteria for registration, the financing of new development and monitoring of performance. As outlined earlier, registration criteria can be used to control the kinds of organisations able to form co-operatives. The central government quangos also intervene at both a general and detailed level in development proposals. Thus, they may insist on particular small design changes or force associations to demolish and rebuild properties rather than rehabilitate existing ones.

In addition, the co-operatives' finances, organisation and structure, policies and procedures are all subject to monitoring, usually on a three year cycle. Regular guidance on these issues is given by the central government quangos and this is used as a basis of comparison during monitoring. In general, monitoring is concerned with policies and procedures rather than the quality of the service provided. The views of tenants are rarely sought.

The sanctions available to the central government quangos are potentially draconian. As a last resort they can close down a co-operative. At a less dramatic level the quangos may withhold new capital finance from a co-operative. In addition, individual committee members or even whole committees can be removed and new members appointed.

Clearly the constraints operating on co-operatives vary considerably between different co-operative forms. Par-value co-operatives have greater powers than tenant management co-operatives, where ownership is held by another body which retains an interest in the property and a corresponding level of influence over the affairs of the co-operative.

Co-operatives are clearly not autonomous agencies, but it would be equally wrong to think that they had little influence over their members' housing circumstances. Despite the efforts of some public landlords to adopt tenant participation, it is clear that co-operative members have greater formal powers than tenants in public rented housing. Even in estate management boards, which represent the most developed non-co-operative form of participation structure at an estate-based level, tenants' representatives only share responsibility with their landlord.

All types of co-operatives have substantial power and responsibility over housing management issues. For example, they can decide on appropriate repairs policies and procedures and are responsible for deciding how it should be implemented. They can decide how rents are collected and arrears recovered, and can develop an allocation policy which reflects local circumstances. They can deal with estate management issues and with the enforcement of tenancy conditions. Co-operatives have powers over the appointment of staff and consultants and over the establishment of offices and community facilities. In addition, many co-operatives have influence over the elements of any improvement and modernisation programme. All of these powers and responsibilities are constrained to a greater or lesser degree, but they give local organisations a substantial degree of influence over the management of their area.

However, this does not necessarily imply that co-operatives are run by the membership as a whole. Most co-operatives are run by an elected committee whose members spend on average nine hours per week on co-operative business (McCafferty and Riley, 1989). Most co-operatives have means of keeping their members informed about the co-operative through newsletters, public meetings, informal personal contact and so on. Some staff and committee members are severely critical of what they see as a lack of commitment from members in their co-operative. In a study of Liverpool co-operatives, Walker (1991), after reviewing the evidence of low participation by ordinary members, concludes:

such low levels of participation by the general membership ... lead one to question whether the general membership is, in fact, in control of the decision-making process.

(pp. 169-170)

These concerns largely reflect what is often perceived as a poor attendance at co-operative meetings. In the Liverpool co-operatives the average attendance at general meetings was estimated by co-operative workers to be about 35-40 per cent (Walker, 1991). In a Department of the Environment survey of 21 co-operatives in England only about 20 per cent of co-operative members were involved in activities such as organising social events, distributing information or maintaining communal areas (McCafferty and Riley, 1989). The rate of activity in Glasgow Community Ownership co-operatives was somewhat higher, although even here a third of all members did no work at all (Clapham, Kintrea and Whitefield, 1991).

Despite their lack of involvement a large majority of members are happy with their role in the co-operative. For example, in the Glasgow Community Ownership schemes 68 per cent of members were satisfied with the information they got from the co-operative and 72 per cent said that the co-operative listened to its members. In an area of council housing taken as a comparator only 17 per cent were satisfied with the information they received and only 20 per cent said that the landlord listened to its tenants (Clapham, Kintrea and Whitefield, 1991).

In summary, co-operatives are not autonomous, although they have substantial powers over important issues of housing management and sometimes housing development. But they are a far cry from an idealised picture of co-operative endeavour in which all members participate fully. Rather, co-operatives are usually run by a small number of committed members and by paid staff, with most of the members taking little part in co-operative activities. An important issue here is whether active mass involvement is the appropriate touchstone for judging co-operatives. Control can be exercised without mass involvement if members have the information to enable them to keep abreast of developments, and the formal or informal structures exist which enable them to participate if they wish to. The experience in Glasgow and the results of the DoE research show that in the vast majority of cases these conditions do exist.

Good housing managers?

Good housing management can be defined in two ways. Either it can
be defined in relation to ideas of 'good practice', or by means of
measures of effective performance. Good practice is usually concerned with management policies and processes whereas effective
performance is more concerned with the outcomes of the policies
and processes. These two elements are considered in turn.
There has been some controversy over the housing management
policies and processes employed by co-operatives. Clearly, housing
co-operatives manage housing differently from other organisations
largely because of their relatively small size and their well-developed
resident involvement. Therefore, co-operative housing management
tends to be more informal and personal than in housing associations
and local authorities (Satsangi and Clapham, 1990). This means that
procedures and policies are less likely to be written down than in
other organisations, resulting in more flexibility and less standardisation. Each case can be dealt with on its own merits. This approach
runs counter to the conventional idea of 'good practice' in housing
management which lays emphasis on standardisation, written procedures and impersonal management with the primary objective of
achieving fairness of treatment through the minimisation of personal
discretion. This approach has brought some co-operatives into
conflict with the Housing Corporation which has consistently taken
the view that co-operative housing management should be assessed
in the same way as management by other organisations.

In addition, in its evidence to the DoE Review, the Corporation
reported that 39 per cent of co-operatives in England compared to
only 19 per cent of other associations received monitoring ratings
which required follow-up action of some kind (Housing Corporation, 1988). Many of these actions stemmed from a lack of written
policies and of systematic procedures. Other criticisms included a
lack of clear aims and forward plans and no precise roles being laid
down for management committees and staff. The Corporation also
pointed to a lack of financial control in some associations.

The co-operative movement disputes the relevance of many of
these concerns and argues that the Corporation does not recognise
the differences in the way co-operatives function compared to other
housing organisations and makes no allowance for the strengths of
the co-operative way of working.

Disagreements about co-operative management policies and practices have particularly focused on the letting of vacant properties. Co-operatives are more likely to use discretionary systems of allocation in which decisions on the letting of property are based on an assessment of applicants' personal circumstances or other characteristics (Satsangi and Clapham, 1990). The Commission for Racial Equality has expressed concern about the potential for racial discrimination in co-operative allocation policies (Commission for Racial Equality, 1991).

Nevertheless, in both Glasgow and Liverpool all the co-operatives operated points schemes in accordance with the wishes of the local authority and of the Housing Corporation and Scottish Homes (Clapham, Kintrea and Whitefield, 1991; Walker, 1991). Most published the criteria for selection of new tenants. Personal elements of the process common in other co-operatives were retained and some discretion still existed. Applicants were interviewed by committee members although it is unclear what influence the interviews had on the allocations made. In most instances the main concern seemed to be to inform prospective residents about the co-operative to impress on them the obligations which membership entailed and to welcome people to the co-operative rather than to choose between different applicants. But, it is difficult to find conclusive evidence about the impact of co-operative allocation policies or about the justification for Housing Corporation criticisms. This is an area which deserves further scrutiny. However, co-operatives defend themselves by pointing to their unique character but also to their good service performance.

In relation to the second means of defining good management, there is now an increasing volume of research on the effectiveness of co-operatives compared with other landlords (for a wider review see Clapham, 1992, and Clapham and Kintrea, 1992). The most direct evidence on this issue comes from an evaluation of the first six Community Ownership schemes in Glasgow. Table 3.2 presents the results of tenant satisfaction ratings on three general indicators of performance, taken before the creation of the Community Ownership schemes in 1986/87 and afterwards in 1989. The six individual schemes were at different stages of development when the surveys were carried out. In general, the 1986/87 survey was carried out at a time when Community Ownership status had been approved, but not yet created and so the properties were still being managed by

Table 3.2 Tenants' satisfaction with housing management in community ownership schemes in 1986/87 and 1989

Location	Proportion satisfied or very satisfied with housing management 1986/87	1989	Proportion saying landlord is efficient 1986/87	1989	Proportion satisfied with speed of repair service 1986/87	1989	Proportion saying service is better than that provided by council 1989
Broomhouse	36	86	26	85	83	85	71
Calvay	19	60	22	68	35	65	51
Castlemilk East	–	78	–	73	–	77	81
Possil	27	60	24	60	17	85	66
Rosehill	25	79	28	73	34	75	61
Southdeen	34	68	34	74	15	81	61

Source: Clapham, Kintrea and Whitefield (1991).

Glasgow District Council. The exception was Broomhouse where a
repairs co-operative existed at the time of the earlier survey, thus
explaining the high satisfaction level for repairs. In Castlemilk East no
early survey was possible because the area was largely abandoned
and derelict and only a few interviews were possible. At the time of
the 1989 survey all of the Community Ownership schemes had taken
over management of the dwellings, although they were at different
stages of their development programme.

It can be seen from Table 3.2 that satisfaction ratings increased
substantially between the two dates in all areas and across all three
indicators. The overall picture of a vastly improved service is
reinforced by answers to a question designed to get residents to
make a direct comparison between the service they received in 1989
and that provided earlier by the council.

The response varied between different areas, but in all schemes a
majority said that they currently received a better service. A similar
picture emerges if housing management performance in 1989 in
the Community Ownership schemes is compared with provision by
Scottish Homes and Glasgow District Council in two other similar
areas of the city (Table 3.3). These two large landlords were
outperformed by the Community Ownership schemes and this
result could not be explained by reference to greater management
and maintenance expenditure nor by the existence of a more

Table 3.3 Effectiveness of different landlords

	Ranking of effectiveness	Ranking of context	Total repair and management cost (£)
Broomhouse	High	10	220
Castlemilk East	Medium	6	700
Possil	Medium	1	452
Southdeen	Medium	2	155
Rosehill	Low	7	142
Calvay	Low	3	373
Scottish Homes	Low	7	n/a
Glasgow District Council	Very low	4	374

Source: Clapham, Kintrea and Whitefield (1991).

difficult management task. (See Clapham, Kintrea and Whitefield, 1991.)

The picture in Glasgow is supported by research in Islington by Power (1988) and in Liverpool by Walker (1991). Therefore, the weight of the evidence points to the conclusion that, despite criticisms of the management practices and procedures of some co-operatives, in general they are more effective housing managers than other landlords such as councils or larger housing associations in that the service provided is more highly rated by those that receive it. Further, there is no evidence that the enhanced performance is associated with higher management or maintenance costs, although this is an area which needs further scrutiny because of the difficulties involved in accurately recording and comparing costs.

Building better communities?

One of the reasons that co-operatives are supported by policymakers and residents is that they will help to regenerate rundown housing areas. Thus, co-operatives are looked on to provide a mechanism for improving the physical appearance of areas, and for creating a sense of community.

The experience in Glasgow and Liverpool shows that co-operatives can be an effective mechanism for enabling residents to be involved in housing development, whether new build or modernisation. For example, in the Glasgow Community Ownership schemes, residents were involved at various levels from decisions about the overall design concept of the improvement, to the detailed specification of improvements for their own homes, including kitchen layouts, fuel types and colour schemes. Surveys indicated that the majority of residents in most schemes had been at least consulted about improvements (Clapham, Kintrea and Whitefield, 1991). On the whole, though, this involvement did not mean that the Community Ownership schemes turned out to be radically different in their design from similar local authority modernisation schemes. Usually residents are not actually conceiving their own designs, but reacting to limited choices brought to them by professionals. Nevertheless, satisfaction with houses developed by co-operatives is very high. For example, Thomas and Hedges (1988) report that 94 per cent of residents in Portland Gardens (a co-operative scheme in Liverpool) were satisfied with their houses. In the six Glasgow Community Ownership schemes 90 per cent or more of residents were satisfied with their houses after improvement (Clapham, Kintrea and Whitefield, 1991).

Co-operatives have also been successful in sustaining or recreating a sense of community and changing the attitudes of residents towards their area. For example, in the Glasgow Community Ownership schemes, the proportion of those who reported that crime was a big worry dropped in all areas after the creation of Community Ownership. The proportion of residents saying that there was a good community spirit increased dramatically (Clapham, Kintrea and Whitefield, 1991). A sense of community was generally seen in these areas as a fairly superficial neighbourhood friendliness, where people chat to each other and some socialising takes place at the local level. However, it was often also seen as a means of social control, where social networks are the basis of collective responsibility for the neighbourhood. The co-operative was seen as a means of ensuring collective responsibility and control over issues such as the upkeep of common areas and the behaviour of children and young people. It provided a focus for feelings of community.

Conclusion: the future for co-operatives

In this short review it is impossible to do justice to the evidence on the impact of housing co-operatives (for a fuller review see Clapham and Kintrea, 1992). Nevertheless, it is clear that co-operatives have made substantial achievements in involving residents in the running of their own housing; in providing an effective housing management service; and in renewing housing and providing a focus for concern about community and an instrument for dealing with neighbourhood problems. At first glance, therefore, the future for co-operatives may seem bright, but further growth is crucially dependent on central government support.

The development of co-operatives in England is fraught with difficulties, some of which are inherent in the co-operative concept, and make it difficult to take advantage of stock transfer mechanisms to form co-operatives out of existing council housing. Clearly, it is easier for local authorities to pursue voluntary transfers of the whole or large parts of their stock to a housing association rather than to invest substantial effort in creating a large number of small co-operatives. In addition, the policies of the Housing Corporation have made it virtually impossible to form new par-value co-operatives. Any further growth in England seems likely to be confined to TMOs formed with the help of Section 16 finance for setting-up costs.

In Scotland the Community Ownership programme seems set for some further growth, viewed as it is by central government as a form of second-best privatisation and by Labour local authorities as an acceptable alternative to council landlordism. But at present, the Right to Manage seems to be taken less seriously by the Scottish Office than the DoE and there is no equivalent of Section 16 funding to support would-be TMOs. Therefore, Scotland seems set to diverge substantially from England in both the rate of growth of co-operatives and their form.

If the growth of co-operatives is to be further stimulated, the difficulties involved in the development of co-operatives need to be reduced. Much could be achieved through the more generous funding of existing mechanisms such as Section 16 support for potential tenant management organisations and capital and revenue funding from the Housing Corporation and Scottish Homes. The Right to Manage arrangements in England seem to offer some hope of expanding TMOs. Other measures which were put forward by the now defunct National Federation of Housing Co-operatives include the codification and simplification of the legal provisions relating to co-operatives. The creation of specific co-operative housing legislation could help to consolidate and simplify the law and help housing agencies and residents' groups to come to grips more easily with the development of co-operatives.

The National Federation of Housing Co-operatives also pressed for a national co-operative development agency, separate from the Housing Corporation. Clearly the Housing Corporation is responsible for many of the obstacles which prospective co-operatives in England have to overcome. A separate development agency would probably increase the profile of the co-operative movement, ensure that its needs were recognised and met, and enable appropriate support to be channelled to local authorities or others setting up new co-operatives.

However, such an agency could create problems. It has been noted earlier that central government exercises considerable control over ownership co-operatives through Scottish Homes and the Housing Corporation. Whilst par-value co-operatives enable local residents to exert considerable influence over their housing circumstances, they also strengthen the hand of central government at the expense of the local authority. A national co-operative development agency would need to take notice of grassroots demands for more autonomy and create the conditions for a greater degree of resident control, as well as showing responsiveness to local needs and demands. In order to achieve this it would be better to break up any national agency into semi-autonomous regional offices able to make their own decisions about capital investment and policy. Indeed, a more satisfactory model might be to establish a series of autonomous or regionally-based co-operative development agencies on the Norwegian model which would be directly answerable to members in their home territory. Regional organisations could combine both financial viability with effective, local accountability.

These kind of measures have been suggested for some time and the failure of central government to address the issues involved reveals a political ambivalence about housing co-operatives. They have been supported by Conservative governments primarily as a means of reducing the role of local housing authorities. The latest proposals on the Right to Manage further emphasise this trend. Although housing reforms have been surrounded by a rhetoric of improved service to tenants and consumers, and greater resident involvement, these are clearly not the primary reasons for the changes. Therefore, evidence that co-operatives achieve a better and more responsive service is ignored because the role of local authorities can be most effectively reduced by large-scale transfers of stock to housing associations. Support for co-operatives has only been given where other mechanisms for large-scale transfer have met resistance or run out of steam, as in Scotland.

Nor is the weak support likely to change much if there should be a change of government. The Labour Party nationally has adopted an equivocal stance towards co-operatives based on deep-seated divisions within its ranks. Some members regard co-operatives as a form of privatisation and a betrayal of council housing. Others are more committed to co-operative housing and some see it as a superior form of tenure. National policy has been a compromise between these positions. Although in policy statements there is a nod towards co-operatives, they are given little emphasis and few firm commitments have been made to change the context within which they work.

So, despite the recent interest in housing co-operatives and the clear benefits which they can bring, their growth is likely to be constrained by the lack of political will to create a framework within which co-operatives can flourish. Nevertheless, the current slow and uneven growth of co-operatives seems set to continue, despite the difficulties involved, as co-operatives can offer clear benefits to residents, central government and local authorities.

References

Bell, T., Bevington, P. and Crossely, R. (1990) 'Estate management boards: the way forward for council tenants', Housing Review 39(4), July–August, 95-98.

Birchall, J. (1991) 'The hidden history of co-operative housing in Britain', Working Paper 15, Department of Government: Brunel University.

Clapham, D. (1992) 'The effectiveness of housing management', Social Policy and Administration 26(3), 209-225.

Clapham, D., Kemp P. and Kintrea K. (1987) 'Co-operative ownership of former council housing', Policy and Politics 15(4), 207-220.

Clapham, D. and Kintrea, K. (1987) 'Importing housing policy: housing co-operatives in Britain and Scandinavia', Housing Studies 2(3), 157-169.

Clapham, D. and Kintrea, K. (1992) Housing Co-operatives in Britain: Achievements and Prospects, Harlow: Longman.

Clapham, D., Kintrea, K., Millar, M. and Munro, M. (1985) 'Co-operative housing in Norway and Sweden', Discussion Paper No. 4, Glasgow: Centre for Housing Research.

Clapham, D., Kintrea, K. and Whitefield, L. (1991) Community Ownership in Glasgow: an Evaluation, Edinburgh: Scottish Office.

Commission for Racial Equality (1991) Achieving Racial Equality in Housing Co-ops, London: Commission for Racial Equality.

Confederation of Co-operative Housing (1993) 'Memorandum' Appendix 10 of House of Commons Environment Committee, Second Report: Housing Corporation, Vol. II Minutes of

Evidence, London: HMSO.
Department of the Environment (1989) Tenants in the Lead: The Housing Co-operatives Review, London: HMSO.
Department of the Environment (1993) Section 16: Aims and Objectives: Background, Progress, London: Department of the Environment.
Duncan, P. (1991) Co-operative Housing: Beyond Customer Care to Consumer Control, Coventry: Institute of Housing.
Housing Corporation (1988) Evidence to DoE Co-ops Review, London: Housing Corporation.
Housing Corporation (1991) Criteria for Registration of a Housing Association, London: Housing Corporation.
Housing Corporation (1993) Housing Co-operative Strategy, London: Housing Corporation.
McCafferty, P. and Riley, D. (1989) A Study of Co-operative Housing, London HMSO.
More, A. (1991) 'The new financial regime for housing associations: an initial assessment of the new funding system on housing associations and housing co-operatives activity in Scotland', Research Report No. 17, Edinburgh: Scottish Homes.
Ospina, J. (1987) Housing Ourselves, London: Hilary Shipman.
Pearson, L. (1988) The Architectural and Social History of Co-operative Living, London: Macmillan.
Power, A. (1988) Under New Management: The Experience of Thirteen Islington Tenant Management Co-operatives, London: Priority Estates Project.
Satsangi, M. and Clapham, D. (1990) Management Performance in Housing Co-operatives, London: HMSO.
Scott, S., Clark, A., Clapham, D., Goodlad, R., Kintrea, K., Parkey, H., Rodger, D. and Williams, M. (1994) The Guide to the Right to Manage, London: HMSO.
Thomas, S. and Hedges, A. (1988) 'Co-operative re-housing; the view of Portland Gardens residents', Research Memorandum No. 108, Birmingham: Centre for Urban and Regional Studies, University of Birmingham.
Walker, R. (1991) 'Housing co-operatives: paths to tenant control and resident satisfaction', Unpublished PhD Thesis, University of Reading.
Ward, C. (1974) Tenants Take Over, London: Architectural Press.
Ward, C. (1985) When We Build Again Let's Have Housing That Works, London: Pluto Press.
Ward, C. (1990) Talking Houses, London: Freedom Press.

4

The origins, evolution and impact of the Estate Action initiative

Ricardo Pinto

Introduction

The Estate Action (EA) initiative is a long-standing but relatively unresearched Department of Environment (DoE) housing scheme. When launched, it created a furore within the housing policy community because of its then mixture of far-reaching and radical objectives. This chapter seeks to demonstrate that the design of the initiative was influenced by both political and managerial considerations; that it has been criticised for being somewhat bureaucratic and inefficient, but that this has improved as the initiative has evolved over time; and concludes that it has had substantial impacts which have touched such areas as housing management style, capital finance, privatisation, central–local relations, tenant involvement and the general direction of housing policy with respect to the interplay of developments in housing management and ownership, at both the central and the local levels. The conclusion calls, with some amendment, for the continuation of the EA scheme but also highlights the major threat to the initiative posed by the recently unveiled Single Regeneration Budget.

Context: origins and aims

The initiative that was launched in 1985 contained a mixed set of criteria. On the one hand, EA was to facilitate innovation via the creation of housing co-operatives, trusts and private sector involvement in line with government housing policy and, it could be said, to facilitate the continued contraction of the council housing sector (see chapter 1). On the other hand, it was also to encourage

authorities to improve their management structures, tenant consultation procedures and help improve their estate security and environment. In other words, these were measures designed to counteract
the management difficulties faced by housing authorities and thus
improve the circumstances for council tenants living in the most
unpopular housing estates in England. This section analyses the
background which resulted in the initiative's final shape. Since there
are neither debates in parliament nor published reports on the
creation of the initiative, of necessity, this account relies on first
hand information obtained from interviews with key individuals
involved in the creation of the initiative.

Management concerns: The civil servants' priorities

When the DoE officials behind the formation of this housing scheme
were interviewed, it became clear that the principle issue which was
stressed was that of management, rather than the range of options
designed to generate the disposal of council housing stock. The EA
scheme represents the culmination of a set of DoE studies which
delved into the development of what became known as 'difficult-to-
let' estates and how best to cope with the problems which arose. One
of the key reports (Burbidge et al., 1981) was stimulated by the fact
that with the ageing of the stock, many housing authorities were
finding that large portions of their housing stock were becoming
increasingly difficult to manage, as witnessed by the fact that the
worst of such properties had to be boarded-up and even demolished.
It stressed management organisation as a key issue behind the
difficulties, rather than the simpler explanations which stressed
design or location of estates. It also noted that peripheral cottage
estates as well as high rise, inner city estates were experiencing acute
management problems. The report was important in that basically it
represented the first official recognition of the widespread existence
of such estates; provided quite a thorough explanation of the causes;
raised awareness of the problem; and made recommendations which
began to focus on the issue of management presence and style
(Burbidge et al., 1981).

An earlier DoE report had also stressed the weakness of the
management presence on the ground. Andrews (1979) spent a year
experiencing and examining the way the management functions
were carried out by housing professionals on this type of estate. The
result was a series of recommendations which proved influential in

focusing attention on the issue of estate based management. Andrews made several key points (1979):

• the key housing management functions should be controlled locally;
• housing managers should be responsible for their own area and budget;
• the housing brief should be extended and staff better trained; and
• local staff should be accessible to, and work with residents.

This gave rise to the third stage, namely the creation of Priority Estates Project (PEP) in 1979 which provided the final impetus towards more intense, localised management arrangements (see chapter 1). With the aid of DoE pump-priming funds, pilot schemes were formed throughout the country, some of which were pre-existing local management projects which local councils had already begun to experiment with. Such schemes began to spread throughout Britain and bring about major organisational changes and achieving positive results, as discussed in chapter 1. EA was the culmination of the previously mentioned DoE interest, research and experience, not least its managerial bent.

Targeting, riots and privatisation: the politicians' priorities

Until 1985, the Conservatives had failed to establish a view on public housing, other than that it ought to be sold off at discount under the Right to Buy legislation. In certain respects, as will be discussed below, the thinking behind the creation of EA served to focus and extend housing policy. Following hard on the heels of EA were to come the more radical and overtly anti-municipal housing proposals such as Tenants' Choice, Large Scale Voluntary Transfers and Housing Actions Trusts, CCT in housing management and the other transfer options.

The government's starting point in creating EA was a critique of the established council housing management arrangements and the proposal of alternative ways of managing and organising the council housing stock. It was designed to encourage housing authorities to evaluate the adequacy of their arrangements and to point out alternatives. The second Thatcher administration was keen to reach the parts which the then existing housing programmes were not reaching. In particular, it was anxious to forestall any repeat of the inner city riots which had been sparked off in run-down council

estates with high concentrations of unemployment, poverty and
sterile environments (see Scarman, 1982): 'The origins [of EA] ...
were essentially political. There was a desire by politicians for
something to be done for the inner city ... or to be seen to be doing
something' (DoE Official).

A further political motive was that ministers were concerned
because local authorities did not appear to be investing their housing
resources where it was felt, they ought properly be investing in
namely, run-down estates. The Housing Investment Programme
(HIPs) statistical returns indicated to the DoE that too little was going
towards this part of the housing stock. Therefore, given its emphasis
on targeting resources on where they were most needed (as opposed
to the blanket HIPs approach which enabled local authorities to
determine their local priorities and allocate resources accordingly),
EA was designed in such a way as to focus funds to a limited number
of authorities deemed to experience disproportionate housing
stress.

Two other factors were important. First, at this point in time,
severe pressure was operating upon the Treasury to allow local
authorities to spend more on their deteriorating housing stock. The
AMA (1983), the Audit Commission (1986) and even the DoE's
(1987) own study supported the estimate of a housing disrepair
backlog of £19bn which was accelerating at the rate of £1bn per
annum. The Treasury was forced to relent and, by sanctioning the
creation of EA, threw into reverse the important Conservative
nostrum that additional resources would not be directed at social
housing. Secondly, and in support of the argument that EA ushered
in a new phase of housing policy, the politicians sought to add to
and boost the Conservative's council housing privatisation drive:
'Ministers were sold on the idea that if estates could not be let, there
had to be other alternatives – the obvious one being disposal to
willing private sector developers' (DoE Official).

The final product: EA unveiled

In seeking to accommodate these various strands of thought, the
initiative that was finally launched in June 1985 was rather mixed in
nature. It sought to:

* develop new or relatively untried solutions to the problems facing
  run-down estates, including transfers of ownership and/or manage-

ment to management trusts, involving tenants, or to tenants' co-operatives;

- encourage authorities to adopt, where appropriate, one or more of a range of existing disposal solutions such as sales of tenanted estates to private trusts or developers and sales of empty property to developers for refurbishment for sale or rent;
- encourage authorities to improve the management and maintenance of their own estates by establishing local autonomous estate based management schemes on PEP lines;
- advise ministers of the need for new machinery, incentives or legislative change to promote the full range of solutions.

(DoE, 1985).

EA's aims were a radical departure in an age unaccustomed to Housing Action Trusts and other 'exit' options. The notion of voluntary disposal of whole or even parts of housing estates was novel and the local authority reaction was suitably vociferous. Housing authorities chose to concentrate their critique on the privatisation element and EA was projected as being entirely about transferring stock to housing association, co-operatives, trusts and private sector developers. This was certainly the main fear of the majority of authorities targeted by EA and by their representatives such as the Association of Metropolitan Authorities. The reaction was so severe that some local authorities experiencing the most severe housing disadvantage vowed never to participate despite being courted by EA.

The second main line of criticism related to the financial arrangements, namely the issue of 'topslicing' and the degree of centralisation and control exerted by this mechanism of targeting financial resources. Local authorities were furious with the fact that the initial £50m worth of EA HIPs were actually resources which were withdrawn (or top-sliced) from the mainstream HIPs allocation and then transferred to EA Central, to be disposed of on the basis of its criteria and priorities. This perceived evil is accentuated by the fact that whereas HIPs can be used by authorities as they see fit, EA HIPs can only be used in DoE-approved ways. The other initial reactions, shared by the press and the limited academic attention alike, related to the fact that this additional resource was considered paltry in relation to the identified degree of council housing disrepair (Balchin, 1989); the conviction that such a mechanism inevitably results in an unacceptable degree of centralisation; and that the government and the DoE had chosen not to consult either the authorities or their representatives in creating the scheme.

Structure and organisation

EA (or the Urban Housing Renewal Unit as it was originally known) was initially only targeted at run-down estates in 69 authorities and encouraged the following types of housing scheme:

The key ingredients are a responsive, comprehensive and *effective local management* ... including the development of tenant management cooperatives to encourage the *fullest possible tenant involvement* ... encourage local authorities to *involve the private sector* in the upgrading process, both to generate additional resources and to widen the tenure mix.

(DoE, 1986, p. 6, Emphasis Added)

The EA scheme so articulated, was intended to be of benefit to local authorities, their tenants, the private sector and the government. Since the late 1970s, councils had seen their capital allocations rapidly reduced in real terms (see Table 1.2) yet EA provided one of the few extra source of funding. Rapidly escalating resources each year provided an incentive (the EA HIPs allocation currently stands at £356m). Capital allocations would be available, but only if the bids conformed to the DoE guidelines. The initiative offered several advantages for the government, not least the fact that research had established the need for attention to be focused on problem estates; a highly visible (albeit minimalist at first) way to begin dealing with the looming backlog of disrepair; a potentially excellent vehicle to further the aim of privatisation and diversification of the public housing stock; and also the political virtue of being a good vehicle for continuing criticism of council housing management practices whilst enabling the government to demonstrate how things should be done.

In terms of the finance, although the government gained control over these schemes, it did not actually cost anything by way of grants. The EA HIPs were merely annual capital determinations by the government of how much extra local authorities could be allowed to spend in addition to the general HIPs allocations. Authorities then had to raise the actual finance in the usual way. In terms of the administration, the bids, resources and implementation of the EA initiative, a complex structure was created by the DoE which involved the formation of an in-house EA Central team, the Regional Offices and the local authorities.

It is evident from the discussion above that the EA system involves a number of different agents. The Treasury decides the housing allocation on an annual basis and requires that such resources be spent within the financial year. EA Central (based in Marsham Street) formulates policy, oversees and co-ordinates the whole process and makes final decisions on bids submitted by authorities for schemes to be funded with EA HIPs. It also leads the process of retaining or increasing EA resources, relative to competing DoE schemes. Nine DoE Regional Offices and the Merseyside Task Force, prioritise their authorities' bids for schemes seeking to utilise EA resource, liaise with local authority officers and monitor schemes. The local authorities (through departments such as housing and planning) consult tenants, generate bids, erect and implement the schemes which successfully gain EA approval. The council tenants themselves and the Tenants' Associations are expected to be fully involved and finally, the Direct Labour Offices (DLOs) or contractors undertake the building work. Additionally the private sector may be involved in partnerships to renovate properties and authorities may contact their representative associations in an effort to influence the operation of the programme.

These interactions are illustrated in the Figure 4.1. There are two stages in the application process (Forms A and B) requiring increasingly detailed information; a Quarterly Financial (C) and an Annual Assessment Form (D). This gives an indication of the degree of co-ordination, complexity and cost involved in generating EA proposals. Even if bids conform to EA criteria and receive support, the allocation must be spent before the end of the financial year or the allocation will be lost. Having set the context, the remainder of the chapter moves swiftly to discuss the existing evidence on the impact of the EA initiative.

Implementation and evolution

The initial research on the EA initiative related to the nature of the implementation of EA-funded schemes and was the result of a national postal survey of 81 local authorities in England (representing a 75 per cent response rate) which had experience of bidding for

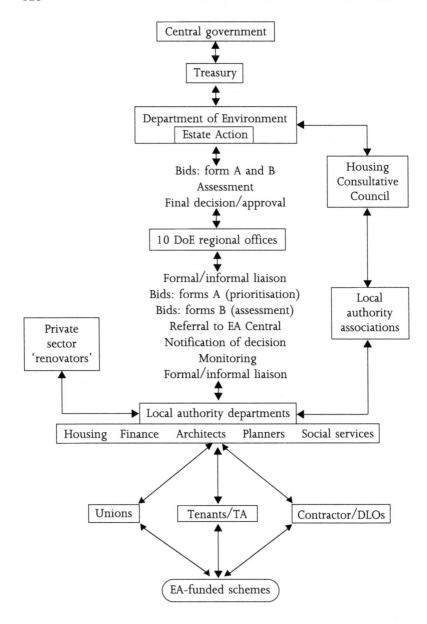

Figure 4.1 Estate Action agents and policy contect
Source: Pinto (1993a).

EA funding and of implementing the schemes. This section summarises
the main findings of this work, which is presented from the local
authority perspective (for a fuller discussion see Pinto, 1990; 1991).
This is followed by an analysis of the way both EA Central and the
DoE Regional Offices have adapted their procedures in response to
criticism. This lays the groundwork for the subsequent analysis of
the impact of the initiative at national, regional and local levels.

Implementation: central–local interaction

The discussion above has indicated that local authorities question
whether EA HIPs are really additional as opposed to topsliced
resources and greatly mistrust the privatisation and diversification of
tenure motives. In addition, the survey demonstrated that local
authorities appear to be principally involved with EA because it is
one of the few legitimate ways of supplementing their basic
allocations, even though they disapprove of having to confine their
proposals to the priorities defined by EA. Ninety two per cent argue
that EA's main appeal was the fact that it enabled more schemes to be
developed by local authorities than would otherwise be the case, rather
than finding merit in EA's stated objectives per se. The local
authorities surveyed also maintained they would have implemented
such schemes much more effectively if the topslicing and reallocation
mechanism (EA and its structure) did not exist. This section analyses
the key reasons why this conclusion was reached by local authorities.

Deficient EA timetabling arrangements

According to the survey results one of the prime factors inhibiting
the smooth implementation of EA schemes is the programme
timetable which is not well geared to the one that housing authorities work to, particularly with respect to capital programming. Sixty
nine per cent of the respondents felt that one of the chief problems
relates to the inadequate 'nature of the timetable for bidding,
acceptance and allocation of EA HIPs'. Fifty-one per cent of the
authorities stated that the main reason why they experienced delays
was because of the lack of an adequate timetable for bids and
furthermore, 51 per cent also stressed this difficulty by contending
that EA invited authorities to bid 'too late in the financial year and
imposed unreasonable deadlines'. Such a timetable creates major
difficulties, particularly as the EA schemes become increasingly
complex and costly.

Problematic administrative procedures

As discussed earlier, EA's operational arrangements involve a number of different agents. This serves to create severe administrative difficulties for authorities, 74 per cent of which experience unreasonable 'delays from the point when they submitted their bids to EA, to the point when they received final approval'. Seventy-one per cent of the respondents felt that this delay was mainly because of the time it took EA Central itself to process the bids. This has several knock-on effects. Since EA operates on a financial year timescale, delays may threaten effective resource use (as indicated by 87 per cent). Additionally, the two bidding rounds (Forms A and B) have built-in costs, not least for the unsuccessful bidders whose costs have to be written off and lastly, the uncertainty and delay in completing schemes add to tenant frustration according to 78 per cent of the respondents. Whilst it can be argued that such effort is not entirely wasted since local authorities would have to grapple with their problems and come up with alternatives, the above factors point to significant procedural difficulties.

Changing EA criteria and emphasis

A source of constant irritation for the authorities visited and surveyed relates to the criteria of what is permissible for authorities to bid under EA. It was felt by housing authorities that this was constantly changing and that the emphasis placed on certain elements by EA also varied from year to year. Over a third of those surveyed blamed the delays which arose on this uncertainty and a further 31 per cent argued that this occurred because EA's criteria were ill-defined. The level of uncertainty was even greater in relation to the elements which EA will not fund as part of an estate's package of solutions. Only 36 per cent of those applying for funding felt that they knew for certain what EA was *not* prepared to approve. This degree of uncertainty seems unwarranted for a steadily expanding national scheme and the DoE was eventually forced to issue annual guidance on its priorities for the forthcoming year.

Adequacy of tenant consultation

From the outset, EA sought to place the issue of increasing tenant consultation at the forefront of its agenda in the generation of EA schemes. The evidence of the survey suggests that, though positive, this has not been entirely successful. While undoubtedly this has spurred a number of local authorities to alter their attitudes and practices, in actual fact, 69 per cent of the respondents felt that their involvement with EA had not necessarily resulted in 'greater tenant consultation, participation and input into schemes than would otherwise have been the case' in their authority. This appears to be partly because of the way EA itself is structured since 30 per cent stated that they were in a EA-devised system which forced them to 'plan, consult and submit bids too quickly and too late for full and effective consultation to occur'; and others feared raising tenant expectations (35 per cent), while not being in a position to guarantee delivery of the schemes. Approval of proposals rests entirely with the EA machinery.

Although most consultation took the form of surveys (82 per cent) and public meetings (83 per cent), notably only a small proportion of authorities actually consulted their tenants at the initial bidding or 'Form A' stage when the overall plan and costings are submitted to EA (see Figure 4.1). It is only at the 'Form B' stage that tenants are consulted, even though the nature and focus of the scheme is generally determined at the earlier point. This makes sense in minimising disappointment to tenants if the scheme proposal fails, however, it actually works against the principle of tenant consultation, not least because by this stage authorities are having to move very quickly in order to finalise, approve and spend the resources in the remaining time. These factors work against effective tenant consultation.

Evolution: the response of EA Central and the Regional Officers

The discussion above points to difficulties with the EA method of targeting and allocating capital resources for housing schemes. To EA's credit, interviews with the EA Central team, DoE Regional Officers and case study work at the local authority level, all indicate that the EA Central team has sought to accommodate a number of problems. Several noteworthy adjustments have been made in response to criticisms and recommendations put forward by the local authorities. The development of the EA initiative is summarised briefly below and readers are referred to Pinto (1993b) for fuller details.

Some attempt has been made to 'bring forward' the timetable, such that it coincides more closely with authorities' own capital programming. Many of the authorities that were interviewed professed to be happier with this arrangement although the majority still feel that more could be done, not least the introduction of a scheme-based timetable. The EA Central team maintains that this is dictated by the way the Treasury's financial system operates, that no more flexibility exists and that local authorities themselves and their procedures are partly responsible for any remaining problems.

The issue of fluctuating criteria and emphasis has been criticised by local authorities, however, these are defended by both the Regional Offices and by EA Central on the grounds that the initiative seeks to encourage innovation in housing management and other solutions and that as such, it must be free to adapt and point authorities to things they may not have attempted before.

Authorities are also concerned about the administrative arrangements, but these have improved. The Central team eventually came to the conclusion that it could not cope with the volume of work involved in administering the bids for EA support and the continuation (longer than one year) schemes. It has accepted the Regional Offices' contention that they were better placed to deal with these issues and decentralisation of functions has ensued. The Regional Offices now prioritise and decide which bids to approve, interact with and keep authorities informed of developments, monitor the financial situation and development of schemes, and are also in charge of the continuation schemes. EA Central is now able to concentrate on policy development, information dissemination and on persuading DoE ministers of the value of this initiative. This is a rather important development, not least because EA Central must devote a certain amount of time to ensure that it maintains or increases its share of resources within the DoE.

Following on from this, the new arrangements have evolved because of the very fact that the Regional Officers have proven themselves to be aware of the EA 'ethos', have developed very good relationships with their local authorities and are thus in a position to take over from EA Central. Although authorities are still not entirely happy with the arrangements, they represent very encouraging developments which have served to cool the central–local housing relations which used to exist in the initial phase of the scheme. The issue of ensuring effective tenant consultation remains a problem for EA and local authorities.

Impact: national, regional and local assessments

The discussion turns next to the actual impact of the EA initiative in terms of its general effect on the management of run-down estates. Chapter 1 indicated that estate based management, which is the principal type of decentralised management structure which EA has tried to promote, has been highly successful. This section evaluates EA's impact by reference to three levels: the national, regional and local levels. Naturally, in a paper of this size, little more than a flavour of the key findings can be attempted.

The national postal survey: some relevant results

A sub-set of the postal survey data is analysed in this section and the discussion concentrates on key indicators highlighting the nature of EA's impact on run-down estates. Readers are referred to Pinto (1993a) for further details. The survey addressed two main issues in evaluating the degree of effectiveness of EA-funded schemes, the first of which was explored with the local authority housing officers co-ordinating the EA schemes. According to officer evaluations, the EA-funded schemes seem to be working extremely well. If the majority of the estates (67 per cent) have indeed shown substantial improvements (a finding which the DoE Regional Officials that were interviewed fully concurred with), or general improvements (adding up to 98 per cent), then this would suggest that EA is actually achieving positive results and that this DoE initiative seems to justify its rapidly increasing budget, despite the issues discussed earlier. Just as importantly, the results also suggest that targeting resources along DoE-prescribed lines appears to work, an issue which is developed below. Only 2 per cent indicated that there had been no discernible improvement.

In addition, a set of crude management indicators are commonly used in the housing literature such as the level of voids, arrears, crime and transfer requests. These were, therefore, built into the postal survey in order to assess how the EA-funded schemes performed on this basis. It must be stressed that not all authorities completed the questionnaire sufficiently well to be included in the analysis that follows. Although 61 local authorities responded to this part of the survey, only the data from 40 authorities (constituting 53 EA schemes in all) could be included in the analysis, representing a 49 per cent overall response-rate. Despite this caveat, Table 4.1

provides useful indications of the degree of success met by the EA-
funded schemes which have already been implemented.

Based on the management indices chosen, the statistics suggest
pronounced improvements in the management situation of the great
majority of EA-funded schemes. For example, transfer requests have
decreased in 44 per cent of the estates; the average time taken to re-
let property has also declined (in 57 per cent of the cases); as has the
number of dwellings still classified as 'difficult-to-let' (57 per cent).
Similarly positive results are evident as concerns the reduced level of
vacant dwellings (57 per cent); the lower incidence of crime (62 per
cent); and vandalism and graffiti (63 per cent). The management
costs per dwelling have increased in 56 per cent of the cases,
reflecting the more intensive nature of estate based management.
Whilst recognising that these improvements cannot be separated
from wider developments in the authorities concerned, nevertheless,
these findings suggest that 'targeted' EA HIPs encouraging a number
of local authorities to experiment with a number of different
management styles appears to be having a measurably beneficial
effect, which is the key objective as far as the EA schemes and the
tenants are concerned.

The DoE Regional Officers and EA Central

The view that the EA initiative does seem to be achieving positive
management and other results is shared by all the Regional Officers
interviewed 'the message of EA has spread out and some of the
estates have been outstanding successes. They have changed the

Table 4.1 An evaluation of Estate Action schemes

Management indicators	Increased %	Decreased %	No change %	Not known %	Valid cases
Outstanding transfer requests	18	44	22	16	45
Average time to re-let the dwellings	5	57	28	10	42
No. dwellings (still) difficult-to-let	0	58	26	16	38
Current tenants with rent arrears	19	57	18	6	47
Management costs per dwelling	56	0	7	37	27
Vacant dwellings	15	57	22	6	47
Incidence of crime	2	62	30	6	52
Incidence of vandalism and graffiti	2	63	29	6	52

Source: Pinto (1993a).

atmosphere on the estates and local authorities are thinking differently about estate management, upkeep and other solutions.' (RO Interview); and in similar vein: 'EA has been successful. It has confronted a problem which authorities did not have the resources to address. It has been a pat on the back instead of the usual criticism of the DoE and it has highlighted what can be done by targeting resources into certain areas' (RO Interview). One of the many positive quotations obtained from the EA Central team is that: 'There is also plenty of evidence to suggest that the money is producing good results on the ground' (Central Interview). There is clearly little doubt among the Regional Officers and EA Central that the EA scheme has been very successful.

The localities

In addition to the national survey and interviews with EA Central and DoE Regional Officers, Pinto (1993a) discusses in some detail the results of four case studies covering the following types of scheme: estate based management, refurbishment, concierge and a private sector involvement scheme. Discussion on the EA 'impact' entails an analysis of wider effects resulting from involvement with the EA initiative, its policies and methods and is based upon semi-structured interviews with relevant local politicians, housing and finance officers in each case study, supplemented with tenant surveys.

It is not possible to fully explore this research here (but see Pinto (1992a)). Suffice to say that in terms of the impact of EA-funded schemes at the local level, the information obtained indicated, as clearly as is possible in the circumstances, that the schemes were improving the estates. Every single management indicator (such as the reduction in rent arrears and the crime rate) recorded improvements occurring either one year after the completion of the scheme or in subsequent years. The research suggested that this is probably happening in conjunction with other factors which the study did not take into consideration; nevertheless, the results were supported by the local authority housing officers and by the limited tenant surveys which were carried out in the estates concerned. The remainder of the chapter moves the discussion to an analysis of the impact of the EA initiative at the broad, housing authority-wide level.

An overall assessment of the impact of EA

Taken together the national, regional and local evidence constitutes an incomplete but substantive body of evidence that suggests that, not only is the situation improving in all the four case studies and beyond according to the survey results, but more importantly, that these schemes appear to be meeting managerial expectations in what used to be estates which were extremely difficult to manage. As indicated above, it is almost impossible to extricate the pure 'EA' impact from other factors occurring independently of the initiative. For example, to what extent does the improvement simply reflect the fact that these estates were desperately in need of additional investment? Most of them were so severely run-down that any focused and substantial investment in environmental, dwelling or managerial terms would probably have resulted in tangible improvements. Partly for this reason, this section attempts to evaluate the EA initiative's overall impact on housing authorities. This means synthesising the evidence from the four main sources: the postal survey, the DoE Regional Office and EA Central interviews; and the four case studies. To this end, the central point of reference for the remainder of the discussion in this section is Table 4.2. The 'Administrative and Implementation Issues' were discussed earlier but it is worthwhile analysing the remaining categories in some detail.

Management issues

It was argued at the beginning of this chapter that although political motives were important in the formation of the EA initiative, it was the managerial issues that were uppermost in the civil servants' minds. A key concern was to improve the management organisation in 'run-down' estates. Central government does not believe in the traditional, centralised and hierarchical model of council housing management and, in line with its housing objectives of creating a diversified sector of social housing, EA attempts to provide incentives for authorities to experiment and innovate with alternative forms of housing management and ownership, as set out in EA's remit. This section analyses EA's achievements in this context.

1. The general opinion obtained from the survey is that authorities are primarily implementing those schemes and initiatives which conform to their housing policies although some indicate that, were it not for EA considerations, they might have developed them in

Table 4.2 Synthesis of impact of Estate Action

Themes and evidence:	Postal survey	DoE regions	EA central	Case-studies
Administrative/implementation issues				
1. Timetabling arrangements	--	-	+	-
2. Administrative Procedures	--	-	++	-
3. Whether EA keeps changing its criteria	--	+	+	-
Management issues				
1. Impact on number of schemes	+	+	+	+
2. Impact in aiding management innovation	-	+	+	+
3. Impact in aiding decentralisation	+	++	++	++
4. Impact in aiding tenant consultation	--	-	+	-/++
5. Overall impact on housing management	++	++	++	++
Financial issues				
1. Whether EA HIPs is additional or topsliced	--	--	++	--
2. Whether EA results in underallocation	--	-	-/+	-
3. Whether EA results in underspending	--	-	-	-
4. Continuation funding issues	--	++	++	-
5. Quality of EA's targeting	+	++	++	+
Housing policy issues				
1. Whether EA results in more investment	-/+	++	++	++
2. Whether EA influences management styles	0	+	++	+
3. EA's overall impact on housing policy	+/++	++	++	++
Centre–local relations				
1. Degree of conflict	--	+	+	-/+
2. Degree of co-operation	-	++	+	+
3. Degree of privatisation	--	+	+	+
4. Generation of alternative organisations	--	+	+	+
5. EA's impact on local policies/autonomy	-	0	0	-/--

Notes: Code: Very poor (--); Poor (-); Neutral (0); Good (+); Very good (++)
Source: Pinto (1993a).

different estates. A related point is that they believe that if there were to be a further tightening of the financial situation confronting authorities, this degree of freedom might well be impaired in the future. All the available sources of evidence suggest that EA has enabled more schemes to occur than would otherwise have been the case, which is an important finding in EA's favour. About 1,200 schemes involving improvements to approximately 460,000 dwellings have been funded by EA since its inception.

2. As regards helping authorities to *innovate*, the results of the survey suggest that the EA initiative has had little impact and that the great majority of schemes were either 'under discussion for future implementation' or 'in the process of being implemented from mainstream HIPs'. This implies that a large proportion of EA HIPs is simply 'dead-weight' investment, however, both the Regional Offices and EA Central disagree with this conclusion. They maintain that EA has enabled authorities to experiment with innovative management styles instead of simply talking about it, not least because of the provision of additional resources. Since 1986/87, EA resources have helped to fund 228 schemes (19 per cent of all schemes) which have resulted in tenants participating in the management of the estates. This has been principally through housing co-operatives and Estate Management Boards.

3. Evidence from the survey also suggests that the options placed before local authorities together with the additional resources, have forced them to both consider and implement different types of management and ownership schemes. Whether EA really aids innovation, depends on the authorities' attitudes to the initiative. The results of the case studies suggest that there is an element of truth in this argument. For example, some authorities have only been able to put into effect schemes (such as co-operatives and 50 per cent sales to the private sector) because of EA's existence. Therefore, EA appears to have helped both the process of *innovation* and *decentralisation* in run-down estates (see Table 4.2).

4. In dealing with the topic of management efficiency, a key issue of concern is that of *tenant consultation* (see earlier discussion on implementation issues). The local authorities examined in the survey suggest that although improving the level and quality of tenant consultation is a key EA objective, most believe that this has not occurred in their authorities. This is mainly because the 'Authority/ officers were satisfied with the existing levels of consultation' and secondly, as discussed earlier effective tenant consultation may have been impaired by the way EA operates.

Both the Regional Officers and EA Central argue that local authorities may be underplaying EA's impact in this respect and the evidence of the case studies indicates that in EA's first year of operation, the level of tenant consultation was very great indeed. In part, this is because the schemes implemented in the first couple of years would have been the authorities' top priorities. As such, they are more likely to have been researched and the tenants well consulted, although this may not necessarily be the case with subsequent bids. The fact that EA has given this issue so much emphasis, made it a pre-requisite for EA funding, required local authorities to monitor impacts and encouraged them to create Estate Management Boards among other factors, has undoubtedly impacted upon the tenant consultation practices of many authorities. This remains a contentious issue since the evidence consistently suggests that the quality of tenant consultation could be improved even more. The Regional Office and some EA Central officials concur that more attention ought to be given to this issue, although they remain uncertain as to how this can be achieved.

5. It could be concluded that EA is having a positive impact on council housing management. Despite initial fears that the true aim of the initiative was about the disposal of housing stock, the authorities which are experimenting, for example, with security and environmental works, concierges and estate based management, report very encouraging results. This is true of the national survey, local authority staff views, Regional Official and EA Central assessments, tenant opinions and case study schemes. In view of this consistent evidence and despite the implementation difficulties identified earlier in the chapter, targeting resources in specific ways and localities along DoE-prescribed lines does seem to work. The value of this achievement should not be underrated by local housing authorities, though they too can justifiably claim to be the main reason why these schemes have been successful. The 1980s was a decade when the key council housing concerns were related to the issue of management and EA has made a important contribution to the process of understanding how to improve management organisation in the most problematic portions of council housing.

Financial issues

An earlier section introduced the argument that there was a concern amongst politicians and civil servants that the HIPs system of block allocations was failing to provide sufficient resources for what the government saw as a housing priority, namely run-down council estates. In terms of the government's objective of achieving greater financial efficiency in the use of public resources, a key concept is that of 'targeting' resources. Much has been said about targeting but it remains virtually unresearched. The government's most significant targeting mechanism in the housing field is EA HIPs and its experience is useful in that it also sheds light on similar systems such as HATs and City Challenge, and is analysed in some detail below.

1. The existing research has demonstrated that every local authority contends that EA HIPs resources are *topsliced* from mainstream HIPs, centralised and redistributed according to government or DoE determined priorities (see Table 4.2). This has been a criticism of the EA initiative since its inception and the mechanism is resented by authorities who regard this as clear-cut evidence of further centralisation of autonomy. Only the Treasury and EA Central still maintain that EA resources are 'additional'. The housing authorities in the survey and the balance of the Regional Officers' opinions suggest that virtually everyone now accepts the notion of 'topsliced' finance and also, the increased central control that it implies. This perception has never been shaken off and has made EA's role more difficult to implement but even so, the dire local government financial climate has forced a number of authorities that had originally refused to participate with the initiative, to swallow their pride and also bid for EA HIPs.

There is a set of additional problems which can arise from the EA HIPs mechanism for targeting. The earlier discussion made it clear that a side-effect of targeting resources is that (in the case of EA), there are two timetables in operation: one linked to the general capital allocation system and another relating to the targeted resources. These are not necessarily compatible and may prove difficult to co-ordinate and synchronise, with the effect that two important problems can arise which are discussed below.

2. The Regional Offices may *underallocate* the targeted resources. EA HIPs is divided among the Regional Offices to be allocated to the authorities within their jurisdiction, but as discussed earlier, there exist several administrative and timetabling problems with EA's operation which can lead to delays. These have moved local authorities and their representatives to remonstrate against the fact that EA HIPs are not fully distributed to local authorities – they contend that the delays, the timetable, the rapidly increasing resources and bids, all mean that EA is simply unable to prevent underallocation of EA HIPs. The survey results suggest that this does happen and EA Central itself confirms that this occurred in the first year (when about £5m

was underallocated) but maintains this is no longer a problem because the Regional Offices can now over-programme their allocations (by 15 per cent). The existence of a Central Reserve Fund which pools all the potential underspend and allows EA to re-allocate it before the end of the financial year also helps matters.

For their part, the ROs contend that underallocation is almost inevitable, although it is the London RO which is particularly prone to it. Research indicates that certain authorities also obtain 'reputations' based on whether they can achieve spend which in turn affects their success rate in the EA bid process since a 'credibility' factor comes into play. A similar sort of reputation can develop among the Regional Offices themselves. For example, the London RO complains that EA Central does not allow it to invite its authorities to submit bids for resources which become available at the last minute (via the Central Reserve Fund mechanism), which has implications for the authorities excluded and thus for their residents. This particular policy has everything to do with administrative efficiency but little to do with housing need. In other words, those authorities in regions which have proven records of spending at short notice are given the chance to mop-up the potential underspend, whereas authorities in regions with perhaps less enviable records, but proven need, are denied the opportunity of doing so. This implies that not only is there competition *among* authorities for the limited resources, but this also occurs *between* DoE regions.

3. In addition the local authorities themselves may *underspend* EA HIPs. This occurs due to the financial year cut-off. If there are delays in processing bids and issuing approvals, or indeed, if local authorities are inefficient, they may end up underspending their allocations and having to complete the schemes from their 'own' resources. Thirty-nine per cent of the local authorities surveyed underspent, though the amount of resource involved was not quantified. Fifty-four per cent of those that did achieve spend argued that they only managed to do so because they worked 'at risk', meaning that they started on site before receiving formal DoE approval to start with the scheme. One must not lose sight of the fact that under/overspending also occur under the HIPs system (see chapter 1), although the authorities concerned suggest that the problem is much greater with the EA schemes, mainly because of the greater degree of uncertainty and delay. All the evidence from the survey, EA Central and RO inter-

views bears out the fact that underspending occurs. As to the reason, the local authorities blame delays and inefficient procedures on the part of EA while naturally, EA Central and the ROs point in the opposite direction. One of the case study authorities did argue that local authorities had only themselves to blame for this, although this authority only had one EA scheme to programme.

4. A further issue of importance relates to continuation funding. The survey indicates that authorities were very critical of the EA constraint of two years of funding per scheme (see Table 4.2). The EA Central team has sensibly accepted the local authority argument that some estates may require a longer timescale to turn around and now encourages authorities to think in terms of bidding for different phases each year. This enables substantial schemes to be programmed over several years. Another important development is that all of the supervision and monitoring of continuation funding schemes has now been devolved because of the Regional Officers insisting that they were better placed to deal with these aspects. The EA Central team argues that this is no longer an issue but local authorities remain unconvinced. They maintain that there are still no guarantees of 'promised' continuation funding being received and that this hampers their financial programming and threatens the success of the larger 'comprehensive' initiatives which EA hopes to generate in future. EA Central counters that it is almost inconceivable that the Treasury would disband the EA initiative without meeting its continuation funding obligations. This argument does little to assuage authorities' concerns and remains unresolved.

5. It is becoming increasingly common for DoE initiatives to be targeted at specific areas, groups of people, types of housing and so forth by employing the technique of 'topslicing and targeting'. The conclusions drawn from research on EA suggest that these mechanisms may well work in terms of their specific objectives, but that unless careful attention is given to the issues of local authority timetables, council procedures, political processes and consultation, the government's objective of financial efficiency may be compromised. Problems such as underallocation and underspending, not to mention mistrust and reluctant co-operation may derail such initiatives. The importance of consulting with local authorities, their representative associations, the tenants and the Regional Officers cannot be over-stressed.

That said, the government's aim to direct more resources to run-down estates and the view that the EA initiative would be a good vehicle for achieving this has been fulfilled. By originally targeting a limited number of authorities, insisting that bids for EA support could only be made for estates with certain indices of deprivation, securing an increasing supply of EA HIPs allocations from the Treasury and demanding a 50 per cent contribution from local authorities, the initiative has ensured that this aim was met. About £1.6bn has been made available since 1986/87 through EA HIPs to these council estates. In addition, a substantial amount of resources have been levered through the local authority contribution, private sector investment and Housing Corporation funds.

However, the survey results imply that the notion of targeting was not entirely effective in that a number of authorities argued that, given the choice, they would have used the EA HIPs resources in different areas/estates or in different schemes/ways. Both the Regional Officers and EA Central maintain that the policy of targeting has been highly successful. The case-studies reveal that the EA scheme estates were the four authorities' greatest priorities and that even where they were not, the estates were undoubtedly in severe need of additional investment. The local authorities maintain that they themselves would have directed more resources into these estates if their financial situation had enabled them to do so and one of the biggest critiques of EA, in terms of financial targeting, must remain that it evades the responsibility for investing in major structural disrepair. EA Central counters that it is only concerned with management and innovation and that the costs of structural repair must come from the local authorities' own mainstream HIPs, yet various reports alluded to elsewhere have highlighted not only the severe problems which exist, but also the huge level of expenditure which is necessary. The government has yet to come to terms with this major issue.

Housing policy issues

1. This section starts with the level of investment as this links with the previous conclusion that as far as targeting was concerned, EA is succeeding in directing resources towards the areas it considers are in need of them. All the evidence suggests that more investment is undoubtedly now finding its way into unpopular estates (see Table

4.2) and local authorities see this as being one of the essential virtues of the EA initiative. While they argue vigorously that these estates would have been accorded greater priority if centrally determined financial resources had been more directly and freely available, the case studies in particular, leave little doubt that a large proportion of housing resources is being directed in the way the government hoped.

This is not simply because EA HIPs are targeted at particular authorities and tied to public housing estates exhibiting above average problems of various sorts. The way EA has changed over time has accentuated the direction of the authorities' own investment. The survey revealed that, to start with, virtually all the capital allocation was provided through EA HIPs but that in subsequent years, EA began to 'encourage' authorities to meet approximately 50 per cent of the investment from their own mainstream HIPs. This has meant that an ever greater level of commitment (financial, departmental and political) is required to maintain any authority's involvement with the EA initiative. While local authorities bitterly criticise this development (indeed, this has encouraged some to part company with EA), all the same, the great majority have gone along with it and committed their resources accordingly. The tenants in the most run-down estates have benefited from this development.

2. The survey information also illustrates that all local authorities were engaged in EA primarily to obtain additional resources, but that the second most important factor was because of the fact that it advocated decentralised or innovative management structures. The implication of this response is that EA is not affecting local authorities in terms of the management issues because they planned to implement these anyway. EA merely releases the resources to make this possible. Of course, a different perspective was obtained from the ROs and EA Central. The case studies suggest that EA involvement (not least the availability of resources), certainly affected the predisposition of some authorities to undertake initiatives such as private sector involvement and co-operatives. Housing officers in one of the case studies only became convinced of the value of setting up localised management structures and involving the tenants more closely by being involved with EA. EA has certainly begun to affect some authorities' perception of management issues in significant ways.

3. We come now to the *overall effects* of EA identified in the Table 4.2.
Local authorities' traditional attempts at ameliorating the situation in
'problem' estates have often been half-hearted and excluded the
tenants from the proposed alternatives, thus ensuring from the start
that the impact would be limited. For all its administrative, implementation and other deficiencies, the EA initiative has presented
various 'tried and tested' management models to local authorities;
provided capital allocations to carry them out; forced authorities to
consider alternatives and make novel choices; courted tenant consultation; and insisted upon authorities providing firm tenders and
monitoring the financial and management developments closely. It is
for these reasons that Table 4.2 indicates that according to all the
sources of evidence presented in this chapter, EA's overall impact on
management is viewed as having been very positive.

Central–local relations

1. It is clear from the earlier discussion that the initial reaction by
local authorities to EA was one of dismay and *conflict*. Some authorities were so set against the initiative (in particular its principles of
topslicing resources and partnership with the private sector), that
they refused to participate at all. What has happened is that in the
subsequent time, most authorities have realised that it could be
profitable to 'do business' with EA and there has been a steady
diminution in the level of overt conflict and criticism of the EA
initiative. The onus has shifted perceptibly from lambasting the
initiative, to more constructive suggestions of how to improve its
operation which have been channelled to EA Central through the
Regional Offices. The Regional Officers in particular, note that there
has been a complete change in the local authority attitude to EA. The
words 'pragmatism' and 'realism' frequently cross their lips with
regard to their relationship with local housing authorities.

2. This *co-operation* seems to have arisen because most authorities are
predominantly motivated by the fact that EA provides an additional
source of finance, rather than the other aspects that the initiative
seeks to promote. It is apparent that authorities have been forced by
the capital restrictions and reductions to engage in the initiative, but
they appear to have managed to do so mainly on their own terms.
Nevertheless, it is also evident that with time, EA has begun to gain
the upper hand in the relationship. Authorities submit ever more

bids for EA support and even formerly dissenting authorities now actively bid for EA funds. EA HIPs allocations have steadily increased while HIPs allocations have dried-up and capital restrictions further constrain financial flexibility. With so few alternative sources of finance, authorities have had to consider and often implement many of the options offered under EA, particularly in view of the fact that EA expects authorities to contribute financially and develop innovative management styles.

All the local authorities surveyed and the case study authorities agree that EA's 'power' is bound to increase, resulting in further centralisation of control. Local authorities must dance to a central government tune, nevertheless, most have benefited from it and have been able to fulfil their aims (and EA's) without compromising their housing policies. Such a trick becomes harder with time and as EA's expectations of participating local authorities rise. The topslicing and targeting mechanism in conjunction with capital restrictions provide great scope for central direction and control.

3. As regards privatisation, because of the hitherto lack of research, the conventional view regarding the EA initiative has generally been along the lines of Balchin's comments (1989, p. 224):

To ensure that local authorities would not be slow in disposing of their estates, the Department of the Environment set up the Urban Housing Renewal Unit (UHRU) in 1985 both to promote emptying and selling local authority housing (so that it could be refurbished and resold) and to oversee the handing over of estates to trusts. Within a year, 42 local authorities (half of which were Labour controlled) had embarked on 80 estate sale schemes under UHRU, although with only £50m at its disposal in 1985/86 UHRU could not be expected to have much impact on a £20bn repair problem.

Such a view over-estimates the extent to which EA has resulted in disposals to the private sector. Of the 1,200 schemes which have been developed thus far, only 36 per cent have involved the private sector and under 30,000 dwellings have been disposed of this way. It also ignores the fact that the main emphasis shifted almost overnight to the encouragement of a range of management initiatives, but more importantly perhaps, it also misses the more subtle point regarding the extent to which EA has contributed to the acceptance of the notion of privatisation of council estates. Whilst its resources have been limited (but rapidly escalating), EA has played a crucial role in conditioning housing authorities to the concept and value of selling either parts of their housing stock or land parcels.

Whereas such a notion was absolutely taboo when EA was created, the case studies demonstrate that this has gained credibility and even acceptance among many authorities as a perfectly sound option to consider, especially at times of fiscal stress. This is reflected in the previously mentioned allusion by the Regional Officers of the 'pragmatism' demonstrated by authorities of all political back-grounds. It also implies that authorities are increasingly willing to form partnerships with the private sector despite this being the housing authorities' least popular option to undertake under the EA initiative. In terms of the wider housing policy, experience and involvement with EA may also mean that local authorities will look more pragmatically upon such policies as Tenants' Choice, Large Scale Voluntary Transfers and Housing Action Trusts (the next chapter discusses these policies in detail).

4. As regards EA's aims of encouraging innovation and helping stimulate *alternative management organisations* in line with government's social housing policy, the overall conclusion is that EA has also had a degree of success in this respect. The survey results indicate that authorities have generally been pursuing EA schemes which were in line with their own housing policies, some of which involved the formation of co-operatives and concierges. They do confirm that EA has enabled more schemes to take place, which implies success for EA. Both EA Central and the ROs have no doubts that they have been influential in this respect and the evidence from the case studies confirm some authorities' greater predisposition to experiment with alternative management and organisational styles. In the majority of cases this is done willingly but in others it may be because of a lack of alternative, since the authorities do not have sufficient resources to undertake the schemes on their own. None have so far considered the most radical options such as the transfer of stock/estates to Trusts.

5. One of the biggest criticisms of the EA initiative to start with, was the fact that it was believed that the financial mechanism of topslicing and redistribution via DoE determined criteria of what was relevant, resulted in centralisation, a reduction in *local autonomy* and interference with local housing policies and priorities. Such a view comes through very clearly in the survey and in the case studies and

as argued above, there is also the expectation that the level of EA control will accentuate because increasingly more authorities bid for EA support and alternative sources of funding are harder to find or yield less resource.

These arguments have by no means disappeared and remain a thorn in EA's operation. The EA Central team exhausts itself in arguing that EA HIPs is separate from, and additional to, mainstream HIPs – with little success. There is some recognition on the part of the case study authorities that they have complete freedom over the decision on whether to get involved in EA and what to bid for, nevertheless, in both the survey and the case studies, authorities maintain that there has been a degree of compromise in local priorities and a reduction in local autonomy.

Local authorities argue that both these trends will increase in future. The reason why most authorities are not more critical of these issues is because of the latitude afforded by the EA initiative where a great deal can be funded, provided it is presented in the right way and with the appropriate phrases. In this respect, the ambiguity over EA criteria works in the authorities' favour. In addition, the Regional Officers have become adept at advising authorities on the presentation of their bids and with further decentralisation, their knowledge and understanding of local needs and priorities will improve matters even more. A great deal of scope exists within the initiative for local authorities to benefit from EA support without necessarily feeling as if its local policies are unduly compromised. That is precisely why (together with the additional resources) many local authorities which originally refused to participate are now heavily involved to the EA initiative.

To conclude this section, the few housing commentators who have paid attention to the EA initiative have pointed to the fact that its resources are topsliced, that they are inadequate in view of the scale of housing disrepair and that it is anti-municipal housing in nature. This chapter has shown that while the first two issues may be correct, despite its remit, the third is far from clear-cut. The essential point is that it is simplistic to conclude on whether the EA initiative is 'pro-' or 'anti-' council housing. The evidence presented here clearly demonstrates that although the programme is highly politicised, both views of EA are partly true. EA can and sometimes does, work against local determination of housing policy; however, housing authorities can also, and many have, made the initiative work extremely well for themselves and their tenants.

The future of Estate Action

The DoE has re-launched and expanded the Estate Action initiative, yet much can be done to improve the operation and effectiveness of the initiative:

- The creation of a mechanism which would generate more effective *consultation* between the EA Central team, the DoE Regional Officials, local authorities and local authority associations. This would ensure that each party is aware of the main problems, the developments occurring, share best practice and so forth. It would also help reduce mistrust and increase co-ordination.
- Tightening of the *targeting criteria* so that the authorities with the greatest housing problems receive more resources. At present, all authorities are able to submit bids to EA since even rural authorities have housing problems, however, such authorities may have relatively less need and more capital receipts. The initiative could be targeted in a more refined manner.
- Each authority is currently expected to contribute about 50 per cent of the capital costs per scheme. This principle could be retained but there ought to be a *sliding scale of support* according to need and affordability. This would only strengthen the principle of targeting.
- The operation of a strict one year timetable for designing, bidding and implementing schemes often works against effectiveness. This should be replaced by a *scheme timetable* if possible.
- The various bid stages should be *amalgamated* to speed up processing.
- More efforts should be made to ensure full and effective *tenant consultation*.

One of EA's most interesting innovations has been its intent to generate large scale 'Enterprise Initiatives' which will seek to generate additional training and employment opportunities in housing estates. This has been welcomed as a critical issue which should be addressed. Concern with the housing environment, fabric and management are important, but the very high levels of unemployment, the low level of skills and the general dislocation of housing estates from the labour market, are all issues which must be confronted sooner rather than later (see Pinto, 1992a; 1992b). It is important that there is a realisation that the development of comprehensive housing initiatives will not depend simply upon effective co-ordination within the DoE. New, workable relationships must be developed with other government departments, voluntary and community organisations, as well as other critical actors such as developers, employers, Training and Enterprise Councils (TECs) and so on. It remains to be seen how well these links are developed in the 'flagship' housing schemes being encouraged by EA (see chapter 7 for the issues raised).

Since the creation of the EA initiative, several other mechanisms for targeting resources to perceived problems have been created, Housing Action Trusts and City Challenge being the best known examples. The experience of EA and the issues which have been highlighted in this chapter should be instructive to those similar targeting mechanisms in general terms. This is a trend which is going to continue in the future and that local authorities will continue to oppose on the basis that they represent further centralisation of local government functions and erosion of local autonomy. The recent DoE attempt to create Integrated Regional Offices and amalgamate the 20 separate programmes for urban regeneration and economic development into a Single Regeneration Budget (SRB) will affect the EA initiative as from April 1995 (see DoE, 1994). This reform does offer the opportunity for some of the issues highlighted above to be revised but there are a number of implied threats to the Estate Action programme which will also need to be addressed.

EA funds make up about 30 per cent of the SRB's pool of resources, most of which is currently allocated to local authorities which have a large council housing stock. In future, SRB funding will be awarded on a competitive basis to partnerships led by local authorities and/or TECs which can put together attractive and innovative regeneration proposals. Only a small number of the bids for area regeneration (comprising less than 25,000 residents) and/or pilot schemes submitted will succeed. The economic imperatives are likely to predominate in the selection process – social housing will only be one of a number of lesser, secondary issues. The very fact that EA is pooled into the SRB will lead to a radical change in the distribution of EA HIPs. Local authorities, TECs and other bodies such as voluntary organisations can all submit SRB bids and as a result, EA HIPs will no longer necessarily benefit those local authorities that are currently making good use of it, namely those with a large portion of council stock and estates.

The second major concern relates to the fact that, unlike HATs, Urban Development Corporations and City Challenge, the EA resources are not 'ring-fenced' for housing estates. Since housing is not awarded high priority, this means that the SRB process is likely to result in fewer resources being allocated to most deprived local authorities generally, and by extension, that it will not necessarily be council tenants who will benefit from SRB expenditure. Social housing can only retain its share of EA resources if bidding organisations award a high priority to housing but the pressures to be innovative means that this is unlikely to figure as prominently as other, more appealing 'flagship' regeneration initiatives. Since these important issues remain unresolved, attractive as the SRB might be as a much-needed reform, it is likely to undermine one of the most successful housing initiatives of recent years.

Conclusions

Because of the relatively unknown quality of the Estate Action initiative, this chapter has had to skate over a good deal of ground. The Estate Action initiative was created out of a mixture of political and managerial concerns which in turn gave rise to a mixed set of objectives, some of which were very much 'pro-' council housing and others 'anti-' municipal housing in nature. In some ways, the scheme marked an important step forward in Conservative housing policy, a policy which would eventually culminate in more radical legislation such as Housing Action Trusts and Large Scale Voluntary Transfers. The first few sections also paid close attention to EA's complicated administrative structure involving the Treasury, the DoE, Regional Offices, housing authorities and others which results in a number of implementation difficulties.

The initial press, local authority and academic reactions to the EA initiative were hostile. The issues of encouraging disposal of land and housing to other organisations such as social and private landlords and the notion of targeted or topsliced finance, which were seen to be very much geared to ensure further erosion of local decision-making, were particularly singled out for criticism. In the event, even those councils which vowed never to deal with EA have now capitulated, in large measure because of the financial situation confronting housing authorities and indeed, because of EA's positive impact on the ground.

The initial research on EA uncovered severe problems with the implementation of the initiative, not least the timetabling problems, the administrative delays, the changing criteria, the inadequacy of tenant consultation and financial problems. These weaknesses drew severe complaints from local authorities and both EA Central and the Regional Offices have improved their structures and procedures to meet the criticism. Problems remain but the management indicators which are available (at the national, regional and local levels) on the impact of the EA schemes all suggest that pronounced improvements are occurring in some of the most problematic housing estates in England. Both the local authorities and the EA initiative must take a great deal of credit for this achievement.

The subsequent section analysed the overall impact of the initiative on the basis of management, financial, housing policy and central–local issues and found that the influence of the initiative across a wide set of issues is pervasive and that in large measure, EA's objectives have been met. Local housing authorities and their tenants have benefited in the process. The overall impact of the scheme appears to have been recognised by successive Conservative governments who have awarded increasing amounts of resources and placed greater responsibilities on EA. The next phase of the initiative is much more complicated and multi-disciplinary and multi-departmental in nature. It also remains to be seen whether the initiative is up to the challenge of the Single Regeneration Budget. The fact that EA resources will not be a ring-fenced component within a large initiative comprising 20-odd schemes from five different government departments, is likely to mean that EA will lose its distinctive features and may eventually disappear altogether. For local housing authorities, that would represent the loss of a potential enemy, turned valuable friend.

References

AMA (Association of Metropolitan Authorities) (1983) *Defects in Housing 1: Non-traditional Dwellings of the 1940s and 1950s*, London, AMA.

Andrews, C. L. (1979) *Tenant and Town Hall*, London, HMSO.

Audit Commission (1986) *Improving Council Housing Maintenance*, London, HMSO.

Balchin, P. N. (1989) *Housing Policy: An Introduction*, 2nd edn, London, Routledge.

Burbidge, M., Curtis, A., Kirby, K., and Wilson, S. (1981) *An Investigation of Difficult to Let Housing: Vol. 1 General Findings*, London, HMSO.

DoE (1985) *The Urban Housing Renewal Unit*, London, HMSO.

DoE (1986) *Urban Housing Renewal Unit Annual Report 1985-86*, London, HMSO.

DoE (1987) *Estate Action 2nd Annual Report 1986-87*, London, HMSO

DoE (1994) *Bidding Guidance: A Guide to Funding from the Single Regeneration Budget*, London, HMSO.

Pinto, R. R. (1990) 'An Evaluation of the Estate Action Initiative: Aims Versus Achievements', *Housing Review*, Vol. 39(2), pp. 45-48.

Pinto, R. R. (1991) 'Centre–Local Interaction in Renovating Run-down Estates: The View of Local Housing Authorities on the Estate Action Initiative', *Local Government Studies*, January–February, Vol. 17(1), pp. 45-62.

Pinto, R. R. (1992a) *Linking Problem Housing Estates to Labour Markets: A Model of Employment and Training Initiatives*, Centre for Economic Performance, Working Paper No. 264, London, LSE.

Pinto, R. R. (1992b) *Duration of Unemployment and Housing Tenure: An Analysis of the Labour Force Survey*, Centre for Economic Performance, Working Paper No. 263, London, LSE.

Pinto, R. R. (1993a) *The Estate Action Initiative: Council Housing Renewal, Management and Effectiveness*, Aldershot, Avebury.

Pinto, R. R. (1993b) 'An Analysis of the Impact of Estate Action Schemes', *Local Government Studies*, January–February, Vol. 17(1), pp. 37-55.

Scarman, Lord (1982) *The Brixton Disorders April 1981*, London, HMSO.

5

Tenants' choices: sales,
transfers and trusts

Alan Murie

The language of housing policy in the 1980s shifted significantly away from collective housing shortage, housing needs and house condition, and towards individual tenants' rights and choices. The emphasis was on the problems of monopoly control by local authorities, demunicipalisation and enabling exit from the council sector rather than on choices facilitated by expanding the provision of rented and other housing and intervening to raise housing standards.

Debates about choice within the welfare state predated the election of a Conservative Government in 1979 and Labour's Housing Bill which was under discussion in the House of Commons before the 1979 general election included new measures to enhance tenants' rights. These were measures to extend rights in tenancy. The rights which were subsequently embodied in the Housing Acts of 1980 included a Tenants' Charter to increase rights in tenancy, but in addition increased opportunities for exit from the council sector. The tenants' rights and choices which have subsequently dominated debate in the 1980s have largely involved opportunities for exit from the tenure. In the early phase of policy they formed part of a concerted policy to expand home ownership. The Right to Buy introduced in the Housing Act 1980 has remained the single most important measure affecting the social rented housing sector in Britain since then. It has remained the flagship of Government's housing policy and both small and major additions to legislation have been designed to maintain its effectiveness in transferring ownership. Since 1986, however, the Right to Buy has been complemented by the introduction of other exit options. The phase of policy following legislation in 1988 has been marked by measures to encourage tenants to consider changing landlord. Tenants' Choice, voluntary transfers and Housing Action Trusts form key elements in this approach and a Right to Manage has also been promoted. In discussing these schemes, this chapter focuses initially on the Right to Buy and then on the new tenants' choices emerging in the late 1980s. It presents a summary of policy objectives and activity and concludes with some reflections on the emerging pattern and on possible future development.

The first phase: Right to Buy

Both the Right to Buy and other developments in relation to tenants' choices and rights emerged out of a long period of policy development. These are not products of a new right philosophy and their emergence from local and national experiments and discussions is fully presented elsewhere (Murie, 1975; Forrest and Murie, 1988; Malpass and Murie, 1990). The immediate environment for legislative developments in the 1980s involved a preoccupation with the expansion of home ownership and a linked concern to restrict public expenditure on housing. The Right to Buy fitted both of these concerns admirably and represented a major element in the Conservative Party's electoral strategy and attempts to change the allegiance of a key sector of the electorate. The policy was not expressed as one for the social rented sector. There were no targets for sales and no apparent vision of what the remaining public sector would be. The aims were about tenants' choices, demunicipalisation and rolling back the state and there was a belief that the financial implications would be advantageous. The Housing Act 1980 and The Tenants' Rights etc. (Scotland) Act 1980 involved major changes in policy and practice towards council housing. In particular they included a statutory right to buy replacing local discretion. This applied to the bulk of secure tenants with three year's tenancy and to all council properties with the exception of some dwellings for the elderly or disabled and some other smaller categories. Consistent with its policy commitments the government, both in drafting legislation and associated regulations and in other actions, has sought to minimise the numbers of properties and persons excluded and to maximise sales. The legislation sought to limit local discretion and it set down a statutory procedure for sale, for determining valuation and discount and for a right to a mortgage. Very strong powers for the Secretary of State to intervene in local administration were also put in place and were used (see Forrest and Murie, 1985). Other contemporary policies and especially those related to rents and subsidies reduced the advantages of renting and increased the relative attraction of buying. Subsequent legislation in 1984 widened the scope of the Right to Buy, increased maximum discounts and further strengthened central government's position relative to local government. The more critical change however was that introduced in the Housing and Planning Act 1986 which introduced higher discounts for flats and a more rapid acceleration to this maximum of 70 per cent.

Some commentators, throughout the 1980s periodically pronounced that the Right to Buy had run its course – pent up demand was exhausted and there was little capacity for a significant continuing level of sales. The experience repeatedly confounded these predictions. At the outset of the process in 1979 the stock of dwellings owned by local authorities and new towns in Great Britain was 6,521,000. By the end of March 1993 some 1,653,150 dwellings had been sold to sitting tenants, mostly under the Right to Buy. In England and Wales sales rose to a peak in 1982 and fell away sharply to about half that rate in 1985. In Scotland sales rose more slowly to a peak in 1983 and did not fall as sharply. A variety of factors then contributed to a surge in sales to a new peak in 1989 (Table 5.1). In addition to these sales to sitting tenants, a further 367,477 council and new town dwellings were sold in this period.

The surge in sales to sitting tenants in the late 1980s was affected by improved economic circumstances, rising rents and house prices and the higher discounts introduced in the legislation of 1986. In the early phase of the Right to Buy a low rate of sale was associated, among other things, with a relatively large stock of flats (see Dunn, Forrest and Murie, 1987). After 1986 sales of flats increased significantly and this particularly affected the overall rate of sales in Scotland (Murie and Wang, 1992). By the end of 1992 over 150,000 council flats had been sold in England and Wales and over 60,000 in Scotland. The regional variation in sales of all council houses has remained marked throughout the period. The lowest rates of sale (excluding voluntary transfers) between 1979 and the end of 1991 were in the Northwest of England (20.8 per cent), Yorkshire and Humberside (21 per cent), the North (21.7 per cent) and Scotland (21.9 per cent). The highest rates of sale were in the South East (31.4 per cent), the South West (28.7 per cent), the East Midlands (28.3 per cent) and the Eastern region (28.1 per cent).

Table 5.1 Right to Buy and other sales to sitting tenants by local authorities and new towns in Great Britain, 1979–92

Year	Sold to sitting tenants
1979	4,140[a]
1980	83,175[a]
1981	108,980
1982	213,581
1983	152,359
1984	114,794
1985	102,395
1986	98,655
1987	115,081
1988	174,500
1989	195,120
1990	132,692
1991	76,746
1992	69,288

Note: [a] Includes other sales of existing dwellings, local authorities only.
Source: Housing and Construction Statistics, 1978-88; 1980-90; Part 2, No. 49, 1992, HMSO.

There can be no doubt that the Right to Buy and sales to individual purchasers has effectively extended choices to many council tenants and has transformed many areas of council housing. Many of those who exercised the Right to Buy had sufficient resources to buy houses elsewhere. The choice provided under the Right to Buy presented different elements – an extremely preferential discounted purchase price and the opportunity to buy what in most cases was an established home which the family was reluctant to leave. In this sense the choice did not test attachment to home and area. Tenants could exit the tenure and the financial regime without leaving the dwelling. The normal trade offs involved in housing and house purchase decisions did not have to be faced. It may be argued that decisions to exercise the Right to Buy represent exit from the state sector. Alternatively, such decisions could be seen to represent statements of commitment to the dwellings and areas created by state investment in housing. Both perspectives, however, must take into account the conscious attempt to generate sales by manipulating the pricing of renting and buying to favour house purchase.

The Right to Buy and other sales of housing merit three other comments. First, its success in generating capital receipts enhanced its appeal to central government and the Treasury Capital receipts from the housing programme amounted to £17,580 million in the ten years after 1979. They represented 43 per cent of all the government's privatisation programmes and a key element in the public expenditure, and fiscal policies of government.

Second, the sale of flats under leaseholds rather than removing local authority involvement in these properties left them with responsibility in respect of management, maintenance and repair. Leasehold management and service charges began to emerge as important areas for local policy especially in London boroughs.

Third, the choices provided under the Right to Buy are inevitably unequal. They are choices for existing tenants which in the long term reduce those of new tenants; they are choices which are less generous for those in less desirable and saleable dwellings; and they are choices which generate much more substantial cash gains in areas of higher house prices and for those in the most desirable dwellings.

If the Right to Buy dominated housing policy in these years it was by no means the only element in policy. Schemes to make it easier for council and housing association tenants to move to other districts were introduced and a range of low cost home ownership policies were often targeted on council tenants in particular. In addition the housing legislation of 1980 had introduced a tenants' charter which strengthened tenancy rights and established a legal form of secure tenancy.

During this period of policy there were other significant developments in the ownership of public sector housing. Important transfers were made between local authorities (including the transfer of GLC stock to London boroughs and transfers to other local authorities of some properties in areas beyond the boundaries of landlord authorities). The stock of New Town housing continued initially to be transferred to the local district council. There were important developments in the sale of vacant properties to the private sector and some new departures such as the establishment of the Stockbridge Village Trust to take over Knowsley's Cantrill Farm Estate. New measures in the legislation of 1986 speeded the process of disposal to the private sector (see Usher 1987; 1988). At the same time the government resisted further transfer of new town housing to local authorities.

By 1986 a shift in the emphasis of policy was apparent. The

Housing and Planning Act 1986, as well as making the right to buy more attractive, introduced measures to facilitate other forms of privatisation. The emphasis shifted to sales to private developers and other landlords. The legislation was a precursor to the 1987 election slogan of the 'Right to Rent' and the measures contained in the Housing Act 1988 to change and revive the private rented sector. The Right to Rent involved further deregulation of private renting and a more substantial role for housing associations and legislation in 1988 and 1989 was designed to carry this through.

This legislative package also introduced a new financial regime in England and changed tenancy arrangements in the private and housing association sectors throughout the UK. For this chapter however it is the introduction of Tenants' Choice and powers to establish Housing Action Trusts which are most important. Local authorities were no longer to have the major role in new building for social rented housing – it was housing associations which inherited this role. But, more than this, government aimed to reduce the existing dominant role of local authorities in the sector through creating new routes for exit.

The second phase: Tenants' Choice

The background to Tenants' Choice, voluntary transfers and HATs is best outlined through reference to the policy statements emerging from government in 1987 and 1988. These are dealt with in some detail before discussing the policy outputs.

The Conservative Manifesto 1987 (Conservative Party, 1987) introduced the Choice of Landlord scheme under the heading 'Rights for council tenants'. It stated that where council estates were badly designed, vulnerable to crime and vandalism, were in bad repair and, where rent arrears were high it is often difficult for tenants to move. 'If they are ever to enjoy the prospect of independence, municipal monopoly must be replaced by choice in renting.' Two key paragraphs outlined what this involved:

We will give groups of tenants the right to form tenant co-operatives, owning and running their management and budget for themselves. They will also have the right to ask other institutions to take over their housing. Tenants who wish to remain with the local authority will be able to do so.

We will give each council house tenant individually the right to transfer the ownership of his or her house to a housing association, or other independent, approved landlord.

(Conservative Party, 1987, p. 14)

The problems of council estates were ownership and management by local authorities – a view asserted by a range of other commentators (Henney, 1984, 1985; Power, 1987).

The Secretary of State for Environment in a speech in 1987 (Ridley, 1987), juxtaposed choice and improved management and conditions and explained the merits of releasing capital tied up in council housing so that it could 'be turned over, over and over again in order to transform housing conditions'. But neither tenant control nor the release of substantial funds were stated to be necessary components of 'choice'. Later in the same speech Mr Ridley outlined social and community problems and stated:

We must therefore find ways of enabling more balanced, mixed communities to develop; to remedy some of the physical difficulties in the way of decent living conditions on such estates; to secure better all-round standards of service; to help tenants to help themselves. Our priority is to put the tenants first as customers, as they should be.

He went on to outline the rights for tenants to transfer:

First that in order to move towards more diverse communities and to give tenants an effective voice in determining their own future we will introduce a right for local authority tenants to choose to transfer to other landlords. Tenants in blocks of flats or maisonettes will be able to transfer collectively. Tenants living in separate houses will have the right to transfer individually. New landlords might for example be tenant co-operatives or housing associations or private landlords approved by the Secretary of State. No one who is content with his or her landlord and is happy with the service they get will be forced to transfer; they may choose to stay as council tenants. For example tenants in a block of flats might become sub-tenants of the new owner with the local authority as their immediate landlord.

The wider assumptions behind the approach were indicated in a later speech Mr Waldegrave, the Minister of Housing. He stated that he could see no arguments for generalised new build by councils and expressed the belief that there should not be much property in council ownership at all.

It is an oddity confined largely to Britain amongst European countries that the State goes landlording on this scale. The next great push after the Right to Buy should be to get rid of the State as a big landlord and bring housing back to the community. If you want to buy and can buy, so much the better; if, for example, flats are more likely to continue to be rented, then the landlords should be the sort of social housing organisations we see overseas. They can represent tenants more closely; they are not caught up in the electoral swings and cycles of party politics; they can be single minded about housing and as skilful about it as only specialists can be; they can in many cases be smaller and more local.

While British Housing Associations could operate to this model local housing authorities could concentrate on their front line housing welfare role, buying the housing services they need, or subsidising those who need help, and undertaking the wide range of regulatory enforcement, planning and other tasks which are the essence of the public sector. The White Papers outlining legislative proposals placed considerable emphasis on problems in housing estates. The Scottish White Paper (Scottish Office, 1987) stated:

The problems of disrepair and bad management in some areas have extended beyond housing to affect the quality of life as a whole. As the quality of the housing and its environment has declined, crime and violence have increased; many people have left for better opportunities elsewhere; local enterprise and employment have disappeared; and whole communities have slipped into a permanent dependence on the welfare system from which it is extremely difficult for people to escape. Providing a choice for those who are public sector tenants through lack of alternatives is one part of the solution to these problems. Another is to improve the position of those who wish to remain as public sector tenants.

(paras 1-11 to 1-12)

And in England, (DoE, 1987):

the system of ownership and management ... is often not in the tenant's best long term interest. In some areas the system has provided good quality housing and management. But in many big cities local authority housing operations are so large that they inevitably risk becoming distant and bureaucratic. Insensitive design and bad management have alienated tenants and left housing badly maintained. As the quality of the housing and of its environment has declined, so a wide range of social problems has emerged; crime and violence have increased; many people have left for better opportunities elsewhere; local enterprise and employment have disap-peared; and whole communities have slipped into a permanent dependence on the welfare system from which it is extremely difficult for people to escape.

(para. 1.9)

The Scottish White Paper referred to recent improvements in the status and rights of tenants in the public sector and presented the right to form co-operatives or to transfer to new landlords of their choice as a logical next step in moving forward to give tenants a greater positive role in securing the housing conditions and quality of community life to which they aspire. The intention to introduce arrangements to allow council tenants to choose to transfer to other landlords would:

offer a remedy for tenants who receive a poor service from their council. Exposing councils to healthy competition should also contribute to a better general standard of services even for tenants who do not transfer.

(DoE, 1987, para. 5.9)

Similarly in Scotland:

tenants who are not satisfied with their housing conditions or the standard of management offered by their present landlord should not have to wait for improvements if they can obtain a better service more quickly from another landlord. The Government intend to introduce new rights for tenants to choose to transfer their tenancy to other landlords. As transfers take place, authorities will be able to concentrate more effectively on providing an improved service for the remainder of their tenants.

(Scottish Office, 1987, para. 6.9)

Subsequent papers reiterated the options and elements of choice, the landlords involved (local authorities with statutory powers to provide general housing for rent, new towns but not housing associations or charities or co-operatives) the excepted housing (as with the Right to Buy, dwellings let in connection with employment, especially built or adapted for the disabled or handicapped, dwellings particularly suitable for and used for the elderly) and excepted tenants (non-secure tenants). Landlords would have to be approved before they could take on tenants under Tenants' Choice. While landlords might be registered housing associations, co-operatives or other independent housing bodies, they could also be private firms. The approval process would aim to ensure that new landlords were financially stable and capable of managing their homes to a high standard while giving value for money. Local authorities and other public sector landlords were excluded from being 'new landlords' under the scheme.

Procedures were also set out for the process of implementing Tenants' Choice including adjudication, valuation and ballot. Inevitably there were problems in this and the ultimate safeguard which emerged was in restricting the agencies able to initiate the procedure and strengthening the scrutiny role of the Housing Corporation, Housing for Wales and Scottish Homes. The form of this supervision was referred to as the social landlords' charter.

The increasing emphasis on a social landlords' charter and the insistence upon all new landlords conforming with this was an important addition to the policy since its first appearance. It also represented part of a stronger recognition of the need for social rented housing. Thus Mr Ridley prefaced a discussion of Tenants' Choice as follows:

Everyone agrees we need subsidised housing for the less well off. There has been something of a debate as to the extent to which those subsidies should be provided for the houses themselves, bricks and mortar subsidies, or for the tenant-housing benefit. We do not think the goal can be achieved solely through housing benefit. This would mean an undesirable increase in the number of people caught in an earnings 'trap' – people for whom there was a disincentive to increase their earnings because by doing so they would lose benefit.

So we are aiming to create a third market, with housing provided below cost for those who cannot afford to buy or rent privately.

(Ridley, 1988)

The Minister acknowledged that since the Bill had been published a great deal of further thought had been given to how the social rented sector would operate in future and to the contribution that private landlords could make. A new code of guidance for housing associations – a tenants' guarantee and procedures for Tenants' Choice and the criteria for large scale disposals of stock had been developed.

Mr Waldegrave outlined a wider concept of social housing which emphasised the need to ensure that those who take over council housing, either at the tenants' request or as the result of voluntary transfer by councils, do not strip the assets and that the housing provided continues to meet needs left unmet by the market and is not sold for other purposes. In the first instance, Government or the Housing Corporation would see that the articles under which the new landlord is established, are compatible with this. As a long-stop landlords who later want to dispose of property which has been transferred to them would need the Secretary of State's consent to do so, and that would help make this commitment stick. He also emphasised the need to make sure that tenants would not find themselves transferred to landlords who, while accepting their continuing role in providing low cost rented housing, drop standards for tenants unacceptably. This necessitates a proper guarantee that transferred property must normally be kept available for renting, but also guarantees decent treatment for the tenants themselves. As far as Tenants' Choice is concerned, the procedures must give tenants real choice and proper information with which to exercise it. In addition Mr Waldegrave considered it important to prevent transfers to new landlords which met all of these tests but might be indirectly controlled by the council. The proposals emerging from this:

Will establish a tenants' guarantee for those in Registered Housing Associations and housing transferred from local authorities, and will establish fair and open landlords, independent of councils, with a commitment to meeting housing needs. We will be opening up a new era in Britain, in which a far wider and more pluralist rented housing sector will come into existence.

(Waldegrave, 1988)

Government's objectives in safeguarding tenants and services involved placing the Housing Corporation and Scottish Homes at the centre of the procedure for tenants' choice – for scrutinising and approving which landlords, tenants and dwellings could be involved. The requirements of the social landlords' charter made it likely that any tenants' choice transfer would be to registered non-profit-making housing associations. The charter also applied to other tenants of housing associations.

These statements form the background to changes in ownership since 1988. By the end of 1993 Tenants Choice had not resulted in a single property moving away from local authority control. The reasons for action not taking place are always difficult to discern and the simplest answer is to argue that Tenants' Choice did not relate to tenants' concerns and needs. Tenants appear to prefer the landlord they know and the images of inefficient landlords which appear to have figured large in Ministerial minds are less dramatic in those of tenants. Publicity given to possible predatory or speculative landlords may have reinforced the fear that a new landlord would be worse. There is some support for this view in the increased uptake of the right to buy associated with the uncertainty surrounding future landlords. It is also the case that many housing associations as potential new landlords were wary of the process and did not wish to conform to a predatory image.

Leaving this aside the Tenants' Choice arrangements have not proved wholly academic. They have provided the framework for large scale voluntary transfers.

Large scale voluntary transfers

In the period when Tenants' Choice measures were under discussion and following the introduction of Tenants' Choice, a number of local authority landlords took stock of their situation and took steps to initiate procedures to transfer their stock. By the end of 1993, 23 transfers had been completed (Table 5.2). This landlord initiated process – Landlords' Choice – received Ministerial recognition in 1988. Ministers would approve such transfers where they followed procedures similar to those embodied in Tenants' Choice and the social landlords' charter. For local authorities actively contemplating major or total disposals, the concern to preserve a rented stock and escape the public expenditure restrictions which limited capital expenditure on their stock were important considerations. Their concern in the light of this was to transfer to a responsible social landlord rather than to a predator landlord who would maximise profits through asset stripping or actions which would reduce the quality of service available to those needing to rent.

Voluntary transfers have occurred on the initiative of individual local authorities using statutory powers (under the Housing Act 1985) for disposals of land and dwellings subject to the Secretary of State's consent. Mullins et al. (1993) point out that these powers were not introduced with voluntary transfers in mind and that provisions in the 1988 Act which elaborated on the considerations the Secretary of State would look at can best be seen as a response to local government initiatives already underway. They also point out that the first completed transfer (in Chiltern) actually predated the implementation of the 1988 Act. These authors comment:

voluntary transfer decisions cannot be understood in isolation from the national policy agenda. Interviews in case study authorities generally located the main impetus to voluntary transfers in reactions to the Government's housing policies. In a number of areas the process started with officer assessments of the implications of the 1987 White Paper for their authorities' future housing role. While implementation decisions were local, their context was clearly the relationship between central and local government,

and the various threats which national policy was perceived to constitute to
local housing services.

(Mullins et al., 1993, pp. 170-171)

Large scale voluntary transfers of local authority housing are subject
to the consent of the Secretary of State but were seen to accord well
with the enabling role which the Government envisages for local
authorities in housing (DOE, 1988). The Secretary of State would
consider each application on its individual merits but would be
unlikely to give approval unless the acquiring body was independent
of the local authority, able to demonstrate that it is a stable and
responsible organisation with a long-term commitment to the
provision of rental housing for those who need it and committed to
providing a good service to tenants. Consent would be unlikely to be
given to disposal to a single purchaser of more than 5,000-10,000
properties and authorities within that range would need to demonstrate the advantages of doing so:

The Secretary of State does not wish to see large public housing monopolies
converted into large private housing monopolies. To ensure that the
management problems which beset over large housing organisations are not
perpetuated, he will in principle prefer local authorities to dispose of their
stock to more than one purchaser. This is also in line with the Government's
objective of providing a wider choice in rented housing. Even in the area of
a small housing authority, it would be undesirable if a disposal created a
single new predominant landlord in the area. The key point is that, so far as
reasonably possible, there should be genuine competition in the local
market.

(DoE, 1988)

Consultation with tenants was necessary and the disposal would not
go ahead if a majority of the tenants affected oppose it. Sales would
be at market value, subject to tenancy and allowing for a repairs
backlog. They should be privately financed, although a residual
portion of the purchase price could be outstanding on mortgage to
the council.

Welsh office guidance also encouraged such transfers but stronger
reference was made to the form of management structure and to
estate based management, tenant participation in management, and
the provision of readily understandable information. Reference was
made to the advantages of arrangements under which tenants could
become members of or shareholders in their new landlords. In Wales
a single purchaser of more than 4,000 properties was unlikely to

Table 5.2 Large scale voluntary transfers by local authorities in England, 1988–92

Local authority	Year of transfer	No. of dwellings
Chiltern	1988	4,650
Sevenoaks	1989	6,526
Newbury	1989	7,053
Swale	1990	7,352
Broadland	1990	3,721
North Bedfordshire	1990	7,472
Medina	1990	2,825
Rochester	1990	8,029
South Wight	1990	2,119
Mid Sussex	1990	4,429
East Dorset	1990	2,245
Tonbridge and Malling	1991	6,382
Ryedale	1991	3,353
South Bucks	1991	3,319
Christchurch	1991	1,542
Suffolk Coastal	1991	5,272
Tunbridge Wells	1992	5,519
Bromley	1992	12,393
Surrey Heath	1993	3,068
East Cambridgeshire	1993	4,266
Breckland	1993	6,684
Hambleton	1993	4,268
West Dorset	1993	5,279
Total		117,766

Source: Hansard, House of Commons, 16.7.92, Col. 1044; Audit Commission (1993).

receive consent. Transfers carried out in the first phase of LSVT policy are summarised in Table 5.2. The 23 transfers have been mainly from smaller shire districts especially in the South. The only comparable transfer completed in Scotland involved the transfer of Scottish Homes' stock in the Borders to Waverley Housing Trust.

At the time of the general election of 1992 it was rumoured that some 150 councils were contemplating voluntary transfer and would go ahead if the post-election situation promised no change and no better prospects for the local authority housing service. No such rush to transfer emerged in the six months which followed the general election. Various factors contributed to this including concern about the housing benefit implications and revised guidance about the size of units of transfer. Other concerns existed over pricing, the availability of private finance and the large amount of borrowing necessary to achieve very limited additions to the housing stock. The government announced revised rules for transfers in 1993/94 and later. The total stock to be transferred was to be limited nationally (initially to about 25,000 units in 1993/94). In addition, in order to secure a diversity of new landlords a benchmark of 3,000 to 4,000 properties per disposal was set. And in order to limit the impact of transfers on public expenditure (through increased housing benefits) not all the proceeds from the sale would remain with the local authority.

Of the completed transfers, one (Bromley) breached the previously indicated maximum for transfer to the single landlord. Only eight would have failed to break the limit regarded as appropriate for Wales. If the local authority could previously be represented as a monopoly landlord in these areas then the new landlords are no less monopolists. Demunicipalisation has not involved any break up of monopoly control. The new landlords have generally been able to embark on repairs and other programmes which will benefit tenants. Inevitably new tenants experience other changes. They have higher rents than their longer established neighbours and have no statutory right to buy. By the end of 1991, 12 proposals for voluntary transfers had been rejected by tenants and a further 21 had been dropped prior to ballot (Mullins et al., 1992). In such cases the choice can be offered again. But where the decision to transfer was agreed by tenants and the transfer has taken place Tenants' Choice ceases to apply and neither new nor existing tenants have any choice of landlord remaining.

In evaluating the early experience it has also been argued that the transfers which have taken place raise concerns over a lack of awareness of what is involved in a transfer and difficulties for tenants in making an informed choice. Central to these problems is that the financial and administrative arrangements do not operate on a level playing field (the restrictions on what local authorities can spend and can do, distorts the choices on offer). It is also argued that valuations and therefore the viability of the whole package are sensitive to assumptions about future rents, management and maintenance expenditure, right to buy sales and tenancy turnover. The sensitivity to assumptions adds a perception of risk which increases the premium charged by those financing transfers and, by effectively lowering the price which can be paid, makes them less attractive to the local authority (and the Treasury). The absence of any mechanism to make adjustments in the light of how far actual experience diverges from assumptions results in long term financial advantages or disadvantages which will affect tenants. (see Gardiner et al., 1991). These are real issues for the transfers which have taken place but these are all in areas where even with these complications loan debt could be written off following transfer. The inner London boroughs and large urban authorities are not often in this position and transfer in these areas may prove impossible whatever government decides to approve.

These questions have been modified by the new arrangements applying to transfers since the first phase referred to here. As well as the concern not to transfer large blocks of stock to single landlords, central government is to take 20 per cent of any balance arising from a transfer once housing debt has been paid off by means of a levy. This levy relates to the effects of transfer on housing benefit and the loss of HRA contributions to Housing Benefit when transfers occur. By 1993 the government had approved 12 additional transfers under these rules and 11 of these relate to the whole of the local authority's stock. These new arrangements make LSVT less attractive financially to local authorities but do not alter the basic issues for existing and new tenants in relation to rents, repairs and other investment.

Housing Action Trusts

The final element in the patchwork of tenants' choices involves Housing Action Trusts. The legislation for these trusts was included in the Housing Act 1988 and applied to England and Wales only. HATs were presented as a new method of tackling the growing problems of disrepair and neglect of local authority housing in urban areas. It was designed to supplement the initiatives being developed through Estate Action and Priority Estate Projects. The model for HATs was the Urban Development Corporations set up in a number of cities under the Local Government, Planning and Land Act 1980. HATs would be established in designated areas to take over responsibility for local authority housing, renovate it and hand it on to different forms of management and ownership (DOE, 1987). The HATs were to be corporations appointed by the Secretary of State to take over large rundown estates and secure repair and improvement and proper and effective management and use of the housing stock. Following this, they would transfer ownership to new private or voluntary sector landlords. In the initial formulation HATs were a response to failed local authority management. Neither local authorities nor tenants were to be consulted, there was to be no tenant ballot, boards would be appointed by the Secretary of State with no intent of representative status and transfer back to the local authority was not envisaged. The original proposals placed wide powers with the Secretary of State and his appointed board and little or no power with tenants or the local authority.

The first six areas identified by Central Government for HATs (Lambeth, Leeds, Sandwell, Tower Hamlets, Sunderland and South-wark) were announced without consultation before the legislative process was completed. These were intended to be the forerunners of a larger programme but local authority and tenant opposition in these six cases halted progress. Some of this opposition focused on the lack of any provision for balloting tenants. Although government subsequently accepted a House of Lords' amendment which introduced such provision, the damage was already done (Woodward, 1991; Gregory and Hainsworth, 1993). The evidence of overwhelming opposition to HATs in Lambeth and Leeds meant that neither went to a formal ballot. Tower Hamlets was withdrawn on 'technical' grounds and Sandwell received Estate Action money instead. Only Sunderland and Southwark went to a ballot and both rejected HATs by majorities of over 70 per cent. After two and a half years on the statute book the HAT powers remained unused. Faced with this rejection Ministers would use the resources earmarked for HATs on other programmes but were prepared to consider sympathetically any proposals for a Trust which other councils or tenants brought forward (Gregory and Hainsworth, 1993).

The failure of the initial conception of HATs is evidence of ministerial misunderstandings of the position of council tenants. Valerie Karn's account of the policy process identifies that tenants far from feeling rescued were alarmed at the prospect of HATs. Even after the right to a ballot had been conceded tenants were concerned that after a HAT had been created there would be no control over rents and the future of estates. Feasibility studies identified these problems and recommended that government needed to drop the confrontational approach to local government, that illustrative plans should be distributed before ballots and that a lengthy consultation process was needed. In addition, HAT budgets were increased. However, making HATs more acceptable in these ways did not secure support and lack of certainty and lack of trust in central government proved key factors. As a result, the HATs which eventually emerged were local authority HATs – HATs set up in a manner acceptable to local authorities and tenants (Karn, 1993).

The first local authority to enter into negotiation with Government was Kingston upon Hull. Hull agreed that provided a series of conditions were met it would actively support a HAT proposal to tenants on its North Hull estate. The conditions involved keeping the Department of the Environment out of the consultation process, making the HAT board acceptable to local people, setting up the HAT board before the ballot and asking Government to commit itself to a detailed reassurance about the return of homes to local authority control if tenants so chose. After gaining agreement on these conditions the local authority, proceeded to market the HAT with its tenants. The proposal was approved (not overwhelmingly) by tenants (see Gregory and Hainsworth, 1993). Following Hull two other districts (Waltham Forest in 1991 and Liverpool in 1992) have negotiated acceptable proposals which have been approved by tenants.

In 1994 it seemed likely that further HATs would emerge. Whether or not they do, any HATs that are established are a long way from the original Ministerial conception. The Minister of Housing had agreed that ballots of tenants would proceed in Birmingham and in Tower Hamlets with a view to setting up new HATs. HATs will continue to be initiated and orchestrated by the local authority and to be devices to capture additional capital allocations. Most critically they will operate in a similar way to other methods of carrying out improvements to council properties. They will sit alongside (or within) the Estate Action programme, representing partnerships between central and local government – more like the Partnership Schemes in Scotland than the confrontational HATs originally proposed.

Discussion

The elements of policy presented in this chapter have been in operation for different time periods and their scale of impact has been very different. The major aspects of this have been discussed separately in each case. From these more specific considerations a number of general issues emerge. Firstly in terms of the scale of impact the most important element of tenants' choice has been the right to buy. HATs and Tenants' Choice have had very limited numerical impact. Large scale voluntary transfers have had more impact but in 1993 the future prospects are unclear. This ranking of relative importance also relates to other issues. Both HATs and voluntary transfers have been landlord initiated. Rather than shifting the initiative and control in council housing they could reasonably be regarded as merely new policy devices through which the state manages neighbourhoods, property and people. The empowerment of tenants is not yet self evident and it may be that these new mechanisms are better seen as representing landlords' choice. This does not mean that tenants' and landlords' choices are necessarily opposed. In contrast to this the rights associated with the Right to Buy represent more clear cut individual choices which, once exercised, place the tenant in a different tenure with different legal rights.

The different scale of impact raises a second fundamental point. The White Papers, Ministerial Statements and other policy documents which introduced the 1988 policy package were confident statements appealing to an exploited and dissatisfied tenantry. The expectations of a rush to exit were clear. In practice there was resistance rather than a rush. Policy had to be altered and sweeteners introduced to persuade tenants to exit. HATs and LSVT have been packaged to guarantee existing tenants (who have a place in decision making) attractive elements with protection over rents. The costs of these enhanced tenancy packages are postponed and borne by newcomers who will not have a choice of landlord once they become a tenant (and may not have had one previously). Even the Right to Buy has this feature. Discounts in 1980 were as high as 50 per cent but were raised in 1984 and again in 1986. Tenants of flats were less prominent among purchasers before the enhanced discounts (up to 70 per cent) of 1986.

It was important to government that tenants took up choices and proved they preferred to exit and, to ensure the desired result, the balance of advantage for tenants was shifted. The meaning of tenants' decisions and the nature of the policy has to be understood in this context. It also raises another point. For some tenants the package on offer meant short term gains from buying. Rents could be more expensive than mortgage repayments. But if circumstances changed through unemployment or loss of income or relationship breakdown the problems could be greater. And as maintenance and repair costs increased the advantages were eroded. The attention given to some flat purchasers whose short term gain translates to high service charges on a property which is difficult to sell and has declined in value highlights this element and the difficulty of evaluating the gain to the tenant compared with those to government.

Leaving the Right to Buy aside, the experience with other policies presented within the language of empowerment and choice draws attention to different elements in the objectives of these policies. The various statements emanating from government have different emphases and three different formulations of objectives can be identified.

1. Providing the right to choose by definition alters the position of tenants. However the right is exercised, the objective is an end in itself and is achieved at a stroke with the royal assent to legislation.
2. Providing the right to choose provides the capacity to alter the pattern of ownership of rented housing. It may bring in new organisations including tenant co-operatives or may merely redistribute between existing owners (say from councils to the independent sector). It could actually reduce the number of landlords and increase the average size of social landlords. The objective is achieved if the pattern of ownership is changed whether or not a greater variety of landlords operates.
3. Providing the right to choose is a means of changing the quality of life and the standards of service experienced by those living on less desirable and less well-managed estates. This is by far the most ambitious interpretation of the objective and the one most relevant to consumers in that it provides some change in their material circumstances. It is far and away the most difficult to evaluate. If the right to choose a landlord was widely exercised but only or principally by those in the 'best' and 'best managed' parts of the council stock it would arguably have failed to achieve objectives. In contrast, if it was only used to a limited extent but had affected the 'worst' and 'worst managed' council estates, it would have come nearer to achieving objectives. Ironically, it could be argued that if it failed to result in any transfers of ownership but did trigger a real change in management style and service delivery in the council sector in general and the worst

parts of it in particular, it would almost certainly have achieved most in terms of changing conditions for tenants. It is not evident however that Ministerial thinking was focused on service delivery rather than on the assumed means of achieving this.

When the experience is evaluated against these objectives different conclusions arise. Additional rights have been provided through legislation. However it is also important to recognise that the same legislation means that new tenants of housing associations (and new tenants in districts where stock has been transferred to such associations) will be assured tenants and have higher rents and fewer right than previously or than tenants in the council sector who remain secure tenants. Assured tenants in particular lack the Right to Buy. The extension and exercise of choice for one group of tenants reduces the choices for their successors and determines the regime they will have to cope with. It is also important to avoid overstating the effect of new rights on the practice of housing management. In the private rented sector the existence of rights has not meant that tenants have been protected (see e.g. GLC, 1984). And in the public sector local authority management practice did not generally operate in ways which antagonised tenants or was significantly changed by measures affecting management in the 1980s. While it is true that council tenants had few legal rights it is naive to present this as the test of quality of service. Birchall's view that 'public-sector housing has always been deeply flawed because it has always, as a matter of course, excluded the interest of the users' is an inadequate assessment and bears no relation to the comparative experience of other tenants with legal rights (Birchall, 1992, p. 163).

In terms of altering the pattern of ownership and control of social rented housing significant changes have been achieved in specific localities through LSVT and HATs but not nationally. However the changes achieved represents demunicipalisation without the introduction of a plurality of alternative landlords and the landlords involved may be less accountable to tenants. Evaluation in terms of the quality of service is premature. Areas affected by HATs and voluntary transfer have escaped the constraints which prevent local authorities from investing at the rate they would prefer and real benefits have accrued. New tenants will pay higher rents but there is no reason to expect any general dissatisfaction with the quality of service. Moreover it may reasonably be argued that the environment of tenants choice and transfers has contributed to the growing concern with service delivery. Throughout the 1980s and earlier some local authorities have given great attention to the quality of service. Many local authorities did develop decentralisation, provision of more information and consultation with tenants and setting standards and targets for performance. Various factors have contributed to this and central government's interest has added weight to an underlying trend. These developments (leaving aside ideas of a right to manage and the impact of compulsory competitive tendering) may give tenants more effective power and choice. In this case however the achievement will have been to increase the 'voice' of the tenant and power to affect the service received from the existing landlord. The emphasis of government policy has been rather to encourage 'exit'.

In all of this the emergence of the Social Landlords' Charter is an enormous advance on the arrangements initially drawn up. It offers a prospect of eliminating gross exploitation. It places the major emphasis on how the Housing Corporation and others exercise very substantial discretionary roles. However, the Charter falls a long way short of a comprehensive protection for tenants. It appears to fall between two models – that of a code of practice and that of a legal contract. There must be doubts about how far it will prevent asset stripping or other less committed landlords from being approved. The phraseology of 'normally' continuing to let properties does not rule out an erosion of the rented stock through this. The more paranoid scenarios are that less responsible landlords can work through more responsible ones and their true nature emerge later; or that control and management of approved landlords can change; or that unexpected financial pressures will contribute to some less enlightened management practices. The implications for those needing to rent – of Tenants' Choice leading to a declining stock as a result of this, and of declining security – are important. The scale of the problem depends initially on how far tenants use the choice and subsequently on how far the social landlord's charter can be and is enforced.

Where established housing associations are involved there may be a reasonable degree of confidence in how they will operate. However this will not always be so and the powers of the Housing Corporation after approval and especially after transfer of property are critical. The most problematic situation arises when properties have been transferred. After transfer all tenants will have binding tenancy terms which can be enforced contractually. While, for example, the Housing Corporation will be able to assist tenants in certain ways, enforcement will be through legal processes initiated by tenants.

There are clear expectations about contractual rights for tenants in respect of exchange of tenancies, taking lodgers or sub-tenants, carrying out improvements, providing information and setting up clear procedures and frameworks, especially in relation to rents and repairs. However, unless the language of undertakings is judged to be enforceable in the Courts and unless tenants are able to use the Courts effectively, it must be doubtful if it would represent an effective Tenants' Guarantee. This is particularly the case where a landlord is less than committed to the spirit of the document or is under financial or other pressure to adopt a different approach. Furthermore, landlords' responses to difficult tenants or tenants with arrears of rent is likely to escape such constraints and reflect other pressures. It would be preferable if different and speedy procedures existed to enable the Housing Corporation or some other body to act on behalf of tenants and to prevent landlords from breaking under-takings.

It may be argued that as a long term consumers' charter these arrangements are seriously deficient in other ways:

• they provide a once and for all choice with no opportunity for tenants' review;
• by excluding public agencies from the competition as new landlord they significantly reduce the range of potential new landlords and the potential for local authorities to revise their own procedures through experience as bidding new landlord;
• only council and new town tenants have Tenants' Choice – housing association and other types of tenant are excluded. Where housing association tenants feel their landlord is remote, too large or unresponsive, they do not have the same options;
• a growing distinction will emerge between two groups of tenants: (1) those who were secure tenants at the time of transfer who have exercised choice of landlord and who retain the Right to Buy and – if they stay with the existing landlord – the rights of secure tenants; and (2) those who have had no choice of landlord, have never been secure tenants and will not be entitled to the Right to

Buy. They will also not have the rights of secure tenants but of assured tenants.

Tenants' Choice and voluntary transfer are choices made by one generation of tenants which reduce the rights of the next generation. Depending on this and how far it progresses, it reduces the portion of the housing stock easily transferred through sitting tenant purchase. As a result, it closes down one route into home ownership. For some households this will directly reduce the likelihood of their becoming home owners. From this perspective it does not seem to be a good development for all consumers.

Any full commentary on these developments would refer to other elements. Briefly these include the changing nature of central–local government relations involved. Central government's stance is more interventionist with more specific powers, used more often and operating against a background of financial and other measures which prevent local authorities from developing the service as they think fit. The anti-municipal stance of central government and the absence of a level playing field between alternative providers of rented housing affects what is on offer to tenants. In this environment local authorities have developed their own internal organisation and policies. They have also developed a range of partnerships with private and voluntary sector organisations and begun to develop new relationships with tenants – using legislation to support tenants and develop tenants' organisations. The implications of sales and transfers of stock have been profound for some local authorities and important for all. At the same time they have had a profound impact on housing associations – adding to other pressures to review and change their role. Finally, in the whole policy area the issue of capital receipts remains central. Government has not used the capital receipts generated from sales and transfer to increase housing expenditure and feed back into the quality of the rented housing sector or the local authority housing service.

Future developments

In 1993 a number of elements are in place which affect the future of rented housing. The economic situation and pressures on public expenditure mean that new capital investment in local authority housing will continue to be severely restricted and rents are likely to rise. The Government's housing programme of 1987 and 1988 has been overtaken by an unexpected recession and unprecedented problems in the home ownership sector. Its policy preoccupations have moved on. Nevertheless, Government seems likely to maintain its anti-municipal stance and desire to reorganise the tenure structure. Against this background the Right to Buy is likely to continue to recruit purchasers. Rising rents, uncertainties about tenancy arrangements and any future economic upturn are likely to increase the rate of sale. Existing HATs are likely to continue as they are now as an additional mechanism to achieve renewal on large council estates. The financial provision for HATs is being terminated and incorporated into the Single Regeneration Budget. As a result the number of HAT areas will be small. Whether properties will be returned to council ownership subsequently will depend on various circumstances applying at that time.

There is no reason to believe that tenant initiated tenants' choice will blossom in the future. The evidence of underlying dissatisfaction with council housing is limited and relates to a range of factors and the Government's view of tenants' desire to exit is exaggerated. Rising rents and discussions about compulsory competitive tendering may destabilise the situation and affect tenants' views of the range of choices. However the most uncertain additional element concerns the impact of landlord initiated proposals through voluntary transfers. Tenant reaction to such proposals is likely to continue to be mixed. However the terms of voluntary transfers can be made attractive to tenants. As with HATs, these are unpalatable choices for the local authority when its own capacity to invest is limited and the best way of preserving a rented stock and improving services to tenants involves transfer. In this situation what will be crucial is Government's (the Treasury's) view of the cost of transfer. If the housing benefit costs are not deemed excessive, transfers in the English shire counties may prove significant. Outside these areas they are less likely. Other public sector landlords including Scottish Homes are likely, in any event, to maintain their policies of disposal.

The framework in particular of the Right to Buy and landlord initiated choices are likely to continue to provide active choices for some tenants. However the Right to Buy in the long term reduces opportunities and choices in the rented sector. Transfers which in the long term are designed to reduce further losses from the rented stock through the right to buy will reduce the consumer choices of individuals as tenants albeit to increase those of applicants for rented housing unable to buy. The simplest way out of this tension and to maintain real choices for more tenants is to maintain building and acquisition programmes to meet rented demand and for these to operate alongside policies which give individuals maximum choice over ownership and control of their dwelling. The reluctance to contemplate an investment programme based on these principles inevitably dilutes the extent and reality of tenant choice.

There is a final element in discussion of these policy developments. These are policies which have been built on the view that the nature and extent of the council housing system is a key element in contemporary housing problems and that changing ownership control and management would resolve a wide range of problems in council estates. This analysis of problems in council housing received at least partial support from accounts of changes and problems in council housing which took insufficient account of the long term restructuring of housing, the increasing concentration of households with least bargaining power on council estates, changing social and economic circumstances of households and the implications for turnover and community development. The resulting policies with their emphasis on management or ownership fall far short of policies which will resolve the problems articulated in the White Papers of 1988 and experienced by those unable to buy dwellings.

References

Audit Commission (1993) *Who Wins? Voluntary Housing Transfers*, Occasional Paper No. 20.

Birchall, J. (ed.) (1992) *Housing Policy in the 1990s*, Routledge, London.

Conservative Party (1987) *The Conservative Manifesto 1987*, CPCO, London.

Department of the Environment (1987) *Housing: The Government's Proposals*, Cm 214, HMSO, London.

Department of the Environment (1988) *Large Scale Voluntary Transfers of Local Authority Housing to Private Bodies*, DoE, London.

Dunn, R., Forrest, R. and Murie, A. (1987) The Geography of Council House Sales in England 1979-1985, *Urban Studies*, Vol. 24, pp. 47-59.

Forrest, R. and Murie, A. (1985) *An Unreasonable Act*, University of Bristol, Bristol.

Forrest, R. and Murie, A. (1988) *Selling the Welfare State*, Routledge, London.

Gardiner, K., Hills, J. and Kleinman, M. (1991) *Putting a Price on Council Housing: Valuing Voluntary Transfers*, Discussion Paper WSP/62, London School of Economics, London.

GLC (1984) *Private Tenants in London: The GLC Survey 1983-84*, GLC, London.

Gregory, P. and Hainsworth, M, (1993) Chameleons or Trojan Horses? The Strange Case of Housing Action Trusts, *Housing Studies*, Vol. 8, No. 2, pp. 109-119.

180 HOUSING MANAGEMENT AND OWNERSHIP

Henney, A. (1984) *Inside Local Government*, Sinclair Browne, London.
Henney, A. (1985) *Trust the Tenant: Devolving Municipal Housing*, Centre for Policy Studies, London.
Karn, V. (1993) Remodelling a HAT: The Implementation of the Housing Action Trust Legislation 1987-92 in Malpass, P. and Means, R., *Implementing Housing Policy*, Open University Press, Buckingham.
Malpass, P. and Murie, A. (1990) *Housing Policy and Practice*, Macmillan, Basingstoke.
Mullins, D., Niner, P. and Riseborough, M. (1992) *Evaluating Large Scale Voluntary Transfers of Local Authority Housing, An Interim Report*, HMSO, London.
Mullins, D., Niner, P. and Riseborough, M. (1993) Large-Scale Voluntary Transfers in Malpass, P. and Means, R., *Implementing Housing Policy*, Open University Press, Buckingham.
Murie, A. (1975) *The Sale of Council Houses*, University of Birmingham, Birmingham.
Murie, A. and Wang, Y. P. (1992) *The Sale of Public Sector Housing in Scotland 1979-1991*, School of Planning and Housing, Heriot-Watt University, Edinburgh.
Power, A. (1987) *Property Before People*, Unwin Hyman, London.
Ridley, N. (1987) *Conservative Proposals for Housing*, 19.5.87, Conservative Party News Service, London.
Ridley, N. (1988) *Speech to Institute of Housing Conference*, 17.6.88, DoE News Release.
Scottish Office (1987) *Housing: The Government's Proposals for Scotland*, Cm 242, HMSO, Edinburgh
Usher, D. (1987) *Council Estate Sales: Studies of Local Experiences and Future Prospects*, SAUS, University of Bristol, Bristol.
Usher, D. (1988) *Housing Privatisation: The Sale of Council Estates*, SAUS, University of Bristol, Bristol.
Waldegrave, W. (1988) *Speech to CIPFA Services*, 8.6.88, DoE News Release, DoE, London.
Woodward, R. (1991) Mobilising Opposition: The Campaign against Housing Action Trusts in Tower Hamlets, *Housing Studies*, Vol. 6, No. 1, pp. 44-56.

6

The changing role of local authority housing departments

Matthew Warburton

Introduction

Since 1979, the role of local authorities in housing has changed dramatically. They have virtually stopped building new homes, and now rely on 'enabling' new social housing through housing associations and other agencies. Most now focus their efforts on managing and improving the homes they built before 1979, although some authorities have transferred all or part of their stock to housing associations or Housing Action Trusts. They have become used to selling houses under the right to buy and developed skills in leasehold management where flats have been sold. They have taken over full responsibility for administering housing benefit, and adapted their allocations policies in response to a rising problem of homelessness.

As the role of local authorities in housing has changed, so have the structure, culture and practices of local authority housing departments. In 1979, the typical housing department was centralised, segmented into specialised divisions, had no mechanisms for tenant consultation and involvement and never used the word 'customer'. Now it is more likely to be decentralised, organised into areas rather than specialisms and believe itself to be 'customer conscious' to a fault. Instead of a development section responsible for planning, commissioning and managing a programme of new council housebuilding, it will have a section responsible for enabling housing associations and developers to provide new homes to which the local authority may have nomination rights.

The indicators of performance used to judge local authorities have also changed. Authorities were once judged by the number of slums they cleared and the number of new homes they built. Now the emphasis is on management performance and the level of tenant satisfaction.

Council tenants have changed, too, under the impact of the Right to Buy and the elimination of new council housebuilding, as well as broader economic and social changes. Compared with 1979, council tenants are now on average older, more likely to be elderly or single person households rather than families, less likely to be economically active and more likely to be receiving income support or in the lowest income decile. Further, the gap between the top and bottom 10 per cent of the income distribution widened significantly during the 1980s, further accentuating the differentiation between council tenants and the rest of society. The precise relationship between social deprivation and the difficulty of the housing management task is unclear, but there seems little doubt that the management task is harder now than it was in 1979.

Change is disruptive, and the pace of change has been unrelenting. Since 1979 there has been on average, a major housing Act every other year, three Acts on housing benefit and innumerable other pieces of legislation with minor housing implications. The level of Government intervention in the way councils manage housing has been unprecedented. Much of this legislation has been introduced, according to the Government, in order to improve the efficiency with which councils deliver services, or their accountability to tenants. Yet one cause of the poor performance which is claimed as the justification for intervention may be the disruption caused by responding to every new piece of legislation. On this view, time is the great healer, and what councils need now is a breathing space to reap the benefits of the changes which have been made, and the opportunity for a measured evaluation of the success or failure of the Government's interventions.

This opportunity will not, however, be granted. Between April 1996 and April 1998, all English local housing authorities will be required to expose the greater part of their housing operations to competitive tender. They will be prevented from allowing their own employees to manage the authority's housing unless they have won the work in competition. Preparations for CCT now dominate life in every housing department in the country, as well as much professional debate. Whether or not the in-house bid wins the work, no local authority housing department will ever be the same again.

The Government's case for extending CCT to housing management is that it will improve the quality and efficiency of management and 'bring choice and competition within the reach of council tenants ... [who] ... cannot shop around for themselves' (Michael Howard, then Secretary of State for the Environment, quoted in DOE, 1992). This emphasis on choice and competition gives the impression that CCT flows from the analysis presented in the Housing White Paper of 1987 (DOE, 1987), and is in direct line of descent from the measures introduced in the Housing Act 1988 and the ring-fencing of councils' housing revenue accounts imposed by the Local Government and Housing Act 1989. This impression is reinforced by the statement that 'the government considers that its proposals will build upon those developments by maintaining and enhancing good management practice and provide a means by which the poorest performing authorities can raise their standards of management so that tenants receive a better service in future' (DOE, 1992, p. 3).

The argument in this chapter is that CCT has little to do with improving the choice available to council tenants, and its impact on the quality and efficiency of housing management is difficult to predict and likely to vary significantly among authorities. The Government's faith in CCT is rooted in their inadequate explanation of poor housing management performance by local authorities, and their unrealistic expectations of the capacity of competition to improve it.

The Government's view – the failure of a system

The Government's analysis is simply and clearly stated in the 1987 Housing White Paper (DOE, 1987). The distinctive feature of this analysis is its diagnosis of management failure as endemic to council housing. Although it is grudgingly admitted that some council housing is well-designed and well-managed, the argument implies that this is the exception rather than the rule; the good performance of some local authorities has never been used by the Government as a reason to exempt them from the major policy initiatives since 1988, least of all CCT.

The White Paper argues that the council housing 'system of ownership and management' is 'often not in the tenant's best long term interest'. The post-war emphasis on the mass provision of public housing – on quantity rather than quality – had led to 'substantial numbers of rented houses and flats which are badly designed and maintained and which fail to provide decent homes'. Too little attention had been paid to the wishes or the requirements of tenants.

In some areas the system has provided good quality housing and management. But in many big cities local authority housing operations are so large that they inevitably risk becoming distant and bureaucratic. Insensitive design and bad management have alienated tenants and left housing badly maintained.

It is implied that this has led to social and economic decline on the estates concerned:

As the quality of housing and of its environment has declined, so a wide range of social problems has emerged; crime and violence have increased; many people have left for better opportunities elsewhere; local enterprise and employment have disappeared; and whole communities have slipped into a permanent dependency on the welfare system from which it is extremely difficult for people to escape.

(DOE, 1987, pp. 1-2)

In its insistence that 'it is not healthy for the public sector to dominate provision of rented housing', the White Paper is reminiscent of New Right arguments that the defects of public housing are those of a public monopoly (see, for example, Minford et al., 1987). On this argument, where there are no opportunities for council tenants as customers to take their business elsewhere, there is no incentive for council housing managers – who are claimed to be inherently self-seeking bureaucrats – to provide the homes or the services tenants want, or to do so efficiently. Political control of public housing is alleged to make matters still worse – through political decisions to provide 'indiscriminate subsidies from the rates to hold down rents' or to allow 'short term political factors' to override 'efficient and economic management of housing in the long term, leading to unrealistically low rents and wholly inadequate standards of management' (DOE, 1987, pp. 2-3).

The response developed by Government since 1987 has been to restrict political discretion in the financing of council housing, by ring-fencing housing revenue accounts, and to seek to improve the position of tenants as customers of the housing service by strengthening both the 'voice' and 'exit' options available to them (Hirschmann, 1970). 'Voice' options, such as rights to information, consultation and participation, aim to improve the accountability of housing managers to the customers they serve. 'Exit' options give customers the chance to take their business elsewhere. At the heart of Government policy since 1987 has been the New Right conviction that voice is not enough; it is essential to create, through the provision of exit options, a competitive market in rented housing, or something approaching it. Thus Government has sought to promote a more diverse rented sector, through alternatives to council housing, in the form of an expanded private rented sector, a greater role for housing associations and housing action trusts. Local authorities have been encouraged voluntarily to transfer their stock to housing associations. Tenants' Choice offers the alternative to transfer to another landlord, increased discounts under the right to buy, and more recently rents-to-mortgages, make the move to home ownership easier.

In parallel, government has felt itself justified in tightening regulation of local authority housing management, through legislation (e.g. the Right to Repair), through the linking by Estate Action of a growing proportion of investment to improved management and tenant consultation, and latterly by the use of the Minister's discretion in making housing capital allocations to reward what the Government judges to be good management performance.

But the Government also claims to see a continuing strategic and enabling role for local authorities. As the White Paper put it, 'local authorities should increasingly see themselves as enablers who ensure that everyone in their area is adequately housed; but not necessarily by them' (DOE, 1987, p. 3). The Government's commitment to the local authority strategic role is a matter on which a positive or cynical view is possible. A full analysis of the changing role of local authority housing departments would include an evaluation of the extent to which this strategic and enabling role is developing, but there is not space for such an evaluation in this chapter (but for a positive, though qualified, assessment, see Bramley, 1993).

'Problem' estates

The White Paper's condemnation of council housing as a system was a new departure for the Government. Council housing had always had its critics, and there had always been problem estates, but before the mid-1980s these were perceived as exceptions – problems in, not of, council housing. Although there might be issues of inadequate calibre, training or resources, the potential competence of local authority housing managers to deal with these problems was not challenged.

Concern about the design and management of council estates began to crystallise in the early 1970s, although it was not until 1976 that the DOE commissioned a systematic study of 'hard-to-let' estates, and a further five years before the study report was published. In early debates, issues of design and built form were predominant. There was criticism of high rise flats from the first; either challenging their suitability as housing at all or as suitable homes for families with children. Newman (Newman, 1972) was influential in linking management problems to design features, principally the lack of 'defensible space', and his arguments were applied to the British context by Wilson (Wilson, 1978 and 1980). Later Coleman (Coleman, 1985) was heavily quoted in the Audit Commission's important report 'Managing the Crisis in Council Housing' (Audit Commission, 1986).

Once, however, the DOE research on hard-to-let estates was published in 1981 (Burbidge et al., 1981) the analysis took a different direction. The research suggested that hard-to-let estates in fact had no distinctive architectural characteristics and were not peculiar and different from all other estates (although they tended to be larger); problems in managing such estates were not different in kind from those on other estates, they were just much worse. The implication was that there was no separate and different problem of 'problem' estates, but a general problem of poor management, of which the hard-to-let estates were just the most extreme symptom.

The conclusion was that where investment was needed to improve or repair the estates, it would be wasted unless housing management was also improved, and tenants consulted to ensure the improvements were those which were wanted.

Decentralisation

The Government's response to the research findings was to set up the Priority Estates Project (PEP) and continue to focus attention on a small number of individual estates. This provided a valuable test bed for the development of a new approach to housing management; but in the early 1980s the implication that the housing management service needed restructuring as a whole began first to be addressed by those few local authorities which pioneered the decentralisation of housing management, the earliest including Walsall, Islington, Hackney, Lambeth and Glasgow.

The service these authorities and PEP set out to overhaul was typically organised around a centralised housing department, headed by a chief officer, and split functionally into a number of divisions: thus estate management, maintenance, development and rehousing would typically be each in separate divisions. The department would usually be dependent on a number of other departments, both for support services, such as financial, legal and personnel advice, and for the delivery of services such as grounds maintenance, estate lighting and refuse collection on housing estates.

While most Inner London and metropolitan authorities were likely to have a single department responsible for most housing functions, this was less likely to be the case in other authorities. The obvious failing of this functional segmentation of the housing service is that co-ordination of activities at estate level can only be achieved through communication to and from the centre of the organisation. Where problems accumulated on estates, the time lags, bottlenecks and distortions arising in transmitting information to the centre and back rapidly led to paralysis on the ground. In this situation, estate management staff, who were the first point of contact for tenants, were unable to respond to tenants' complaints and requests because key aspects of service delivery, such as repairs and rehousing, were not under their direct control.

These structural obstacles to responsiveness loomed still larger where improvements or major repair works were concerned, and the architects responsible for scheme design were not part of, or even under the control of the housing department as client. Even if the housing management staff were ready and willing to involve tenants in the design of a scheme, they had no capacity to carry tenants' wishes into effect unless the housing department had won a clear role as client to the design service. If the architects themselves were ready to consult and listen to tenants, they seldom had much experience of working on the estate. Kirby et al. (Kirby et al., 1987) highlight the problems authorities faced in acting as an effective client in relation to services delivered on estates.

If the organisation of the housing service was inadequate to the task of managing housing at the start of the 1980s, an explanation is needed of why and how this came about. Power (Power, 1987; 1988) offers a persuasive account summed up in the phrase 'property before people'. The argument is that in the first half-century of council housing, and particularly in the 1950s and 1960s, the emphasis on building new homes meant that more priority was given within local authorities to designing, constructing and letting new houses than to the task of managing and maintaining them. These priorities determined the professional pecking order within chief officer groups and ensured that the housing service was colonised by and divided among the established Town Hall professions — architecture, finance, building works. In the course of this colonisation, the early insights of Octavia Hill into the task of managing 'difficult' tenants and properties were forgotten.

When local government was reorganised in the early 1970s, the guiding philosophy was to create larger authorities to achieve economies of scale in service delivery and attract a higher calibre of staff and elected member. In housing the argument was that reorganisation should create authorities of sufficient size to justify the creation of a comprehensive housing service bringing together all housing functions in one department. Too, often, however, the creation of new, comprehensive housing departments simply brought together the old departments under a single chief officer. Problems of integration and co-ordination remained as intransigent as before.

Other accounts, while sharing many of the features of this analysis, stress that these failings were not peculiar to housing. Hoggett (Hambleton and Hoggett, 1984; Hoggett and Hambleton, 1987; Hoggett, 1990) draws the connections between the dysfunctions of public sector bureaucracies, generally, and the eclipse of the integrated firm and Taylorist principles of industrial organisation in the private sector. He identifies the essential dysfunction within the bureaucratic form as the 'tension between the principle of ordered hierarchy and centralised command on the one hand and the necessary impulse towards an extended division of labour on the other' (Hoggett, 1990, p. 10). The difficulty facing a council housing chief in co-ordinating the input of several different specialist sections to service delivery on an estate is essentially similar in nature to the problem faced by Ford in securing delivery of components and materials at the right place and time on the assembly line. Where uncertainty and rapidly-changing conditions become the norm, the bureaucratic system cannot cope.

In housing, the response, as pioneered by PEP, among others, involved the establishment of local offices, with devolved responsibility for all relevant management and maintenance functions. In the early days, PEP saw these becoming a focus for tenant pressure, creating an informal 'voice' mechanism, with the additional possibility of the 'capture' by tenants of the neighbourhood manager as an advocate for the estate within the bureaucracy.

While PEP focused on work with individual 'priority' estates, several authorities sought from the early 1980s to decentralise their whole housing management operation. Arguably, the identification of an estate as a priority focused the attention of the bureaucracy and of members on it, encouraged the appointment of the best staff to it, and helped to create the conditions for improving management over and above the managerial changes advocated by PEP. It was quite possible for conditions on priority estates to improve while elsewhere in the authority things got worse. The decentralisers, on the other hand, had the much more ambitious objective of transforming housing management – and in some cases other services too.

Management and politics

Hoggett (in Hoggett and Hambleton, 1987) draws a distinction between consumerist and collectivist objectives in decentralisation. The first emphasises getting closer to the consumer in order to improve the responsiveness of local government service provision; the second gives primacy to the democratisation of service provision. He argues that both strands can be identified in the decentralisation initiatives of the first half of the 1980s, though the latter were less well developed.

The first involves a managerial strategy concerned with devolving decision-making as far down the organisation as it will go, stripping out middle layers of management to improve cost-effectiveness, shorten lines of communication and bring operational decision-making closer to the consumer. But while operational decisions are devolved, policy and strategy remain firmly under the control of the centre. Tenants are seen as customers, individuals with the right to be respected, views to be listened to, needs to be met, and levels of satisfaction to be surveyed from time to time, but not as citizens with the right collectively to influence or determine the policies which affect them.

Decoupled from its organisational manifestation as decentralisation, this approach can be seen to lead to the 'customer care' philosophy which has been taken up by many housing departments, whether or not decentralised. It can be recognised to be the public sector equivalent of the new corporate paradigm which emerged in the private sector in the 1970s, summed up by Murray (Murray, 1983) as 'the decentralisation of production and the centralisation of command', and recommended by management gurus (especially Peters and Waterman, 1982) as the 'tight/loose' system of organisation.

This 'tight/loose' approach to management implies considerable freedom for the front-line manager to decide how the service will be delivered, but within the context of a budget and policy framework dictated from the centre. This raises interesting questions about what matters ought properly to be reserved to the centre and what should be devolved. As a theory drawn from the private sector where organisations are assumed to be competing in a market where customers can choose whether or not to consume that organisation's service, the theory does not address the possibility that 'customers' should have rights to influence the policy framework set out from the centre.

This managerial approach can be contrasted with a political agenda whose objective is to pass down policy-making to the local level, involving tenants as citizens rather than as customers in those decisions about service delivery which, in accordance with the principle of subsidiarity, it is appropriate to take at local level. Early examples include Islington and Tower Hamlets, more recently joined by Rochdale and Kirklees, where each area or neighbourhood has been given considerable autonomy over the operation of the housing service in its area. This approach raises exactly the same kinds of questions about which decisions should be reserved to the centre; in Tower Hamlets there has been hot contention between centre and neighbourhoods over issues such as allocations policy. The difference from the consumerist approach is that these issues are seen to be what they are – political issues to be resolved by political debate, in which tenants as citizens can and should become collectively involved.

More than a crisis of management

Work by DOE researchers, PEP and others showed how the bureaucratic and centralised housing department could not cope with the growing number of hard-to-let or difficult-to-manage estates. But an explanation is also needed to show why management difficulties spread to a rapidly increasing number of estates from the mid-1970s on.

As Power notes, (Power, 1987) management problems were not a new phenomenon: problem tenants and problem estates were mentioned in the minutes of the LCC before 1914, and again became an issue in the 1930s when the focus of local authority activity shifted to slum clearance. But in the 1920s and the first two decades after 1945, the shortage of housing was such that council housing was a privilege primarily for skilled and white collar workers and their families, while the poorest continued to live in the private rented sector.

As the local authority housing stock grew and aged, so did the range of tenants. The characteristic housing management response was to allocate the best properties to the 'good' tenants and the worst to the worst. Tenants were graded according to housekeeping standards and other social characteristics, and the promise of promotion to a better council house was used as a carrot for prompt payment of rent and compliance with the tenancy conditions. The stick was the threat of eviction unfettered by security of tenure or homelessness responsibilities.

Consequently, it can be seen why, despite the fragmentation of the typical housing department, and the dominance of building professionals over housing managers in the council pecking order, this system of 'bureaucratic paternalism' (Hambleton and Hoggett, 1984) worked, after a fashion. Crudely, so long as there was a continuing supply of new and desirable homes, any problems in providing a quality management and maintenance service to tenants in their existing homes could be resolved by moving them to a new one; those who were not moved did not 'deserve' a better service.

However, by the 1970s, skilled and white collar workers aspired to owner-occupation, and an increasing number of stable, employed and relatively prosperous council tenants moved out of council housing into owner-occupation. The shortage of rented housing was eliminated in some areas permitting the emergence of 'hard-to-let' estates, while the decline of the private rented sector and the enactment of the Housing (Homeless Persons) Act in 1977 meant that new lettings were increasingly to the poor and economically inactive – who were more numerous in any case now that the post war boom had ended.

The reorientation of the housing service from new build to rehabilitation and management accelerated after 1979. With drastic cuts in both new build and spending on rehabilitation, housing managers could no longer so easily offer a move to a new home to tenants in poor accommodation who paid their rent. The practice of allocating new tenants to the less popular estates, and making them 'serve their time' before making any offer of a new home, was called into question once its equal opportunities implications were examined, particularly in authorities where new tenants were disproportionately black or Asian. Nor did the threat of eviction carry such weight once the Housing Act 1980 introduced security of tenure for council tenants, and duties towards the homeless meant that councils could not always wash their hands completely of those they evicted. Any effectiveness the old paternalism still had quickly collapsed once housing managers were deprived of both the carrot and the stick.

Unpopular estates did not all share the same built form or design characteristics; what was unpopular in a given authority tended also to depend on location and to be defined relative to what else was available in that authority. Hence there were popular high-rise developments in some parts of London, and unpopular cottage estates in some northern authorities. But the unpopular estates did tend to be in need of capital investment in repairs or improvements. One attraction for the government of the PEP approach to housing management was the suggestion that improved management could substitute to some extent for capital expenditure. But even the most ardent PEP proselyte would not pretend that it could do so completely and indefinitely. The government's often-repeated assertion that problems on estates could not be solved simply by throwing more money at them did not imply its converse: that they could be solved without spending any more money at all.

By 1986, the Audit Commission was ready to declare that a crisis existed in council housing (Audit Commission, 1986). As contributory causes, they identified, in addition to poor management and faulty design and construction, underinvestment, a shortage of housing and increasing homelessness, and rents too low to finance adequate spending on management and maintenance. Underinvestment was clearly a problem to be laid at the government's door, since its primary cause was the cuts in capital allocations imposed from 1980: it was not until the mid-1980s that the flow of receipts from council house sales enabled council capital spending on housing to level out and even increase slightly towards the end of the decade. Similarly, the shortage of housing for rent was a direct consequence of the cuts in the capital programme. The Commission's view on rent levels, which is shared by the 1987 White Paper, reflects an approach to rent-setting which conflicts with that adopted by many local authorities. After a 30 per cent real increase in rents in 1980-82, caused by the withdrawal of housing subsidy, and the shambles caused by the over-hasty introduction of the housing benefit system in 1983, many local authorities found it difficult to justify further substantial rent increases because they felt tenants could not afford them. It is undeniable, however, that the effect was therefore inadequate levels of spending on management and maintenance.

The Commission were careful to point out that, in their view, the 'most serious problems' were concentrated in 'perhaps 30 authorities' out of over 400, and these could not be tackled without new investment as well as better management; in other authorities problems were not insuperable, 'given sound management' (Audit Commission, 1986, p. 6-7). With this qualification, the gap between the Commission's claim of a crisis and the opposite conclusion of the Centre for Housing Research is largely presentational. The Centre for Housing Research study, carried out for the DOE (DOE, 1989a, 1989b), was based on fieldwork conducted shortly after the Commission's, although the report was not published until 1989. The Centre concluded that:

social housing and its management in England was not in a state of crisis. ... We suggest that a more informed debate on policies for social rental sector housing should drop the widespread assumptions that there is a pervasive crisis in managing council housing and take as its starting point that there are good and bad managers amongst local authorities.

(DOE, 1989a, p. 1)

This conclusion was too late, however, to divert the government from the course set by the 1987 White Paper.

It becomes clear from this study that it is impossible to make sensible judgements about the relative effectiveness and efficiency of housing authorities without some concept and measure of the degree of difficulty of the management task. In other words, crude comparisons between authorities of the percentage of properties which are empty, or the level of rent arrears, tell little about the relative performance of these authorities without a measure of how difficult it is to fill the empties or collect the rent. Although this claim can sound like special pleading on behalf of poor performers, it should be obvious that an authority which is still able to operate door-to-door rent collection without fear of attacks on staff is in a very different situation from an authority which is not. Apart from the impact on rent collection rates, new management problems arise for the latter authority, like unauthorised occupancy and the sale of rent books, which are relatively simply policed by rent collectors in the former. Other examples can easily be given.

This point was confirmed by the Centre for Housing Policy (DOE, 1993b), revisiting the housing management performance of local authorities and housing associations in 1990/91. They found that important changes had occurred since 1984/85 (the year surveyed by Centre for Housing Research). For example, decentralisation of housing management was much more widespread than in 1984/85. More organisations were using a range of different methods to keep tenants informed of changes in housing management. The use of recognised good practices in the prevention and recovery of rent arrears had also increased significantly. But there was often not a straightforward relationship between practice and performance. In many aspects of housing management, a large proportion of both high and low performers were pursuing good practices; while in some aspects more low than high performers were good practice organisations.

They comment:

thus while London boroughs and metropolitan authorities were in many cases more likely to be pursuing progressive policies or implementing good practices and were spending more than the average for district councils on general supervision and management, these were not sufficient to outweigh the greater degree of difficulty of housing management which they faced. The fact that district councils were more likely to be high performers overall than London boroughs or metropolitan authorities was not necessarily because they were employing better housing management practices. Indeed in many cases they were less likely to be making use of recognised good practices. Rather district councils were more likely to score as high rather than low performers because of the degree of difficulty of the management task (as measured by levels of socio-economic deprivation) which they faced was much less than that which London boroughs and metropolitan authorities generally faced.

(DOE, 1993a, p. 28).

To the extent that the degree of difficulty of the management task is associated with social deprivation among tenants, it is likely not just to vary among authorities, but to have increased within authorities over time, as the characteristics of council tenants have changed during the 1980s. Comparing the situation at the beginning and end of the 1980s, council tenants were:

• older (the percentage of households with at least one member over the age of 60 increased from 36 per cent to 46 per cent between 1977 and 1987;
• more likely to be elderly or single person households (the proportion of family households declined from 31 per cent to 24 per cent between 1977 and 1987);
• less likely to be economically active (the percentage of economically active households fell from 60 per cent to 38 per cent);
• more likely to be receiving income support; and
• more likely to be in the lowest income decile.

Added to this, the ratio of the mean income of those in the highest and lowest income deciles increased substantially during the 1980s, as did the relationship between income support and average incomes. These statistics show an increasing concentration of the socially deprived in local authority homes.

The overall picture is, therefore, neither one of systemic failure – many housing authorities are performing satisfactorily or better – nor is poor performance attributable to poor management alone. Rather, some authorities have significantly improved their performance, in others it has worsened, in still others it has remained about the same. Many of the latter have significantly improved their management systems and their efficiency, but they have been running in order to stand still – as their management has improved, so the management task has become more difficult.

Unified housing departments

The Centre for Housing Research (DOE, 1989a and 1989b) note that 'for large authorities, apart from dealing with problems of size, the major task is likely to be keeping control over a wide range of functions in a single department. ... For small authorities, the major problem is likely to be keeping control over functions exercised by separate departments'. The case for a unified housing service is a continuing theme in debate about housing management, often closely linked to the case for housing management as a distinct profession. As noted above Power (Power, 1987) included the split of responsibility for housing management among separate departments as a key part of her explanation of management failure. The Audit Commission (Audit Commission, 1986) argued that 'a unified housing function is much to be preferred'. Yet the Centre for Housing Policy found that in 1991 'most local authorities [still] did not manage their housing in this way. On average, a third of housing management functions were managed by departments other than the housing department' (DOE, 1993a, p. 11). As was the case five years earlier, the functions most often carried out by departments other than housing were housing benefit payments, repairs and rent accounting.

The Audit Commission's support in 1986 for a unified housing service conflicts to some extent with their later, but equally forthright support for a clear separation of the client and contractor functions in the context of CCT for housing maintenance and other functions. While the client function should clearly be in the housing department, it should not matter where departmental responsibility for the DLO lies, or indeed, from the Commission's point of view, whether the contractor is a DLO or a private builder, since the client–contractor relationship is not mediated through a departmental chain of command, but through the housing maintenance contract.

If this is right, it can be argued that the need for a unified housing department is mitigated to the extent that clear contractual or quasi-contractual service level agreements can be established between housing, as the provider of the front-line service to tenants, and other council departments acting as contractors, agents or support to the housing department. Of course, within the local authority, these agreements cannot be formal contracts, since the local authority cannot contract with itself, hence they can be relied on only to the extent that there is political and managerial commitment to them.

However, this claim is countered by the argument below that organisational separation of client and contractor roles is less appropriate for delivery of an innovating and developing service.

The progress of organisational change

The early experiments in decentralisation were nearly all politically initiated and driven, with the political agenda seen as at least equal in importance to the managerial agenda, although with hindsight it is possible to see that the managerial objectives were rather more often achieved than the political ones. The authorities involved were all inner London boroughs or metropolitan districts with relatively large stocks, of which much was in need of repair or improvement, high levels of social deprivation, active tenants movements and established structures for tenant consultation. Those involved were convinced that housing management needed fundamental restructuring, often together with other council services.

In the early years, attention focused on the not inconsiderable task of financing and providing the decentralised offices and recruiting or redeploying staff to work in them. Policies, procedures and the financial and IT infrastructure necessary to support the new ways of working tended to lag behind.

Decentralisation cannot operate effectively without much wider changes in the way the housing service is organised and delivered. The authority's centre must be prepared to let go of responsibilities it has traditionally exercised, in order to give enough autonomy and operational responsibility to the area managers. Management by objectives has to replace management by rules. Where decentralisation involves cutting out layers of management to create shallower and wider hierarchies, the centre can only maintain control through much more developed and explicit objectives and standards, and fast and accurate management information. The area manager cannot function effectively without access to information held centrally or by other council departments, whether on rent arrears, housing benefit, allocations or repairs. Decentralisation relies on adequate financial and information systems.

It takes an appreciable time, measured in years rather than months, to put these systems in place and make them work. Even in those authorities which started the decentralisation process earliest, it would have been unreasonable to expect the full benefit of the changes to be reaped much before the late 1980s. Cole et al. (1991, pp. 153-4) argue that by the end of the 1980s politicians and officers both shared a more chastened view about the political potential of decentralisation. A number of earlier ambitious initiatives had foundered, and local authorities had 'increasingly adopted more modest proposals for action, in the hope of meeting a number of more limited objectives, rather than risk achieving none at all'.

Meanwhile, in the mid-1980s, the Audit Commission and, under the influence of PEP, the government, had swung into support of managerial decentralisation, and it ceased to be seen as associated with political radicalism, whether left or populist. Thereafter, more and more housing departments were reorganised on decentralised lines, but change was more likely to be managerially initiated and managerially driven. The idea of using decentralisation to strengthen the 'voice' of tenants, and involve them in the decision-making processes of the authority, was often either rejected by politicians in principle, or deemed inappropriate given the low level of tenant organisation in the authority. These authorities tended to emphasise the rights of tenants as customers rather than citizens.

As the new approach to management became more developed and better articulated, it also became possible for authorities which, for whatever reasons, were not committed to radical decentralisation, to take parts of the total package – devolution without decentralisation for example – and develop them to meet their local needs as they saw them.

Overall, therefore, plotting the progress of decentralisation in local authority housing management is not straightforward. Authorities have widely differing concepts about what is involved in decentralisation; there is a wide variation in the size of decentralised areas, and the range of functions devolved to them. And, as suggested above, the effects of the management revolution initiated by the decentralisers and PEP spread much further than those authorities which have reorganised to an area basis. But comparison of the findings in successive research reports (Audit Commission, 1986, DOE, 1989a and 1989b, DOE, 1993a and 1993b) suggests that, between 1984 and 1991/92, there was a steady increase in the proportion of authorities organised on an area basis and the range of functions delegated to the areas.

The Government's role

Thus, by the mid-1980s there had been significant progress in many authorities towards new methods of organising housing management which drew on contemporary management thinking in the private sector but, to a greater or lesser extent, wove into it an attempt to give tenants a greater collective voice in the way the housing service was delivered. The 1987 White Paper can be read either as the Government losing patience with the slowness of progress being made, or as initiating an attempt to point developments in a different direction, emphasising 'exit' over 'voice' options for tenants.

The Government may seek to justify its intervention through the housing legislation of 1988 and 1989 by claiming that local authorities needed to be spurred to improve their performance. The analysis above suggests that this claim is not justified. Poor management performance was only a serious problem in a proportion of authorities, many of which had already initiated attempts to tackle the root causes, and in any case these problems were compounded by underinvestment, to which the solution was in the government's hands. In the remaining authorities, there was little to suggest that fundamental problems existed, least of all a systemic failure of council housing.

The 1987 White Paper launched the slogan of 'choice' for local authority tenants, by which it meant the opportunity to 'exit' by one means or other from council housing, putting pressure on the authority by enabling tenants to issue a real threat to take their business elsewhere, and if necessary to carry it out. In the short term, the Government promised, tenants would get the right to transfer the ownership of their home to another landlord under Tenants' Choice; in the long term, the creation of a pluralistic rented sector would, it was said, offer genuine choice and create competition between landlords for tenants' custom. Both promises are, arguably, illusory. Tenants' Choice has turned out to be an onerous, one-way jump into the unknown; it is not surprising there has been little take up. A pluralistic rented sector would be just as likely, were it created, to become a segmented and stratified market, where tenants get what they can afford, and real choice is available only to those who can afford to pay.

Large Scale Voluntary Transfer (LSVT) is another 'exit' route, not foreshadowed in the 1987 White Paper, but developed by local authorities. But such transfers have neither been initiated by tenants nor primarily motivated, to date, by a concern for their welfare. Rather, it has been the prospect of substantial capital receipt which has motivated such transfers. As Perry (1991) showed, only a small proportion of these receipts has been re-used to the benefit of tenants.

Compulsory competitive tendering

Compulsory competitive tendering was applied to part of or all housing maintenance work by the Local Government, Planning and Land Act 1980, and extended to grounds maintenance and estate cleaning, as well as other blue collar services, by the Local Government Act 1988. It will be extended to housing management in phases between 1 April 1996 and 1 April 1988.

CCT works by specifying a 'defined activity'. After a given date, a local authority is not permitted to carry out work falling within the defined activity through its own employees unless they have won the work in competition. The 'defined activity' for housing management embraces the operational landlord role – activities such as rent collection and arrears recovery, letting and managing tenancies, receiving repair requests and managing empty properties, caretaking and concierges – but excludes strategic, policy and enabling functions. Thus the authority will remain responsible for rent-setting, allocations policy and maintenance planning, as well as managing homelessness, the sheltered housing service (in most cases), housing benefit, renovation grants and housing advice. An authority may, however, arrange if they wish for most of these services to be carried out by a contractor, whether by including them in the housing management contract or a separate contract.

Authorities are required to expose to competition 95 per cent by value of the work falling within the defined activity. If, at the end of the tendering process, the authority decides to give the work to the in-house bid, the in-house team or Direct Service Organisation (DSO) must carry out the work as if there were a contract between it and the rest of the authority specifying the service to be provided and the payment to be made for providing it. The DSO must keep a trading account and show a trading surplus, including a 6 per cent return on any capital employed. Where the return is not achieved, the authority can be required to close down the DSO.

In doing all of this, the authority must not act 'anti-competitively', as determined by a court on the instigation of an aggrieved contractor, or by the Secretary of State in response to a complaint or on his own initiative. Guidance on the avoidance of 'anti-competitive behaviour' embraces virtually every aspect of the process, from the size and scope of the contracts offered, through the way in which the service is specified, to the maximum length of contract, to the criteria used in the selection of the winning bid. Where an authority is judged to have acted anti-competitively, the Secretary of State has wide powers to intervene, including powers to prevent the DSO from carrying out the work and to require the contract to be re-tendered.

In addition to the government, a range of academic and professional opinion has reacted favourably to the extension of CCT to housing management, sharing the government's view that competition will improve the quality and efficiency of service delivery. There are, however, a number of reasons to doubt this assessment.

Favourable assessments of the impact of CCT tend to start from the observation that developments in the private sector have increasingly replaced the 'employment organisation' by a 'contractual organisation'. Corporations such as Ford which once directly employed all those involved in building their cars have now taken a leaf from the Japanese book and sub-contract large parts of the process. Peters and Waterman recommend organisations to 'stick to the knitting', that is, stick to what you do best and sub-contract the rest. Consequently, it is argued, local authorities improve quality and efficiency by taking a leaf from the private sector book and contract out housing management to those who do it best.

One reason for thinking that housing management is not like the supply of engine parts for the Ford Fiesta is that the housing service does not stand still; housing policy changes frequently under the impetus of new legislation, local political changes, professional advice and tenants' representations. The capacity for the service to change cannot easily be captured in the service specification – too general a specification leads to loss of control over costs, but if it is too precise the danger is that the service is set in concrete for the duration of the contract, or alternatively that contract variations must be negotiated, again with the risk of loss of cost control. Although the contractor will acquire the relevant day-to-day knowledge about the job which is the essential raw material for improvement and innovation, he will have no incentive to use it, except for financial advantage.

The disadvantages of the commercial relationship between contractor and council are magnified in CCT by the requirement for the authority to re-tender the work at the end of the contract period regardless of the performance of the contractor. This creates further incentives for the contractor to go for short-term profit by screwing the maximum financial advantage from the contract while it lasts, and to maximise secrecy about the job in order to obtain a competitive advantage from a monopoly of information when the job is next re-tendered.

This is not how successful private sector firms handle subcontractors, particularly where quality is paramount and the subcontractor is expected to come forward with product improvements and innovations over time. Leading firms like Sainsbury or Nissan do not rely on regular competition among potential suppliers to maximise quality or economy. The relationship they seek is a long-term one with a group of 'most favoured suppliers'; in exchange for an indefinitely long contract, subject to satisfactory performance, they demand the right to extensive involvement in the way the work is done – the supplier has no secrets from them.

A further characteristic of these relationships is that the purchaser is normally much larger and more powerful than the supplier, and the supplier is encouraged to work only for that client, creating a relationship in which the supplier is so dependent on the client that failure to retain the contract would be fatal, creating further incentives for the supplier to perform. But local housing authorities vary widely in size and market power, and some markets created by CCT, such as buildings cleaning are dominated by a handful of major contractors. It is too early for reliable prediction of the structure of the market for housing management, but it is possible that a few major private sector or housing association providers will emerge, which will tend to dominate, rather than be dominated by, most local housing authorities. It cannot be assumed that local authorities, particularly smaller authorities, will be able to secure sufficient commercial leverage over housing management contractors to ensure cost-effective, high quality service delivery.

This is not to deny that CCT will have benefits. The most important is that the imposition of a firm deadline will focus attention on the need to set clear service standards and procedures, and force authorities to reach service level agreements specifying the relationships between housing management and the corporate support services. Authorities should have been doing this anyway and many have made significant progress, but there is nothing like a deadline to concentrate the mind.

However, the chosen deadline is so soon that many authorities will not be able to complete the process satisfactorily. There are particular concerns about the ability of IT suppliers to respond to the demands imposed by CCT in time. And if authorities enter the CCT process with inadequate specifications and systems, the risk is much greater than that the DSO will not win the work. The risk is that such authorities will lose control of both the quality and the cost of the housing service because the contract and the arrangements for monitoring it will be inadequate. The government claims that CCT is being introduced to 'provide a means by which the poorest performing authorities can raise their standards of management so that tenants receive a better service in the future' (DOE, 1992, p. 3). Yet these authorities may well be those which fail adequately to prepare for CCT in the short time available; an inadequate specification could well perpetuate poor performance for the life of the contract.

The extension of CCT to housing management is presented by the government as a further extension of 'choice' for tenants. In fact, choice for tenants has nothing to do with it. Local authorities will be required, regardless of tenants' views, to invite competitive bids to carry out housing management, and give the work to the in-house team only if they win it in competition. Although authorities will not be required simply to accept the lowest tender, and are being encouraged by government to involve tenants in the process of shortlisting the contractors who are invited to bid and deciding on the winning bid, the ability of tenants genuinely to influence the process is tightly constrained by the requirement on the authority not to act 'anti-competitively'.

The government may argue that the likely benefits of CCT outweigh these potential difficulties. It is therefore worth examining whether the benefits could have been achieved without the need for CCT. Did CCT have to be universally applied to all authorities? Many authorities are already improving their performance under existing stimuli, others could have been persuaded to do so with the threat of CCT if a required standard of performance were not achieved by a given date. An alternative which would significantly have enhanced the choice genuinely available to tenants would have been to allow tenants the option to demand a ballot to vote for an unsatisfactory service to be exposed to competition.

The removal of the requirement to retender at the end of the contract period, and its replacement with an option to retender or renew without competition for a further period, would significantly alter the incentive structure facing the contractor in favour of quality of service and the pursuit of a long-term relationship rather than a short-term payback.

The limits of CCT

If the analysis above is right, CCT will not bring the benefits claimed by the government, either in terms of improved effectiveness of housing management services or the efficiency with which they are delivered. But even if the analysis is wrong, it remains the case that better housing management cannot be a long-term substitute for better housing. It may be necessary to ensure and safeguard the benefits of investment, but cannot substitute for it.

Finally, the question must be posed whether the continuing residualisation of local authority housing, and its consequent effects on the degree of difficulty of the management task, will wipe out the benefits both of investment and improved management – whether or not as a result of CCT. The effects on the 'manageability' of local authority housing of the increasing proportion of tenants suffering social deprivation and the increasing acuteness of such deprivation are the subject of much speculation but little firm evidence. The steps taken directly to tackle deprivation and to limit the concentration of the most deprived tenants on particular estates, may be more significant for the future prospects for housing management and local authority housing departments than the changes brought about by CCT.

References

Audit Commission (1986) *Managing the Crisis in Council Housing*, London, HMSO.
Bramley, G. (1993) The Enabling Role for Local Housing Authorities: a Preliminary Evaluation, in Malpass and Means, 1993.
Burbidge, M., Curtis, A., Kirby, K., and Wilson, S. (1981) *An Investigation of Difficult to Let*

Housing: Vol. 1, *General Findings*; Vol. 2, *Case Studies of Post-War Estates*; Vol. 3, *Case Studies of Pre-War Estates*, London HMSO.

Cole, I., Arnold, P. and Windle, K. (1991) Decentralised Housing Services – back to the Future, in Donnison, D. and Maclennan, D. (eds) *The Housing Service of the Future*, Harlow, Longman.

Coleman, A., (1985) *Utopia on Trial*, Shipman, London.

DOE (1987) *Housing: the Government's Proposals*, CmD 214, London, HMSO.

DOE (1989a) *The Nature and Effectiveness of Housing Management in England: Summary Report and Recommendations*, London, HMSO.

DOE (1989b) *The Nature and Effectiveness of Housing Management in England: Report to the DOE by the Centre for Housing Research*, University of Glasgow, London, HMSO.

DOE (1992) *Competing for Quality in Housing*, London, HMSO.

DOE (1993a) *Managing Social Housing: Summary and Recommendations*, London, HMSO.

DOE (1993b) *Managing Social Housing*, London, HMSO.

Hambleton, R. and Hoggett, P. (eds)(1984) *The Politics of Decentralisation: Theory and Practice of a Radical Local Government Initiative*, SAUS Working Paper 46, Bristol, School for Advanced Urban Studies, University of Bristol.

Hirschmann, A. (1970) *Exit, Voice and Loyalty: Responses to Decline in Firms, Organisations and States*, Cambridge, MA, Harvard University Press.

Hoggett, P. (1990) *Modernisation, Political Strategy and the Welfare State: an Organisational Perspective*, Studies in Decentralisation and Quasi-Markets No. 2, Bristol, School for Advanced Urban Studies, University of Bristol.

Hoggett, P. and Hambleton, R. (eds) (1987) *Decentralisation and Democracy: Localising Public Services*, SAUS Occasional Paper 26, Bristol, School for Advanced Urban Studies, University of Bristol.

Kirby, K., Finch, H. and Wood, D. (1987) *The Organisation of Housing Management in English Local Authorities*, London, Department of the Environment.

Malpass, P., and Means, R. (eds) (1993) *Implementing Housing Policy*, Buckingham, Open University Press.

Minford, P., Peel, M. and Ashton, P. (1987) *The Housing Morass: Regulation, Immobility and Unemployment*, Hobart Paperback 25, London, Institute of Economic Affairs.

Murray, F. (1983) The Decentralisation of production – the Decline of the Mass Collective Worker, *Capital & Class*, 19.

Newman, O. (1972) *Defensible Space*, London, Macmillan.

Perry, J. (1991) A Wasted Opportunity, *Housing*, 27: 9.

Peters, T. and Waterman, R. (1982) *In Search of Excellence: Lessons from America's Best-run Companies*, New York, Harper & Row.

Power, A. (1987) *Property before People: the Management of Twentieth Century Council Housing*, London, Allen & Unwin.

Power, A. (1988) *Council Housing: Conflict, Change and Decision Making*, Welfare State Discussion Paper No. 27, STICERD, London, London School of Economics.

Wilson, S., (1978) Updating Defensible Space, *Architects Journal*, 11 October.

Wilson, S., (1980) Vandalism and Defensible Space on London Housing Estates, in Clarke, R. and Mughen, P., *Designing Out Crime*, London, HMSO.

7

Housing management in transition: a case study of Hackney

Keith Jacobs

Introduction

It has been almost customary, certainly since 1988, to see central Government housing policy directed at local authorities in stark terms; extending home ownership, reducing local authority housing stock through a number of initiatives such as the Right to Buy and Tenants' Choice; and changing the internal organisation of housing departments by introducing compulsory competitive tendering.

The purpose of this chapter is to provide a localised view of the impact of these policies. This is done by focusing on the efforts undertaken by the London Borough of Hackney to implement its own particular management policies within the parameters of Government legislation and financial restraints. There are good reasons for taking such a localised perspective. As other contributions in this collection have shown, local authorities are still able to determine policy directions within certain constraints.

By concentrating on central government policies it is possible to overlook the extent to which local authorities themselves can and do affect the outcome of policy. This means that specifically charting a council's endeavours to meet local need, manage its housing stock and develop new initiatives can provide important insights about authorities' own potential to affect Government policies. A local case study can also bring to the fore a whole range of issues which are often missed from more 'top down' approaches to housing policy; for example, the extent to which bureaucratic difficulties, tenant action and public perceptions have shaped the housing policy responses of the Council.

This chapter's main theme is to evaluate such responses and in particular the borough's most recent housing management initiative known as the 'Comprehensive Estates Initiative'. Following a synopsis of the political changes that have taken place and the genesis of these initiatives the Council's endeavours are evaluated under three key themes – *housing management, partnership* and *tenant participation*. The picture which emerges is of an authority which, through its new initiatives, has had considerable success in redefining its external relationships with central government and the private sector. Despite this it is having difficulty in securing the desired outcomes for tenants and the organisation itself. Hackney's dilemmas provide a clear indication of some of the serious problems which many other authorities can expect over the coming years.

Hackney as a focus of enquiry

Over the last few years Hackney has been under the watchful eye of writers and the media. Works that spring to mind include Patrick Wright's (1991) *A Journey Through Ruins: The Last Days of London* and the television documentaries last year by World in Action on *Homelessness* and the Channel 4 documentary series *Summer on the Estate*. Further back in the early 1980s Hackney was the subject of Paul Harrison's (1983) *Inside the Inner City*. The reason for the interest in Hackney is not just because it is a London borough close in proximity to both Fleet Street and Wapping. Hackney is, according to the DoE latest Local Conditions Index, England's third poorest local authority, and yet within the locality there are large enclaves of terraced Victorian houses occupied by the middle classes. Hackney's ethnic population includes Orthodox Jews, Caribbeans, Asians, Turkish and Greek Cypriots, Kurdish refugees, Africans and Irish people (LBH, 1993a). Recently it has been the destination of many people seeking political asylum, particularly from Turkey and Eritrea. The politics of Hackney have frequently veered towards nonconformism and radicalism. It was the scene of some of the biggest poll tax disturbances in 1990 and the Council has acquired a poor image for its inability to manage its housing stock. Quite simply one can find in Hackney almost all the issues and juxtapositions of change and continuity which are normally associated with a declining inner city area.

Currently, the borough has the highest rate of unemployment in London – 25.5 per cent of the economically active population (LBH, 1993b). Much of the economic activity pursued by its many small business outlets are related to the fashion and clothing sectors. Wages in these sectors are low and there is little job security. Average income is currently around £11,900 which is nearly £8,000 less than the inner or greater London average (LBH, 1993b). It is difficult to see how Hackney's economy can dramatically improve given the unwillingness of firms to relocate in inner city areas. Hackney Council's other main problem in its efforts to attract and maintain jobs is impeded by the poor transport links with the rest of London. There is no underground connection and much of the borough's population relies on infrequent trains and buses. While car ownership levels are the lowest in England (61.7 per cent of households have no car (LBH, 1993a)), the area is often heavily congested with commuter traffic. In terms of notoriety, Hackney occupies a similar status to areas like Moss-Side in Manchester – those which are generally perceived to be the most disadvantaged in attracting jobs.

The legacy of the 1980s

No account of housing management policies can be presented in isolation from the broad political and economic difficulties which have confronted the borough over the last 15 years. The period is important as the decisions which were taken remain a significant influence on contemporary policy issues.

The mid-1980s was an extraordinary period of turbulence for local government. Authorities, including Hackney, saw themselves as the vanguard for opposition to Government policies particularly rate capping legislation. (Lansley, Goss and Wolmar, 1989; Gyford, 1985). From the Government's own perspective there were good reasons to attack Labour authorities; an important source of the Conservative Government's appeal was its anti-bureaucratic rhetoric (Hall, 1988). The Conservatives throughout the 1980s successfully castigated Labour councils as being profligate and inefficient. A significant part of the political critique relied upon conjuring up an historical imagery portraying Britain in the 1970s under a Labour Government as a bleak and meagre society. Images of trade unionists picketing alongside rubbish lying strewn across desolate inner city wastelands were evoked to justify the Government's legislation affecting local authorities. The notion of the 'loony left council' became an evocative image of political discourse.

The solution paraded by the Government to the defects of collective provision was privatisation and a return to market forces. This would not only extend consumer choice but also undermine the dependency culture which, it was argued, was reinforced by the welfare state. The erosion of local government autonomy became a hallmark of the Conservative administration under Margaret Thatcher (Marsh and Rhodes, 1992; Cochrane, 1993). For example, the 1984 Rates Act gave the Secretary of State power to 'ratecap' high spending councils. The Local Government Act 1985 abolished the Greater London Council and Metropolitan County Councils. The 1988 Local Government and Finance Act brought in the Community Charge or Poll Tax. As the first chapter of this book makes clear, the 1988 Housing Act and the 1989 Local Government and Finance Act had particular implications for local authority housing, with new controls on capital spending and the ring-fencing of the housing revenue account preventing authorities from subsidising their housing expenditure from general rate funds.

Housing departments, as Matthew Warburton has argued elsewhere in this book, have been cited as evidence of local government malaise. The Government took the opportunity to castigate inner city Labour housing departments as being inefficient, reckless and holding primary responsibility for the state of disrepair. While this can now be seen as an attempt to deflect criticism from the decisions taken in the early 1980s to cut local authority capital spending programmes, the image of unresponsive housing bureaucracies struck a chord within the popular imagination.

Labour authorities such as Hackney, while continuing their protest at the spending restrictions, took a number of practical initiatives in an effort to improve their services and standing among the electorate. Quite why practical initiatives were seen as the best strategic solution to the Council's difficulties is discussed later in the chapter; at this point it is worth stressing the pressure exerted on councillors to take action. New initiatives, it seems in Hackney's case, were encouraged partly because they provided reassurance that concerns were being taken seriously. As Edelman (1985) has argued there is a symbolic purpose to most policies conveying an impression to the public that problems are being dealt with. In Hackney the symbolic aspect to policy was never far from the surface. By promoting new initiatives, the Council's aim was to win approval from both residents and sceptical critics in the media as well as to distract attention from the shortcomings of its own performance as a landlord and service provider.

Decentralisation

The main housing initiative which Hackney embarked upon in the 1980s was to decentralise the housing management functions of their local services. At the time, decentralisation was seen by many authorities as an essential strategic response. Ian Cole (1993: 151) has written that decentralisation:

was heralded as the final hope for council housing to respond to the hostile onslaught of central Government, and to emerge from the process as a more popular and accessible housing tenure. Decentralisation rapidly became a central feature of organisational change in many local housing authorities across the country.

Hackney, alongside other Labour authorities, embraced decentralisation as a way of simultaneously fending off criticism about its service provision and 'an administrative remedy to an economic problem' (Tomlinson, 1986: 38) that confronted the council as a consequence of cuts in rate support grant. As Tomlinson's account shows, Hackney's attempt to restructure the social services and housing department ran into political difficulties. Unlike its neighbours in Islington, the Council was unable to implement planned restructuring. In part this was due to hostility from within the white collar trade unions and from certain sections within the ruling Labour group. The result was a hybrid form of decentralisation which set up 24 small area housing offices and six district housing offices across the borough. The success of the restructuring depended on adequate information technology to computerise repairs, lettings and rent accounts and a full complement of staff in post. Neither materialised; no computer links were established to area offices and the council, threatened with rate capping, slowed up its recruitment of staff. Decentralisation, despite all the initial fanfare of enthusiasm, soon lost its impetus. Staff working from these offices were unable to satisfy tenants who had been promised improved services by the Council. Other research on decentralisation in Hackney noted the frustrations felt by staff and tenants:

Problems began when tenants and building workers began to feel that, although repairs and maintenance had been shifted to the decentralised bases, the methods and systems in operation still continued in the old centralised fashion. Frustrations mounted, tenants felt repairs were not improving, the repair teams felt they were being starved of work and in any case what work did arrive was only coming through very slowly. In exasperation tenants and building workers occupied the St John's area base in Shoreditch in January 1984.

(Hoggett, Lawrence and Fudge, 1984: 77)

The failure of the Hackney decentralisation initiative and the twenty week occupation of St John's area base had serious repercussions within the Council. For the housing department itself there was frustration that such an important initiative was only half completed. It was in many respects the worst outcome, reinforcing tenants' misgivings of the Council's ability to implement its manifesto commitments. To the wider local government policy community the failure provided evidence that Hackney was poorly managed and inept.

The morale of many in the department which was already low was adversely affected by its poor image. There was additional embarrassment when the Commission for Racial Equality reported that the Council had discriminated against black and ethnic minority tenants by placing a disproportionate number in older properties (Commission for Racial Equality, 1984). The department was shaken by investigations which uncovered fraud in the housing benefit department. The statistics of the late 1980s show the extent of the poor public image: 3,500 of Hackney's properties were either empty or squatted; 800 families in bed and breakfast accommodation (LBH, 1988a); rent arrears were the highest in the country, after Lambeth's. Staff shortages meant that some of the area housing offices were opened for just two hours per day.

The problem can only be partly explained by the shortage of resources caused by the financial regime imposed by central government An additional problem for Hackney was the internal strains within the Council itself. At the core, there was uncertainty about whether decisions taken by elected councillors were effectively implemented at the point of service delivery.

Anthony Kendall, the leader of Hackney Council from 1982 to 1984 in an interview described the difficulties of policy implementation:

Each Thursday afternoon, I would have regular meetings with the Chief Executive and Director of Finance to discuss what we could do. It was easy to come away from those meetings feeling enthusiastic that we were taking effective action to resolve some of the problems. Of course looking back, much of what we came up with was never implemented ... the council's organisational structure made getting anything done incredibly difficult.

(interview with author 31/5/94)

Hackney's difficulties were reported in a Policy and Resources Committee report written by the Chief Executive, Pamela Gordon (LBH, 1988b). The report concentrated on the decision making process within the authority: 'The main failure in Hackney is not so much the tortuous process before a decision is made as the inability to repose confidence in the prospect of decisions, once taken, necessarily being implemented ... the organisation's capacity to deliver action to desired timetables remains weak and unreliable.'

It is no exaggeration to write that the housing department, by the early 1990s was perceived as damaging the reputation of the Council at a national level. In 1991 Hackney's housing department became the subject of three separate television documentaries focusing on the problems of squatting, cockroaches and the tenants campaign on the Kingshold Estate to remove asbestos from the their flats. A senior officer within the Chief Executive's department recalling the early 1990s said 'it was obvious to me that problems weren't being handled in a focused manner by the housing department. There was a multitude of problems exacerbated by the housing department not being effective'(interview with author 19/3/93).

Moreover, Hackney's political relationship with the DoE was strained, primarily because of the resentment caused by rate capping and criticism of its service delivery. Even when the council had received support from the DoE, the effects were short lived. For example under the auspices of the DoE's Priority Estate Project, a local management initiative was established on the Wenlock Barn Estate, but after initial enthusiasm, the project faltered. The department did not co-ordinate Estate Action bids for a number of years. The imposition of DoE conditions were seen as a unwelcome intrusion into the Council's own housing agenda.

It would be wrong to portray the entire housing department in the 1980s as reeling from one crisis to another. Though the period was turbulent and morale low, there were singular successes. Most significant was the acclaim which greeted the Council's rehabilitation on some of its worst housing estates. The Lea View Estate in Upper Clapton received national press coverage after its rehabilitation by the community architects Hunt Thompson Associates and an endorsement visit by Prince Charles. Other estates were improved on a piecemeal basis including some of the properties previously managed by the Greater London Council.

New initiatives

The political problems of the Council and in particular the housing department provided an impetus to the political leadership to turn their attention to the organisational difficulties that beset Hackney. The motivation to change stemmed in part from the concern among some Labour councillors that the party were in danger of losing votes to the Liberal Democrats, as had happened in neighbouring Tower Hamlets. The 1980s publicity generated by the council projecting Hackney as 'Britain's poorest Borough' and a 'Radical Socialist Borough' were discarded. Steps were taken to portray Hackney in a more moderate light, and avoid the adverse publicity which was, in the view of the Labour leadership, damaging to both its electoral prospects and its opportunities for receiving Government funds. Attention of Councillors returned to the management of its services. A co-ordinated budget strategy and the setting up of a number of new flagship initiatives were seen as the most effective ways of changing both the culture of the Council and its standing with the electorate and Whitehall.

The most significant and high profile of these new projects is the housing department's 'Comprehensive Estates Initiative' (CEI). Other new initiatives which have been established include Hackney 2000 (an environmental and regeneration initiative), Hackney Housing Partnership (partnership agreements with local housing associations), and Dalston City Challenge Partnership.

In housing management terms, the Comprehensive Estates Initiative is a valuable project to examine, as it has already become a prototype for other local authorities' regeneration projects. It was established in 1992, with a projected expenditure of £180 million from a variety of funding sources including Estate Action and City Challenge. The main aim of CEI is to address, the social, economic, maintenance and management problems on the Council's five major system built estates. To achieve this, plans were made to attract additional resources 'so as to protect the mainstream housing capital programme' (LBH, 1994). Over the duration of the project it is estimated that a third of the CEI spending programme will be financed by the Housing Corporation, and up to quarter from the private sector. The desire to attract extra revenue from private and Government agencies though significant, is not the whole picture. There are three other important aspects to the housing department's strategy of promoting the CEI and other new initiatives which make it a particularly interesting subject to examine. First, Hackney's new initiatives are intended as quality 'flagships' to establish a new management culture as an example to other more moribund sections of the authority to show what they should aspire to. The hope is that staff throughout the housing department will learn from good practice and in turn improve management performance. Secondly, the new initiatives aim to change Hackney Council's image within Government and the local business community by establishing new partnership arrangements. Third, for Hackney's own tenants, the new initiatives are carefully structured to engender tenant participation.

An assessment

The following section of this chapter evaluates the housing department's current response in these three key areas: management, partnership and participation. In many respects the deliberations of the Council reflects in microcosm, many of the issues which now confront inner city local authorities. So it is possible, by looking at the CEI in some detail, to build up a picture of the policy concerns that Hackney and other local authorities will have to grapple with over the next five to ten years, and assess what these responses will mean for tenants and staff working for local authorities. The research for this assessment was gathered in a number of ways. Those interviewed including Hackney Council, DoE, Housing Association and Housing Corporation staff. Councillors, private sector employees, and tenants, consultants and architects. Observation has been made of a large number of council meetings, tenant open days and AGM's and internal officer meetings. Secondary information was obtained from a variety of sources, including committee reports and local newspaper articles.

Management

The efforts to improve the management performance of staff, by establishing new initiatives such as the CEI has co-incided with the advent of CCT. This has meant that like all large local authority housing departments much of the activity of Hackney's staff is taken up with preparing for CCT. As explained in chapter one, from 1 April 1996, 40 per cent (by value) of housing management contracts must be tendered. The department is undertaking a major restructuring of its functions and creating a split between 'client' and 'contractor' services. For those staff who will constitute the 'contractor' bid, the most important aspect of this is the switch to generic working practices. This switch, in conjunction with improved performance monitoring techniques, investment in information technology and additional training, is seen as the best way to improve the quality of housing management.

Generic working practices require staff to manage smaller numbers of units but to take on the rent recovery, estate management and void management functions. In addition, the management of the transfer and waiting lists are being decentralised to neighbourhood offices. This is intended to improve service delivery, 'Generic working allows greater flexibility to respond to issues that arise, without the need for a member of staff checking the availability of another officer ... thus providing a "one stop service"' (LBH, 1993c). It is also seen as a way of enhancing individual motivation by enabling staff to deploy a variety of skills in the course of their work. It 'can contribute greatly to staff development and job satisfaction' (LBH, 1993c). A senior officer expressed the reason for the changes candidly: 'In Hackney there is a real weakness among middle managers, generic working arrangements will enable us to provide more money for estate managers and help attract and retain better quality staff' (interview with author 25/3/94). Whether or not the restructuring will achieve the desired results is as yet unclear. What is apparent is that the very process of undertaking organisational restructuring has created major upheavals for staff, especially as the move towards generic working within the department was proceeded by the establishment of the Comprehensive Estates Initiative.

Staff working for the council had mixed feelings about the changes to their job description. On the one hand, some expressed satisfaction that the housing directorate was at last prepared to devote some energy to housing management concerns, rather than just concentrating on the more glamorous development aspects of their work. Yet on the other hand, they expressed concern that the real difficulties were not resolvable by simply changing job descriptions, and senior officers were putting forward the changes because it was the least expensive option. The following three excerpts from recent interviews convey some of the different attitudes of housing staff and provide an insight into the culture of the department and the impact the restructuring has had within the organisation.

The first indicates that the CEI has had a beneficial effect within the organisation by providing a focus on housing management:

Once CEI started, people started taking an interest and channelling more facilities into housing management. When I started you were just left to your own devices and you did as best you could. That was it. Now at least senior managers are taking an interest in the work we do.

(interview with author 4/3/94)

The second quotation is more typical of those housing staff who see the benefits of new initiatives not so much for the effects within the organisation but because they have the potential for attracting revenue:

The biggest single problem facing the housing department is repairs. The decimation of the capital programme means that many properties are in a poor state. It is this disrepair which best explains why tenants are so critical of the Council. Changing job descriptions cannot make that much difference unless there are more resources found to tackle the backlog of repairs. The Council is reliant on the Government for capital spending programmes. CEI and other initiatives are ways in which the Council can get more investment into the Borough.

(interview with author 25/3/94)

The third quotation reflects the anxiety many staff have about their role changing as pressure to meet performance targets increases. Housing managers are moving from a welfare role to a job where a large element is social control:

Estate managers will have less properties to manage − 250 rather than the 400 we manage at the moment which will reduce the burden. Yet it will mean that we have to be both social worker and police officer on the estate. I am really worried that we will be expected to proceed with evictions: this puts us in a difficult position.

(interview with author 9/3/94)

Housing managers working in the inner city have good reasons to be concerned about the welfare of tenants. Though the marginalisation of council housing is not a recent phenomenon. The extent to which the economic and social composition of council tenants has shifted since 1979 has been highlighted by Peter Malpass:

In 1981 42% of heads of households renting from local authorities were counted as economically inactive, and by 1990 the proportion had risen to 61%. This was a much faster increase that in the population as a whole, where the proportion rose from 33% to 38%.

(Malpass, 1993a: 58)

The 1991 General Household Survey (DoE, 1993a) shows that the average age of council tenants is higher than the population at large: 55 compared to 51. Single, widowed and separated people are also over-represented on council estates. When compared with owner occupiers, fewer council tenants have educational qualifications (2 per cent have degrees compared to 14 per cent of the owner occupied sector) and, along with housing association tenants, constitute 64 per cent of all households living on incomes below £100 per week. This residualisation of council housing has taken place as a result of the Right to Buy policies and the encouragement of owner occupation. As Alan Murie's chapter (chapter 5) shows, tenants who are able to exercise choice do so by moving out of local authority accommodation into owner occupation. As Malpass observes 'most of the workers who provide the skills most in demand in the British economy are now housed in the owner occupier sector, and this inevitably marginalises social rented housing' (Malpass, 1993a: 59).

The residualisation of council housing is significant because its effects undermine the efforts undertaken by Hackney and other local authorities to improve housing management. Both economic and housing policies have stigmatised social housing as a form of tenure for those unable to afford owner occupation. The tenants who will move into council and housing association properties will, as David Page (1993: 30) has argued, be 'even more economically disadvantaged than those housed previously – although younger and more likely to be economically active, their incomes are lower and they are less likely to have a job, more likely to be unemployed and more likely to be wholly dependent on state benefits or pensions'.

The concerns of staff about the future of council housing has undermined the potential of the CEI to restore morale. The intent that CEI would lead by example, demonstrating to other more moribund sections of the housing department what could be achieved by setting up a new initiative has, it seems, been met by a mixed response. Although most staff welcomed the initiative, some suggested that it had both divided the department and caused resentment:

CEI is a good idea, it has brought about improvements but in saying this, a lot more could be achieved and more could have been done to consult and encourage staff. As it currently operates, CEI is divisive. There are those staff who work on the CEI estates and there are the rest of the housing department who are expected to carry on as before. Many of the staff not on the CEI estates are resentful, as their problems are pushed aside.

(interview with author 9/3/94)

A senior officer conceded that new initiatives could result in a management vacuum in other areas of provision:

Hackney is good at getting initiatives off the ground. 'CEI', 'Voids Task Force', 'Hackney Housing Partnership' and so on. What this does is siphon off the best staff and leave other areas of the department under-resourced. Paradoxically CEI has left others in the housing department in a poor state of morale. The department suffers from a rigid structure and a state of limbo which means many officers are 'acting up'. There are now huge gaps appearing.

(interview with author 25/4/94)

The problems of new initiatives creating management difficulties elsewhere in the department are not of course unique to Hackney. In budgetary terms too, local authorities up and down the country are facing very similar dilemmas. Since 'Estate Action' funding requires a substantial contribution from local authorities mainstream resources. Councils that bid for additional resources from the Government, often have to reluctantly raid other designated budgets normally set aside for housing refurbishment.

All the responses indicate the uneven impact of the changes taking place within the housing department and the widespread anxiety among staff that, while organisationally the service provided to tenants may improve, the future of council housing faces an uncertain future both in terms of the introduction of CCT and the further residualisation of estates. Efforts to improve the quality of housing management and morale of staff will, it seems, be difficult for all local authorities in the current economic and political climate.

Partnership

The second important strategic shift the council has undertaken over the last few years is to foster new relationships with the private sector and Government. As already discussed, the relationship between central and local government has undergone a significant change. Local authorities are keen to promote themselves as active partners with central government and business in regeneration projects (DoE, 1993b). This marked change is particularly noticeable in Hackney. Government Ministers regularly visit the area. The new language adopted by the Council in its dealings with the Government is often consciously non-partisan; a deliberate attempt to portray the authority as consensual. The Council has taken steps with others, to extend its contacts with local business in a new forum known as the 'The East London Partnership' and with the Department of Environment's 'Task Force'.

Business influence in the activity of local regeneration takes place and is encouraged primarily because local government now sees business success as coterminous with its own interests. The view taken by both politicians and officers is that the locality is in competition with other areas for resources. This entails a redefinition of their own role. The Chief Executive put it in these terms: 'Yes, we are conscious of the game we have to play in order to look acceptable to the Government. But there are much wider changes taking place, our principal aim is to bring business and jobs back to Hackney'(interview with author 17/8/94).

Many senior managers and Councillors are convinced that local government can benefit from incorporating the 'enterprise philosophy' propounded by the Conservative Government. By supporting business and working in partnership, local authorities are seen as tackling bad practice, inefficiency and bureaucracy. Central government funding of regeneration programmes requires evidence of collaboration between the public and private sector and local authorities are now expected to be lead partners with Training and Enterprise Councils (TECs) for future regeneration bids.

Within the housing department itself, there are practical reasons to convey a sense of consensus. Words like 'partnership' and 'efficiency' camouflage potential turbulence arising from budgetary restraint. Managers, if they are having to scale down expectations among both the work force and users of services, deploy such terminology to distract attention from controversial decisions. For example 'redirecting resources to improve the quality of services to the public' or 'redirecting resources to priority areas' is less likely to meet opposition than stating the objective of controlling expenditure.

The use of competitive funding to allocate resources, for example 'City Challenge', 'Estate Action' and most recently 'The Single Regeneration Budget' by central government has further proliferated the terminology. Local government officers take it for granted that many bids for public money require an endorsement of the benefits of private sector activity.

There is a lack of public sector management theory to counteract Government plans to open up local government to competition. Public sector organisations have instead incorporated the theories of writers such as Peters (1987) and Moss-Kanter (1989) which reinforce the notion that public sector managers should incorporate 'entrepreneurship' as a key activity. Financial and business management is now a major part of most training programmes. This trend has been actively encouraged by the Audit Commission in their production and dissemination of management literature (Audit Commission, 1992). Paradoxically, despite the residualisation of council housing, many professionals working within housing departments see their own future security contingent on associating with private sector business practice and minimising the welfare dimensions of their work. Tenants, could if this trend continues unabated, be forced to depend on the most junior members of staff 'shouldering' the welfare aspects of housing management work.

Housing departments are especially affected by the commercial activities of the private sector. To examine these trends in more detail, this remainder of this section of the chapter focuses on Holly Street, one of the five CEI estates. The Holly Street redevelopment encapsulates the public/private partnership approach envisaged by the Government. Over the next 5 years, £71.5 million will be spent redeveloping the estate. This figure includes £14 million from the Government's Estate Action Programme, £5 million from the Council housing investment programme, and £10 million through the Dalston City Challenge partnership. £30 million will come from the Housing Corporation who will fund the housing association development. Private sector sales are expected to raise a further £12 million.

The development process, although on local authority land, is being managed by the property developers, Laings, whose specific role is project co-ordinator for the overall development. They won the contract for Holly Street Estate redevelopment through a complex tender process that included the tenants from the Estate Development Committee adjudicating on the contractors' proposals. The modernisation, when complete, will provide a mixture of different tenures, including new housing association properties to be managed by a consortium of local agencies, refurbished local authority dwellings and new homes for sale. The proportion of housing stock on Holly Street managed by the Council is likely to fall from about 97 per cent to around 30 per cent (LBH, 1994) signalling the extent to which the Government's future plans for council housing has already taken root in authorities such as Hackney.

Laings will co-ordinate a number of employment and training projects. The most significant is the commitment to train up to 200 local people in building-related skills. As part of this commitment to training the aim is to secure by the end of the programme 56 jobs for people in construction. Such a commitment is best understood as a symbolic gesture, put in place to demonstrate that the project is not simply just a housing development programme but a holistic attempt to tackle the multi-faceted problems evident on Holly Street.

The formal mechanism that details the agreed arrangements is known as the Principal Development Agreement and was signed by all six developing housing associations, Laings and Hackney Council on 15 November 1993. A large part of the agreement centres on the form of tenant participation. In addition to the tenants' Estate Development Committee, a working party has been set up to co-ordinate a participation strategy and an overall framework to oversee housing management. The primary aim of the agreement is to protect the Council's interests, should there be any major contractual breach. Arbitration mechanisms are in place in the eventuality of any dispute between the different agencies involved in the project.

The Principal Development Agreement in many respects encapsulates the type of public/private partnerships which many housing departments will have to negotiate in the future. The disagreements and tensions which surfaced during the course of the negotiations reflect the uncertainties which exist at various sites where housing departments collaborate with organisations which operate primarily on a profit basis. At its core this tension can be seen as a struggle over finances. The housing department hoped to secure from the agreement as much assistance as it could extract from the private sector to achieve its objectives. The private sector agencies needed to keep expenses to a minimum, yet at the same time they did not wish to appear either overtly opportunistic or exploitative.

Although the interaction that takes place between the central state, the private sector and local authorities reflects broader structural change it would be mistaken to portray these relationships as stereotypical. Each individual development involving negotiations between the public and private sectors are shaped by a number of different processes which are specifically local in nature. The interpretation placed upon the partnership agreement varies. There is no clear consensus among those who partake in the venture as to whether partnership will bring new benefits to the borough. Views expressed ranged from one architect's opinion that 'The Principal Development Agreement' is little more that a gigantic building project which the Council has locked itself into' (interview with author 14/1/94) to the Leader of Hackney Council's more circumspect comment that 'my big worry about a lot of what is called partnership is the possibility that we could end up just concentrating on the aesthetics of improving estates and not have the resources to secure jobs and social regeneration' (interview with author 11/1/94).

In many respects this anxiety expressed by the Leader is well founded. Regeneration is dependent on successfully stimulating the local economy, yet jobs in the construction industry tend to be short term and insecure. According to Falk (1993: 7) 'they also do not relate to the needs of the prime groups in need, namely women with children and ethnic minorities'. Research by McGregor (1990: x) argued that 'construction-led initiatives have produced relatively few employment and training benefits for local people and often these are achieved at a very great cost'.

To compound matters further, the thrust of Government policy appears to be moving away from providing assistance on the basis of need to a system in which local authorities compete via the Single Regeneration Budget for funding. Housing associations who will be providing the vast majority of new build development for rent in Hackney are also required to bid for funding from the Housing Corporation. Those housing associations which can demonstrate that their development programme costs are low will receive funding. In effect, the Housing Corporation's funding regime, as Judith

Harrison's chapter (chapter 2) makes clear, forces housing associations to raise their rent levels in order to make up the shortfall in funding. The overriding concern with physical redevelopment has overshadowed the concerns about both access and affordability. For example, there has been no stipulation placed on the housing associations involved in the Holly Street redevelopment as to the level of rents they will charge. High rents can only compound the difficulties, by encouraging tenants to buy elsewhere. The cumulative effect of the policy paradoxically residualises the new estates, as the properties are occupied in the main by tenants who are reliant on some form of state benefit making the task of housing management more difficult and expensive.

The partnership arrangements entered into by the Council on Holly Street demonstrates, above all else, the extent to which it is severely constrained by external factors. Despite the efforts being portrayed to present these initiatives as acts of mutual consent, councils who wish to retain influence on new build redevelopments face an uphill struggle to extract concessions from other agencies.

Tenant participation

The final issue examined in this chapter is tenant participation, which is now almost universally seen as a holy grail by most people associated with local authority housing. Hackney is no exception to this and enhancing tenant participation has become a central objective of the Council's housing strategy. 'Over the past three years tenant empowerment has become an increasingly important principle underlying Hackney's entire housing strategy ... enabling tenants to play an active role in the development of their communities and the management of their estates'(1993d: 65).

Where, in the past, the Council did little to encourage tenants to partake in the management of the estates, the Council has recently taken the major step of encouraging tenants to vote for Estate Management Boards to oversee the management of estates. The first EMB for Hackney is the Clapton Park Estate, where 93 per cent of tenants decided in favour of the new arrangements in a ballot in which 74 per cent (943 tenants) voted. On the Trowbridge Estate, a tenant management co-operative was voted for by over 95 per cent of tenants in a 94 per cent turnout. Three other estates are in the process of preparing for ballots for TMC's and a further three for Estate Management Boards.

The Comprehensive Estates Initiative is an excellent example of the current preoccupation with participation. The Council has set up a committee structure to manage the complex range of activities. The main decision-making body is the CEI sub-committee which meets on a monthly basis. As well as Councillors, tenant representatives from each of the Estates are co-opted onto the Committee. In the words of the CEI Progress Report (1992), 'It considers regular monitoring reports on decanting, demolition programmes, developments on each estate and reports on negotiations with our partners and all other policy aspects of CEI.' Each of the five estates have an elected Estate Development Committee (EDC) which acts as a steering group on the estate to oversee the programme. The composition of the EDCs include ward Councillors and interested tenants. EDCs have been meeting on a fortnightly basis. In addition, there are sub-groups focusing on specific issues such as publicity and design, which also meet on a fortnightly basis. Alongside the formal meetings, each of the estates have held open days and events to publicise the CEI, all of which have proved more popular with tenants.

Despite the Council's genuine attempts to encourage tenant involvement, tenants are not keen to actively participate. Those who do, 'show signs of being distinctly weary. For example, average attendance by tenants attending Holly Street EDC between May and August dropped to 8 from 10 during the previous four months' (CLAWS, 1993: 7). A recent independent consultant's report on Holly Street drew attention to the extent to which the consultation is geared to the needs of the officers rather than the tenants:

We recognise the ease at which tenant participation in a complex fast moving programme can become geared to the needs and timetables of officers (or developers) rather than the tenants. In such a situation it is often only the 'tenant activists' who have the skills, energy and knowledge base to keep up and exert any influence. This needs to change however for phase 2 onwards if participation is to be more than rubber stamping and a means by which Hackney generally and CEI officers specifically legitimise their role and approach to the project.

(CLAWS, 1993, p. 12)

An explanation of these difficulties which no doubt affect many of the local authorities engaged in estate renewal programmes was put forward by one CEI estate co-ordinator:

The first year of CEI has been all about publicity and rhetoric, selling CEI both within the authority, to tenants and Government. All this was done without the groundwork in place, the resources for tenants, staff structures, training. The problem of the early months of the EDC was simply catching up with the rhetoric and expectations we had raised with tenants. All of us underestimated the amount of support tenants needed. It is unrealistic to expect tenants just to work coherently in the short time available. A real problem is the difficulty tenants had in sorting out among themselves the necessary working arrangements to make consultation feasible.

(interview with author 4/8/93)

A different explanation was put forward by a community worker responsible for supporting tenant participation who voiced concern about the Housing Corporations allocation guidelines for developing housing associations which has discouraged both local authorities and housing associations from promoting tenant involvement in the design of new homes:

It will become a sink estate unless more tenants living here now decide to stay and not opt for a transfer. Participation could only really be effective when people feel secure and had good reasons to make a personal commitment to the area. Most tenants realise that the estate may take on a new appearance, but the new tenants who will move into the estate will have no connection with the estate. Housing Corporation guidelines mean that 70% of the new housing association development will be occupied by homeless households.

(interview with author 23/8/93)

Tenant participation has been pursued in earnest by the Council to counteract charges that it is unresponsive to the desires of tenants. In part this reflects the dominant paradigm that consultation and communication with staff and the public should be part of the vocabulary of many aspiring managers. Hackney, alongside other councils, is keen to demonstrate their concern for the wishes of tenants by encouraging both consultation and participation in decision making.

Academics, when discussing the role of tenants in decision making, tend to agree that consultation and participation are desirable (Power, 1987; Birchall, 1988). There have been very few attempts to locate tenant participation in a wider political and ideological context. The focus instead is practice orientated to show how authorities can incorporate participation into management functions. There are two important implications of this consensus:

first an uncritical treatment of participation as a component of housing management; and second a revisionist historiography to explain failures of council housing which elevate inadequate participation as one of the important reasons for the decline of many housing estates. This partial reading overlooks the significance of structural processes which affected council housing; in particular the impact of poverty, unemployment, demography and cultural change. In its place the history of the last 20 years is viewed as the period local authorities and architects did not consult adequately with tenants. It is still naively assumed that had tenants' views been listened to, the large system-built estates would not have been built.

This interpretation of the recent past is important in understanding the direction and emphasis of housing management approaches. The stress on tenant consultation and partnership is one way in which programmes market themselves as innovative. The Director of Hackney's housing department in an address to tenants at a recent meeting called to discuss plans to refurbish the estate said: 'we need to make sure you are involved so we don't make mistakes' (CEI consultation meeting Nightingale Estate 10/5/93). Tenant participation and partnership are viewed as new ingredients to guarantee the success of the scheme. The Government's Estate Action Programme makes consultation an essential precondition. 'Our policies,' said Sir George Young the Minister for Housing in a speech at Hackney Town Hall, 'have to recognise the need for partnership. People of all backgrounds and from all walks of life, need to be involved in the decisions which affect them. And they want to be involved. The fact is, they are no longer prepared to accept a paternalistic approach, however well meaning'(11/3/93).

Emphasis on tenant participation as a solution to the problems of inner city estates is apparent in most public pronouncements and documents relating to housing management. The concern to seek out the views of the public stems in part from the anxiety many organisations and public institutions have about their own public standing. Local authority housing departments have over the last 15 years been singled out for criticism by the Government as being bureaucratic and inefficient in the delivery of housing services (Cole and Furbey, 1994: 206). High rent arrears, voids and poor maintenance are, its critics concur, symptomatic of the inability of local authorities to manage properties.

The advocacy of participation is central to all forms of estate management, however, the degree to which the lack of participation is actually a cause of the problems is disputed. Writers such as Johnston Birchall (1992: 186) argue that council housing excludes the interests of tenants. The decay to be found on large estates is attributable to the 'underlying problem – that council tenants have not had a place in the structure of control'. Others such as Peter Malpass (1993b) suggest that tenant participation is a convenient issue in which the government can win public endorsement of its portrayal of local authorities as bureaucratic and in so doing deflect attention away from public expenditure cuts and under-investment in council housing.

It is clear that in Hackney, as elsewhere, consultation is presented as the solution to the problems of tenants living on some of the run-down estates. The stress on participation is an area both the Government and the Council can publicly agree on to reinforce the message that both are now working in partnership so it is hardly surprising that Councillors and senior officers should then make so many references to it. Such language also helps anaesthetise the impact of public expenditure cuts on housing programmes by diverting attention away from spending pronouncements and the incapacity of the state to tackle the problems. Instead the solution presented reinforces the importance of individual responsibility and personal endeavour. An important ideological shift is taking place to present the problems of the welfare state as a failure of individual rather than state responsibility thereby undermining the arguments of those calling for extra resources.

Conclusion

From the evidence gathered Hackney, in common with most local authorities, has changed considerably over the last four years in its approach to a range of housing management issues. Despite the considerable achievements, what seems clear is that none of the new initiatives can perform a salvation for council tenants. It is unrealistic to expect or proclaim that any new initiative whether in Hackney or elsewhere will be able to reverse the long spiral of decline which has been a feature of council or social housing over the last 20 years. The great difficulty for the Council and indeed for anyone associated with housing management in the mid-1990s is how to protect neighbourhoods from the consequences of residualisation. In the specific case of housing renewal, the difficulties are even more pronounced as the Government is pursuing simultaneously fiscal and social policies which impact adversely on council and housing association tenants (for example forcing housing associations to raise rent level by cuts in subsidy). Whatever new initiatives the housing department develops in the foreseeable future, the outcome will be constrained by both the Government's policies and the impact of the economy on the locality. This in effect means that the political pressure will be to maximise resources and to keep costs down. The Leader of Hackney Council's description as to what is possible is true for most local authorities:

Resources from central government are not simply awarded on the basis of need. We are in competition with other authorities for funding. We have to demonstrate value for money ... the tension between keeping costs down and maintaining employee rights and good services is something we are going to have to live with for the foreseeable future.

(interview with author 11/1/94)

The Council seems to have had some success in improving its relationships with central government through the publicity and partnerships generated by initiatives such as the Comprehensive Estates Initiative, although criticism of its housing management performance remains. The cost of this success has mainly been felt within the organisation itself. The complex rules and procedures laid down by the Government for funding projects have meant that many of the staff working within the department are effectively working on these initiatives full time and by implication are excluded from the core activities of the department. By definition, large scale initiatives are 'top down' affairs which are dominated by the most senior members of the organisation, often leaving staff outside the orbit of these new initiatives feeling isolated and detached.

In attracting DoE funding, the Council has also had to utilise budgets from its own housing investment commitments which has caused some consternation from those senior officers not involved in the Estate Action bids. From the Government's perspective the tight rules for local authorities have arguably been more effective as a form of intervention than previous policies of establishing local development corporations and quangos which were criticised for undermining democratic accountability. The funding arrangements for the Single Regeneration Budget require the active co-operation of local authorities. In practice this will mean that local authorities are unlikely to publicly criticise the Government while it seeks to attract funds.

As local authorities such as Hackney prepare for CCT there is a fear among some staff that the imposition of the client/contractor split will exacerbate further the divide between senior and front line staff. In Hackney, the contract specifications being prepared are being drawn up centrally with the support of senior neighbourhood managers who are providing 'service profiles' of the existing service. The danger is that the long term success of Hackney's housing department will to a large extent depend on the ability of front line staff to improve their performance in reallocating empty properties, rent arrears and repairs. The new initiatives have certainly placed a heavy responsibility on staff just at a time when many are anxious about their own future. The following comment represents the view of many staff not just in Hackney but elsewhere as well:

Staff morale is much the same as before. Only now housing managers are expected more and more to deliver the changes decided upon from up above. We feel more and more put upon.
(author's interview with housing management staff 9/3/94)

While much of what takes place is contingent on policies put forward by the Government, there is, as the case study illustrates, still scope for housing departments to shape policy and thereby affect political outcomes. In both policy choices and style of implementation, Hackney appears to be taking innovative steps to maximise resources and collaborate with tenants and the private sector. This will lead to some genuine benefits for Hackney's tenants living on the five CEI estates as well as providing a good example to other authorities developing their own housing management role. Unfortunately, the organisational turbulence created by the advent of the new initiatives and CCT can only add to the internal pressures which have bedevilled the department. Hackney's difficulties despite the endeavours of councillors, tenants and staff look set to continue.

References

Audit Commission (1992) *Developing Local Authority Housing Strategies*, London, HMSO.
Birchall, J. (1988) *Building Communities: The Co-operative Way*, London, Routledge.

Birchall, J. (1992) 'Council Tenants: Sovereign Consumers or Pawns in a Game?' in Birchall, J. (ed.) *Housing Policy in the 1990s*, London, Routledge.

CLAWS (1993) *Interim Report on Tenant Involvement in the Holly Street Comprehensive Estates Initiative*, London, Community Land and Workspace Services Ltd.

Cochrane, A. (1993) *Whatever Happened to Local Government?*, Buckingham, Open University Press.

Cole, I. (1993) 'Decentralisation of the Housing Service' in Malpass, P. and Means, R. (eds) *Implementing Housing Policy*, Open University Press, Buckingham.

Cole, I. and Furbey, R. (1994) *The Eclipse of Council Housing*, London, Routledge.

Commission for Racial Equality (1984) *Race and Council Housing in Hackney: Report of the Formal Investigation*, London, Commission for Racial Equality.

Department of the Environment (1993a) *General Household Survey 1991*, London, HMSO.

Department of the Environment (1993b) *Single Regeneration Budget: Note on Principles*, London, HMSO.

Edelman, M. (1985) 'Political Language and Political Reality' *Policy Studies*, Vol. 18, pp. 10-19.

Falk, N. (1993) 'Housing and Employment Initiatives' in *Seminar Proceedings on Housing and Employment*, 11 October, London, Housing Centre Trust.

Gyford, J. (1985) *The Politics of Local Socialism*, London, Allen & Unwin.

Hackney, London Borough of (1988a) *The Hackney Herald*, May–June, London, LBH.

Hackney, London Borough of (1988b) 'Report of the Chief Executive. Changing the Culture of Hackney – the Decision Making Process and Components for a Strategy of Change', *Policy and Resources Committee*, 12 October, London, LBH.

Hackney, London Borough of (1992) *Comprehensive Estates Initiative Progress Report*, London, LBH.

Hackney, London Borough of (1993a) *Census 1991: Ward Profiles*, London, LBH.

Hackney, London Borough of (1993b) *Hackney Housing Affordability Survey*, London, LBH.

Hackney, London Borough of (1993c) 'Generic Working within CEI', *CEI Joint Sub Committee*, 11 March, London, LBH.

Hackney, London Borough of (1993d), *Housing Strategy 1994-7*, London, LBH.

Hackney, London Borough of (1994), *Housing Comprehensive Estates Initiative: Briefing Note*, Housing Policy and Research Section, 22 April 1994.

Hall, S. (1988) *The Hard Road to Renewal*, London, Verso.

Harrison, P. (1983) *Inside the Inner City*, Harmondsworth, Penguin.

Hoggett, P., Lawrence, S. and Fudge, C. (1984) in *The Politics of Decentralisation* (eds) Hambleton, R. and Hoggett, P., SAUS Working Paper 46, Bristol.

Kantor, R. M. (1989) *When Giants Learn to Dance: Mastering the Challenges of Strategies, Management and Careers in the 1990's*, London, Unwin Hyman.

Lansley, S. Goss, S. and Wolmar, C. (1989) *Councils in Conflict: The Rise and Fall of the Municipal Left*, Basingstoke, MacMillan.

Malpass, P. (1993a) 'Housing Management – By the People For the People', *Housing Review*, Vol. 42, No. 4, July–August, pp. 58-61.

Malpass, P. (1993b) 'Housing Policy and the Disabling of Local Authorities' in Birchall, J. (ed.) *Housing Policy in the 1990s*, London, Routledge.

Marsh, D. and Rhodes, R. (eds) (1992) *Implementing Thatcherite Policies*, Buckingham, Open University Press.

McGregor, A. (1990) 'Local Employment and Training Initiatives. Research Report 15, Scottish Homes', Edinburgh – quoted in Turok, I. (1990) 'Property Led Urban Regeneration: Panacea or Placebo?' *Environment and Planning A*, Vol. 24, pp. 361-379.

Page, D. (1993) *Building for Communities: A Study of New Housing Association Estates*, York, Joseph Rowntree Foundation.

Peters, T. (1987) *Thriving on Chaos*, London, Pan Books.

Power, A. (1987) *Property before People: The Management of Twentieth-century Housing*, London, Allen and Unwin.

Tomlinson, M. (1986) 'Decentralisation: Learning the Lessons? The Radical Failure of Decentralisation in Hackney 1981-83', *Planning Studies*, No. 18, School of Planning, Polytechnic of Central London.
Wright, P. (1991) *A Journey Through Ruins: The Last days of London*, London, Radius.

Synthesis and conclusions

Ricardo Pinto

Context: priming the discussion

The introduction to the book and chapter 1 highlighted the point that four successive Conservative governments have had two housing aims in common: promoting an increase in home ownership and striving to reduce the role of council housing. The Right to Buy policy was perfectly suited to achieving both ends and continues to be the most successful housing policy, as well as representing the single most important privatisation programme ever undertaken by the Conservatives. To these basic aims have been added successive Acts of Parliament culminating in the 1989 Housing and Local Government Act, which was designed to control the way local authorities have invested their capital and revenue resources. The council housing provision role has now come virtually to an end and the remaining resources are directed to the refurbishment and maintenance of an increasingly residualised council housing stock.

The government came slowly to the realisation that the above twin strategies did not amount to a balanced housing policy and made a number of efforts to try to staunch the haemorrhage of private rented housing. The recent signs of revitalisation in this sector reflects more the collapse of the private housing market at the end of the 1980s, than the assorted government efforts to deregulate and provide tax breaks to revive private renting. In addition home ownership is no longer lauded by Ministers as it once was due to the arrival of such issues as mortgage debt, repossession, mortgage rescue schemes and negative equity. Nevertheless, this remains a consistent government policy as demonstrated by the continuation of the Right to Buy as well as more recent developments such as Shared Ownership housing and Rents to Mortgages. These will continue to be taken up by the council and housing association tenants who have or can afford this option, but it is clear that, as pointed out by Alan

Murie in his contribution (chapter 5), such opportunities to exercise choice remove that option from other generations of tenants.

The introduction made no apologies for placing council housing at the forefront of this book. The numerous housing developments which have taken place since the 1980s have emphasised the interrelated themes of ownership and management of housing (see Introduction) and these two issues have had a disproportionate effect on council housing. Local authority landlords have been subjected to unrelenting and indiscriminate government criticism which has treated council housing in a monolithic manner with respect to their management role, and it is this which has acted as the catalyst and justification for virtually curtailing investment in this housing option. It has also served as the basis for the argument that local authorities are singularly incapable of performing their management function and thus that there was no need for council housing as a rented housing option. Evidence was highlighted in a number of chapters demonstrating that local authorities were far from ideal landlords (see chapters 1 and 7), however, the concentration on the management role to the exclusion of other factors, not least adequate investment and the context within which the management function takes place, is hardly a fair or sound basis on which to condemn council housing.

The most acute demonstration of the management problem was associated with the growing evidence of 'unpopular' housing estates, though the criticisms of these were increasingly applied to the whole council housing system. The government launched Priority Estates Project and subsequently the Estate Action initiative to demonstrate to local authorities how to improve their management by following certain organisational guidelines. Using the incentive of additional capital resources, government also began to encourage local authorities to diversify their housing stock via sales to private developers and trusts; and the management of council housing by housing associations, concierges, housing co-operatives, Estate Management Boards and other Tenant Management Organisations.

At the same time, the government also came to accept the argument that there would continue to be a need for social housing for those unable or uninterested in joining the increasing ranks of home owners. The property market crash had also emphasised the dangers of pushing owner occupation further down the affordability line to the more marginal households. Alternative landlords such as housing co-operatives and housing associations were increasingly seen as more appropriate social landlords and legislation was duly enacted to ensure that they took centre-stage in the future provision and management of social housing.

The wholesale criticism of council housing management reached fever-pitch in the mid 1980s. This was given added force by reports such as the Audit Commission's (1986) which alluded to a crisis in housing management. A major DoE-funded research project into the relative performance of social landlords which was carried out shortly after the Audit Commission's report, would have shed light on the debates taking place at this point in time. This report was only released in 1989 which is unfortunate because it found no such crisis in council housing management, just a mixture of good and bad landlords. In the mean time the post-1987 housing policies increasingly sought to bring about the end of municipal housing, despite the fact that Ministers must have been aware of the conclusions of the Centre of Housing Research report (1989), via a number of options enabling local authorities (Large Scale Voluntary Transfers), tenants (Tenants' Choice) or the government (Housing Action Trusts and then Housing Management CCT) to choose to opt out of council ownership and management altogether. Housing estates and indeed, the entire housing stock, could be transferred from local authorities but under no circumstances could they be transferred back to local authorities, even if Council Tax payers or tenants felt this to be an appropriate option. Transfers were to be one-way and council housing was set to end. This formed the context for this book but the chapters in this book demonstrate that the dismantling of the council housing system and the alternative social housing system envisaged by the government are not necessarily going according to plan.

Discussion: key issues arising from the foregoing chapters

The essays in this book covered a good deal of the housing ownership and management debate but conformed to three main types. The first set of papers corresponds to the new social landlords. They demonstrated that it has not been easy or painless for housing associations and co-operatives to take over the mantle of provision and management of social housing in the future. The second set covered the range of options for local authorities to transform, transfer or sell their housing estates. Chapter 4 discussed the impact of an influential housing programme which was initiated by central government. The Estate Action initiative (in conjunction with Priority Estates Project) has had a major impact on the debate about the management and ownership of social housing, not least because it pioneered a number of the more radical exit options. The following contribution discussed the range of options which enable tenants of local authorities to exit council housing and enter new forms of ownership: Right to Buy, Housing Action Trusts, Large Scale Voluntary Transfers and Tenants' Choice. The last set of chapters discussed the overall impact of recent policy on local authority housing departments generally and analysed the more recent legislation with respect to Housing Management Compulsory Competitive Tendering. The last chapter analysed how a particularly deprived local housing authority has responded to the challenges of the legislative, financial and socio-economic environment with regard to the housing service. The aim of this section is to bring all these strands together via an analysis of the main findings of the essays.

Housing associations

The contributions in this book were kicked off by an analysis of the government's preferred social landlords. Harrison's chapter (chapter 2) represents an extremely detailed analysis of the housing associations movement from cradle to maturity; with the prospect of the grave thrown in for good measure. Her contribution highlights the different functions that have been performed by housing associations at different times and charts the most significant government legislation up to the Housing Act 1988. The bulk of her analysis is devoted to exploring the various stresses and strains afflicting the housing association system, having reached maturity as the future providers of rented social housing.

A key point is that as a result of the new financial system, Housing Association Grant (HAG) has been reduced from an average of 75 per cent per scheme to about 62 per cent in 1994/95, with the effect that housing associations must borrow an increasing amount from private financial sources in order to develop new housing. This has a predictable but significant consequence, which is that rents must rise in order to compensate for the reduced subsidy. The tensions generated by the pressure to operate increasingly in a business-like manner and yet provide social housing for their traditional tenants and increasingly the homeless, have presented a major and unresolved problem for associations. The steep rent rises which have ensued and to a lesser extent, the duality of different regimes for different types of tenure have given rise to a major debate about the affordability of housing associations.

A further point from this work is the fact that any additional or unexpected costs, beyond certain limits, which arise from proposed housing association developments must now be met from private finance, rather than HAG meeting the shortfall. Introduced by government with the intention of generating efficiency, this measure appears to have had the unintended consequence of resulting in a major decline in rehabilitation schemes. This is unfortunate for urban areas which also happen to experience the greatest housing pressure since their total costs are somewhat unpredictable. It has also resulted in a notable move towards the funding of new build and larger housing association estates since it is easier to predict total costs and extract savings arising from economies of scale.

Recent research has demonstrated that a worrying trend has emerged in some of these large estates. In particular, it suggests that these have begun to experience many of the management difficulties which a number of 'problem' council housing estates experience, not least the skewed demographic structure. The difference is that these trends have begun to afflict some housing associations within five years of being built (see Page, 1993). These findings should go some way towards modifying central government's blanket condemnation of local authorities, especially in the light of the impact of PEP and EA, and act to curb the blind faith in alternative landlord forms which may replicate the circumstances and errors which resulted in criticism of council housing in the first place.

In the second part of her chapter, Harrison assesses the extent to which housing associations have proved to be effective providers of social housing. She notes that although a number of recent studies have estimated that there is a need to build around 100,000 social dwellings per year up to the year 2001 in England and Wales alone, this has not been translated officially into a target for housing associations to aim for. The emphasis remains one of management and ownership not need. Housing associations have only managed to build 141,000 dwellings since the launch of the 1988 Housing Act. This has been partly because of the disruptive change to the new HAG regime, however, Harrison also makes the important point that just as housing associations were gearing up to build the required numbers, the 1993 Budget slashed the resources allocated to housing associations for social housing construction. With these cuts end any hopes of meeting the projected housing needs, as does the privileged position which used to be enjoyed by housing associations relative to other social housing managers and providers.

Housing associations have not performed well in securing affordable rented accommodation for those most in need. As with the government engineered efforts to raise council rents to market levels, low income households in housing associations have fared badly due to the 'poverty trap' generated by rapidly escalating rents as opposed to static or limited pay rises. By virtue of its control over HAG levels, it is government that determines the affordability or otherwise of housing association rents for those who are not covered by the Housing Benefit system. The changes charted by Harrison point to greater dependency on Housing Benefit and a deepening of the poverty trap for those on low incomes. Although housing associations do appear to have been successful in continuing to house their traditional tenants, future provision for special needs and the homeless have not been considered in the 1993 Budget cuts and will present further problems in the future.

Turning back to a key theme in this book Harrison in common with other papers in this collection, notes the salience of the report by the Centre for Housing Research (1989) which undermined the myth of council landlords as remote, inefficient and unreformable versus the caring and efficient housing associations. She notes in particular the new numbers game being played by housing associations which is reminiscent of local authorities at one time, and is leading to many of the management deficiencies experienced by a number of local authorities in the past.

Harrison argues that housing associations are being 'pulled in different directions' and that this will be accentuated by the recent government announcement that HAG will be further reduced in the future. The likely consequences on rent levels combined with measures to promote home ownership (such as shared ownership) results in a contradiction with respect to the policy of making housing associations the future social rented landlords. This leads Harrison to wonder whether the pendulum will, in due course, swing once again away from housing associations to other landlords with regard to the future provision of affordable rented housing and whether they will merely become vehicles for the privatisation of rented public housing.

Following on from this a further point to note concerns the possibility that such transfers as arise from the Right to Manage, Large Scale Voluntary Transfers (LSVT) and Tenants' Choice will result in the same capital and revenue constraints currently experienced by local authorities which, added to their inherent difficulties such as a dispersed housing stock, may eventually culminate in their own demise as owners and managers of rented housing. There is the possibility that although they may currently be the government's favoured means of providing and managing social housing, the government's ambivalent attitude to housing associations means that they may go the same way as local authorities appear to be heading. The government's attitude and commitment to housing co-operatives as the other key form of social landlord was similarly questioned in the next contribution.

Housing co-operatives

Clapham and Kintrea demonstrated in chapter 3 that despite the housing co-operative movement's relatively long history, it has made slow and uneven progress as a form of social housing in Britain. It has received variable political support and has mainly taken root in locations where central and local support was forthcoming, as in certain parts of London, Glasgow and Merseyside. Indeed, it was only as recently as 1974 that local authorities were able to form tenant management co-operatives and the Housing Corporation was allowed to provide HAG to co-operatives. It was the government's desire to reduce the role of council housing, increase tenants' responsibilities and decentralise housing management that attracted it to the options offered by the co-operative housing sector.

A number of Ministerial and policy statements indicated that co-operatives were also seen as the future social housing landlords. This was to be achieved not only via the possibility of setting up new co-operatives, but also by transferring existing local authority housing stock to this, as the government saw it, more independent and efficient system of housing management. Whilst Clapham and Kintrea acknowledge the overtures and direction of recent policy with respect to this sector, they maintain that it faces major disadvantages which mean that it is unlikely to fulfil the government's expectations, certainly not at the scale and pace envisaged.

They contend that the fact that co-operatives are small and unwilling to expand greatly means that the growth of this sector relies on many new organisations being created. However, this is a complex and time consuming process which in turn means that co-operatives suffer a major disadvantage vis à vis other forms of ownership and management. Whereas it is relatively easy for large portions of local authority housing stock to simply be transferred to housing associations, this does not apply to housing co-operatives. Furthermore, a single or a few housing associations are easier to develop than the many co-operatives that would be necessary to transfer large portions of council housing. These imperatives combined with the recent advent of alternatives such as Estate Management Boards (EMBs) which are argued to be easier to form and more suited to large council housing transfers (Zipfel, 1989; Bell and PEP Consultants, 1990), mean that housing co-operatives are ruled out of benefiting rapidly from policies such as Large Scale Voluntary Transfers, Tenants' Choice or even the Right to Manage.

Moreover, Clapham and Kintrea maintain that the financial, legal and institutional framework within which co-operatives operate 'raises doubts about the political desire to support co-operatives as chances to reform this framework have been missed'. In the 1988 review of the operation of housing co-operatives, the government lost the opportunity to radically change the framework for co-operatives. It merely sought to expand the number of promotional bodies and although it did make some financial support available under 'Section 16' funding, even here, the government did not go as far as the political support for co-operatives would imply. Such funding is for existing local authority tenants and both co-operatives and EMBs are eligible for support. Whilst this is in line with government policy against council housing and for tenant empowerment generally, it is not entirely in favour of co-operatives.

The chapter demonstrates other weaknesses which detract from fast expansion of this sector. The movement is heavily dependent on the Housing Corporation to provide housing and revenue funding but 'all the signs are that the Housing Corporation does not support the growth of co-operatives' and the secondary co-operatives which promote new co-operatives have suffered from a poor funding system and managerial problems. These are major deficiencies which are compounded by the new housing association finance system introduced in 1989. As discussed in Harrison's contribution, this Act has had major implications for housing associations but it has been even more significant for co-operatives whose limited assets, among other factors, have resulted in a collapse in the formation of new co-operatives. In Clapham and Kintrea's view this trend is unlikely to be alleviated by the new right for council tenants to set up Tenant Management Organisations. The only sign of hope relates to Scotland where, in contrast to England, there has been rapid growth in par-value co-operatives formed from council housing, although these have been actively promoted by Scottish Homes as well as local authorities.

Clapham and Kintrea acknowledge that if the co-operative move-ment is to flourish when in competition with other forms of social housing, they need to demonstrate that they are effective. The authors proceed to do so in the remainder of their contribution by emphasising three points: that co-operatives have made major strides in involving tenants in the running of their homes; in providing an effective, indeed highly praised, management service; and in renew-ing housing, providing a focus for communities and resolving neighbourhood conflicts. These advantages coupled with the rapid growth in Scotland mean that it is worthwhile seeking to stimulate housing co-operatives via a range of recommendations which they present at the end of their contribution. However, the key finding remains that as far as the rest of the country is concerned, it is highly unlikely that the co-operative movement, regardless of how advanta-geous a form of management it may be, will pose as much of a threat to the council housing sector as might be implied by Ministerial pronouncements, not least because enthusiasm for them has not been translated into an appropriate financial, legal, administrative and policy framework. The likely impact of the other key housing developments affecting the council housing sector such as the Estate Action initiative and the range of tenants' choices are discussed next.

Estate Action (EA) initiative

Pinto's contribution began by highlighting the mixture of political and managerial motives which gave rise to an extremely diverse Estate Action initiative. General criticism of the local authority management style was the basis of the initiative and PEP-style local based management was the main remedy prescribed, but EA went well beyond this. It sought to encourage local authorities to diversify the tenure pattern in council housing estates via the development of and possible disposal of stock to housing associations and co-operatives; as well as the sale of land and housing stock in problem estates to private developers or trusts. As an incentive to local authorities to change their ways and building on the fact that an increasing number of local authorities were already experimenting with a range of these initiatives, the DoE made capital grants available to the local authorities that submitted the best proposals. This system of grant allocation, even when targeted as it initially was to the most deprived housing authorities, introduced a competitive financial system which was to culminate in the City Challenge and Single Regeneration Budget schemes. Certain key themes were evident in EA. It sought to:

• improve housing management;
• involve tenants in the process;
• invest in housing stock;
• diversify tenure; and
• sell land and stock.

The initiative was illustrative of the nature of the central–local relations which existed at the time. Local authorities felt threatened by the government's attitude and legislation to them and were dismayed by the nature of the proposals unveiled under the initiative. The privatisation and diversification of tenure options in particular, were highly controversial at the time. So too was the competitive nature of the scheme where local authorities vied with each other for scarce resources. In addition the nature of the funding system was a source of major contention, namely that the resources were withdrawn from the mainstream Housing Investment Programme system (HIPs) and transferred or 'topsliced' to EA (as EA HIPs) to be handed out for local authority proposals that conformed to central government's housing priorities, rather than local ones.

A key theme presented in this contribution is that the administrative and timetabling arrangement designed to enable the scheme proposals submitted by local authorities to be short-listed and funded, have resulted in major difficulties for the EA initiative, some of which remain unresolved. In particular the timetable was too tight, the criteria for funding changed continually, tenant consultation was not always adequate and resources were being wasted because the above factors resulted in under-allocation and/or underspending of EA HIPs by local authorities. EA has responded to a number of these criticisms, though local authorities maintain that the whole system remains problematic.

A further point arising from the chapter is that according to the available information, major improvements are taking place in the worst council estates: 98 per cent of all EA schemes showed some improvement, 67 per cent of which was deemed to be substantial in nature. These finding are supplemented and corroborated by qualitative information obtained from a range of relevant agents such as EA central team; the DoE Regional Officers; local authority housing officers; and tenants in the estates concerned. The EA-funded initiatives appear to be returning considerable dividends. Of course, these schemes are partly funded by EA but it is local authorities, together with tenants, that designed and implemented them. EA provides broad guidance but it is up to local authorities to interpret them and develop schemes which accord with their own housing priorities. The success of these schemes runs counter to the government's argument that local authorities are incapable of reforming themselves so as to provide a more sensitive and responsive housing management service.

Pinto's contribution (chapter 4) highlights a number of other conclusions with respect to the role and general impact of the Estate Action initiative. Firstly, the overwhelming majority of local authorities participated with EA because it represented one of the few remaining means by which they could gain additional resources. Nevertheless, the research demonstrates that a number of local authorities have adapted their management structures as a direct result of being involved with EA. Secondly, the fact that EA has been able to increase its funding attests to the need for such resources as well as the success of such schemes in helping spread these management arrangements and structures throughout local government. Thirdly, EA has recently achieved the landmarks of having allocated close to £2bn of capital receipts and helped develop about 1,200 initiatives throughout the worst housing estates in England, almost all of which have had a management dimension. These have had knock-on effects in other estates and the general management practices of the participating local authorities (but see chapter 7 for a discussion of some of the implications). The EA principles have encouraged local authorities to diversify their management practices but it must be acknowledged that the initiatives marketed by EA such as concierges and comprehensive estate regeneration, took their cue from developments in local authorities themselves. Fourthly, the more radical aspects advocated by EA such as housing trusts failed completely and there have not been as many sales of land and housing as the government might have expected. Nevertheless, EA has played a critical role in conditioning local authorities to issues such as disposal of stock and has paved the way for subsequent initiatives like HATs. Fifthly, the experience of EA (and PEP) ought to have demonstrated to government beyond reasonable doubt that local authorities could, via greater tenant involvement, new management styles and additional investment, regenerate even their most intractable housing estates. As discussed elsewhere, Ministerial denouncements of council housing actually intensified in the late 1980s and the stage was set for alternative government approved landlords to take over the management role and dwelling stock from council housing.

The next chapter analysed these 'exit' opportunities and argue that they are not turning out to be quite as straight-forward as may have been originally assumed in 1987.

Tenants' Choices

Murie's chapter (chapter 5) emphasises the point that tenants' rights and choices since the 1980 Tenants' Charter have been almost entirely about increasing opportunities for them to exit from council housing. The Right to Buy was the flagship exit option designed to expand home ownership but has been complemented by a range of other potentially more powerful options.

The Right to Buy was not a new policy. It arose from a consensus regarding the need to restrict public expenditure, promote home ownership and the promise of electoral advantage. It has proven highly popular and has resulted in over 1.7 million sales to sitting tenants, thus extending choices for those households but restricting them for existing or new council tenants who face a reduced as well as a residualised housing stock. Other developments also resulted in major changes to the ownership of public sector housing such as the transfer of the now-defunct Greater London Council's (GLC) housing stock to London boroughs; New Towns to local district councils; and the establishment of Trusts. These together with the experience of Estate Action, paved the way for the more radical 1988 and 1989 legislation designed to bring about the revolution in rented housing ownership and management. The government philosophy at the time could be boiled down to the fact that the council housing sector could be not be entrusted with either ownership or management of its stock. The solution was to deprive it of either role and along the way, insert an ill-defined 'enabling' function instead.

The chapter developed in some detail the rationale behind the government's second phase of transfers from council housing (Tenants' Choice) and how the initial proposals were subsequently revised to offer a modicum of safety features such as the need to scrutinise potential new landlords, maintain high standards of management and, not surprisingly, exclude local authorities from presenting themselves directly or indirectly as new landlords. In the event, not a single property was transferred under Tenants' Choice. Tenants it appeared, did not share the government's abhorrence of local authorities as landlords. Previous chapters have indicated that many local authorities were far from ideal landlords and others have pointed to the improvements which have taken place in the time since, which may have influenced tenants' reaction to Tenants' Choice. One of the key reasons for the lack of interest relates to the fact that tenants remained concerned about the possibility of being taken over by predatory landlords. Housing associations preferred to maintain stable relations with local authorities. Since they did not wish to present themselves as aggressive landlords, housing association remained cool about this transfer option. As discussed above, housing co-operatives did not easily lend themselves to rapid growth via this option either but Tenants' Choice did lay the groundwork for the dramatic changes which took place under LSVT.

By the beginning of 1994, 23 LSVTs had taken place representing about 118,000 units, all of which occurred at the initiative of local authorities who were principally motivated by the prospect of evading public expenditure restrictions which applied exclusively to council housing. Whilst rumours abounded in 1992 that a very large number of local authorities would make use of this option, the surge failed to materialise. The government itself has become concerned about the implications of such issues as the Housing Benefit expenditure, transfers to other single landlords and the availability of private finance. Murie points out that the revised rules for transfers for 1993/94 mean that LSVT has become distinctly less financially attractive to local authorities and since they are the ones who must apply to the Secretary of State for permission to generate LSVTs, this is likely to mean that interest in this exit option will cool even further.

Housing Action Trusts (HATs) were designed specifically to tackle what was seen as the local authority failure to deal with their most problematic council housing estates. HATs would aim to regenerate such estates in a comprehensive manner but there was little choice for anybody in the original conception. Tenants and local authorities would not be consulted, let alone balloted on their views. The Secretary of State would simply choose the estates to be designated and appoint a HAT board which would eventually transfer the stock to alternative landlords. Chapter 5 makes it clear that the government failed to take into account the degree of tenant opposition which was generated, with the result that only one of the six original HATs went as far as the ballot and that was decisively rejected by tenants.

The government had to reforge the nature of the HAT concept, allocate much more resource to it, encourage consultation and drop the confrontational approach to local authorities. Partnership between government, local authorities and tenants became the buzz-word of the new approach, with the result that three HATs were quickly voted for by tenants with their local authorities' blessing. These new style HATs are 'a long way from the original Ministerial conception', such that they now meet the needs of tenants first. Government housing policy as directed to achieve the demise of local authorities, has been compromised since tenants now have the option of transferring back to the local authority if they so desire. This precedent means that it is likely to be even harder for large scale demunicipalisation to be achieved.

Murie also highlights a number of points of general relevance arising from this experience of increasing choices for tenants. First, it is LSVT and to a lesser extent HATs that have accounted for the bulk of the transfers from council ownership and both are local authority initiated, which means that the initiative and control remains with local authorities. Second, rather than rush to exercise their new rights, tenants have tended to resist transfers. HATs, the Right to Buy and LSVT have all had to be repackaged in order to make them more attractive to tenants. This undoubtedly presents those tenants with more choice, but at the expense of others who are excluded. Third, different emphases can be identified under the language of choice and empowerment. The objective of providing the right to choose can be seen as:

- an end in itself;
- achieved if the existing pattern of ownership is changed, regardless of whether or not a greater diversity of landlords operate; and
- a way of improving the quality of life and standard of service in unpopular estates.

Murie argues that the government does not appear to be principally motivated by the latter objective. The fact that additional rights are provided to existing tenants also means that future tenants in the transferred properties will have fewer rights. Furthermore, the transfers so far achieved via HATs and LSVT may mean demunicipalisation but have not necessarily resulted in a plurality of landlords. It is impossible to escape the conclusion that these are choices made by one generation of tenants which will reduce the rights and opportunities of future generations. The points made by Murie indicate that the language of choice, opportunity and diversity within which this legislation is couched, does not appear to have been thought through carefully by government. The suspicion lingers that the primary objective was to bring about the end of council housing and the related issues of tenants' choices were merely convenient language.

The concluding sentences of Murie's chapter merit restatement, namely that all the above government housing policies emphasise management and ownership as a means of resolving a wide range of problems confronting council housing but:

This analysis of problems in council housing which received at least partial support from accounts of changes in council housing which took insufficient account of the long term restructuring of housing, the increasing concentration of households with least bargaining power on council estates, changing social and economic circumstances of households and the implications for turnover and community development. The resulting policies with their emphasis on management or ownership fall far short of policies which will resolve the problems articulated in the White Papers of 1988 and experienced by those unable to buy dwellings.

Housing departments and housing management CCT

The discussion in this book takes the developments affecting local authorities as the starting point. It ends with an evaluation of the changing role of housing departments as a means of assessing how they have responded to government-led housing initiatives since 1979, for as Warburton argues 'As the role of local authorities in housing has changed, so have the structure, culture and practice of local housing departments.'

The central thrust of Warburton's forceful chapter (chapter 6) is that the direction of the government's housing policy and the range of initiatives culminating in the housing management Compulsory Competitive Tendering (HMCCT) legislation, is 'rooted in their inadequate explanation of poor housing management performance by local authorities, and their unrealistic expectations of the capacity of competition to improve it'. In substantiating this argument, the chapter takes the reader through the government's view of the failure of council housing system as managers and owners of rented housing stock and the New Right critique of the council housing. It is this analysis which resulted in the efforts to increase 'voice' options (such as information, consultation and participation) and particularly 'exit' options (HATs, Tenants' Choice, HMCCT etc), thus bringing about a competitive market in rented housing. As we have seen, Murie has questioned whether the latter has been achieved with respect to the stock transfers which have taken place thus far.

Warburton argues that it was only after 1987 that the council housing system was condemned. Previous to that point it certainly had its critics, particularly in relation to unpopular council housing estates, but these were seen as the exception. It was following a number of the DoE reports (Burbidge et al., 1981, Vols. 1 to 3) that a general problem of council housing management began to be articulated by government and problem estates came to be regarded as merely the most extreme symptoms of a more general problem.

The government response was to set up PEP and then Estate Action; however, Warburton stresses that by then local authorities were already aware of the fact that 'the housing management service needed restructuring' and were pioneering various models of decentralisation so as to reduce the functional fragmentation of the housing service, improve the repair service, involve tenants more meaningfully and so on. This was to eventually result in the complete decentralisation of the housing service (not just to the estate level as espoused by PEP and Estate Action), emphasising the need to improve the responsiveness of local services as well as the democratisation of service provision. Undeniable management problems existed in inner and outer as well as high rise and cottage estates. New management structures were needed but as the Estate Action scheme demonstrated, additional investment was just as important to ensure that the new arrangements proved long-lasting.

With respect to the general state of council housing management, Warburton reiterates the point that two reports conducted a short time apart pointed to different conclusions. One referred to a crisis of management in about 30 local authorities, which could be tackled through new investment and management arrangements (Audit Commission, 1986). The other could identify no such crisis, just a range of good and bad managers (Centre for Housing Research, 1989). Warburton quotes more recent research (Bines et al., 1993) which underlines the widespread decentralisation of housing management practices and the fact that supposedly good performers may not necessarily be utilising good management practices, in the same way that supposedly bad performers may be utilising the best management practices yet fail to make headway due to the increasingly fraught socio-economic environment facing them and their tenants.

Warburton concludes that there is no systematic failure in council housing management and neither is inadequate performance attributable to poor housing management alone. He notes the research demonstrating that weaknesses remain, in that a number of local authorities still do not have a unified housing department (such as Audit Commission, 1986; Power, 1987), but chooses to emphasise the major progress made by local authorities in decentralising since the early 1980s. The implication is that the post-1987 legislation must be seen either as the response of a government exasperated with the slow pace of change or alternatively, as emphasising the exit options regardless of the improvements which were taking place at the time. In actual fact, Ministers maintained or even intensified their critique of council housing and sought to encourage tenants to take up their new rights as discussed in chapter 5; as well as the more recent transfer options arising from the HMCCT and Right to Manage legislation. Some academic and professional opinion has reacted favourably to the possibility that HMCCT will lead to greater competition which will in turn improve the quality and efficiency of housing service delivery:

The management of local authority housing has developed new, more business-like styles in the last decade. CCT could help to progress these changes if it is seen to be concerned with 'efficiency' and if it is accepted that a supply side response may have to be ensured, then it could generate beneficial changes. Above all, tenants could benefit and have an increased say in service provision.

(Baker et al., 1992, para. 7.24)

Whilst acknowledging this possibility Warburton analyses a number of caveats which remain:

- contractual arrangements may be too inflexible and unresponsive to policy changes, new legislation, local political change, professional advice, tenants' representations and so on;
- need to re-tender regardless of performance may present perverse incentives for contractors to extract maximum short term profits and maximise secrecy in order to obtain competitive advantage;
- local authorities, especially the smaller ones, may not command sufficient leverage to ensure cost-effective, high quality service delivery;
- the timetable for HMCCT is so tight as to result in inadequate arrangements which may lead to inefficiency and other problems;
- choice for tenants is limited by the requirement to invite tenders regardless of tenants' satisfaction with the service; and the requirement for local authorities not to act anti-competitively;
- HMCCT legislation was not necessary because many local authorities were improving their services; others would have changed their practices under the threat of competition or by allowing tenants to vote on whether their housing service should be exposed to competition.

Warburton's conclusions echo those of other chapters in this book in arguing that better housing management is essential to safeguard the benefits of investment, but no substitute for better housing (see also Glennerster and Turner, 1993; Murie, 1994). The difficulties facing the housing system go beyond management, just as social housing was never simply about the landlord role. He also returns to a theme highlighted in the conclusions of other chapters, namely that restricting council housing to the most disadvantaged will result in conditions which become increasingly unmanageable, regardless of whether this takes place under HMCCT or not.

Housing management in transition

The last contribution follows on from Warburton's analysis of developments across local housing authorities as a whole. Jacobs (chapter 7) presents a case study of one of the most deprived local authorities in Britain, the London Borough of Hackney. This qualitative analysis enables a number of policy dimensions to be explored in more detail than would be possible with other methodologies and highlights the point that local housing authorities do have policy options. Councils such as Hackney have in the past been castigated as being the most ineffective and inefficient local authorities of all, the very landlords perhaps that government feels ought to be divested of their housing management responsibilities as allowed by the more radical transfer options. Therefore, this particular case study is all the more pertinent to the debates in this book.

It is worth noting first that after years of simply ignoring the salience of the locality, both of the most influential DoE-sponsored reports comparing the effectiveness of the social housing service, have increasingly pointed to its importance. The Centre for Housing Research (1989) merely noted the need to take into account the 'degree of difficulty' of the housing management service, however, Bines et al. took this much further and explicitly acknowledged that: 'a local authority or housing association facing a greater degree of management difficulty would need to spend more on housing management (other things being equal) than one with a lesser degree of difficulty, in order to achieve the same level of performance' (1993, para. 3.22); and thus proceeded to weight their analysis accordingly in order to take into account the degree of management difficulty. It is this approach which leads Bines et al. to the conclusion that the stock size, location and level of social deprivation are of importance, especially for local authorities, and that these issues were particularly significant for London and metropolitan authorities (1993, para. 14.6). This is merely confirmation of common sense but represents the first formal acknowledgement of this issue.

Jacobs shows at the beginning of his contribution why this must be the case by pointing to the very high level of deprivation in Hackney where, according to the government's Index of Local Conditions (DoE, 1994), the borough tops the extent of deprivation ranks at the finest geographical scale (Enumeration Districts). He proceeds to chart Hackney's transition, in common with a number of other local authorities, from symbolic gestures to an increasing focus on 'practical initiatives in an effort to improve their services and standing among the electorate', not least with respect to the high profile housing service.

The starting point for Hackney's progression was decentralisation. In common with a number of other local authorities throughout the country, Hackney made serious efforts to devolve its housing management functions as a means of delivering a better quality service whilst responding to a fast changing political and economic environment. Jacobs shows that this particular model of decentralisation ran into difficulties which derailed the initiative, thus adding to the frustration of tenants and staff alike and compounding the image of the housing department as being poorly managed. The morale of the directorate was further undermined by a Commission for Racial Equality report highlighting discriminatory housing allocations practices and a series of television documentaries recording the housing directorate's more startling failures.

Jacobs' chapter demonstrates that the 1990s witnessed a turning point which was very much related to new initiatives such as the housing partnership with the Housing Corporation and the Comprehensive Estates Initiative (CEI) which were to lead to a change in the culture of the housing department and a radically improved relationship with the DoE. The chapter then utilises the CEI flagship initiative as the means of demonstrating the changes and tensions which have arisen with respect to three key dimensions: management performance, partnership arrangements and tenant participation. Although Hackney may be an example of a housing authority facing an extreme socio-economic and housing management environment, a number of the developments and issues chime with the experiences of other local housing authorities throughout the country.

With respect to management performance, Jacobs notes the Borough's increasing focus on organisation, management and the role played by new initiatives in attracting resources. Although schemes such as CEI in Hackney have the potential to restore morale, they can also give rise to resentment and tensions within the rest of the organisation. In particular, Jacobs draws attention to the fact that such management improvements are taking place against a deteriorating economic, political and social backdrop. The twin processes of residualisation and polarisation will continue to play a major role in undermining the progress on the housing management front. This is a theme which runs consistently through a number of contributions in this book.

Turning to partnerships, Jacobs charts Hackney's successful efforts to develop a range of partnerships, as increasingly recommended by the DoE. He uses the example of the Holly Street CEI Estate regeneration programme to highlight the advantages as well as tensions which can arise from such coalitions. Although the high profile partnership between the Council, government, private sector, Housing

Corporation and tenants will result in £180m in financial commitment, tensions arise over the need for profits (developers) versus
extraction of maximum concessions (housing authorities and the
community); as well as whether they necessarily result in self-
sustaining economic and social regeneration on housing estates
which are often semi-detached from the local labour market.

Jacobs takes issue with the fact that tenant participation is
increasingly regarded as the 'holy grail' for social housing. Tenant
participation is increasingly seen by the housing policy community
as the means of avoiding past mistakes and counteracting charges of
being unresponsive to tenants' wishes. Jacobs illustrates Hackney's
extensive efforts to develop effective tenant participation mechanisms for the CEI estates, only to be frustrated by low attendance.
Contrary to expectations, tenants themselves appear to be apprehen-
sive of participating and require much more support and resources
such as training than normally anticipated and planned for. Moreover, Jacobs questions whether the lack of tenant participation is the
root cause of management failure and warns against presenting
tenant empowerment as a solution to management problems as this
over-emphasises the importance of the individual whilst drawing
attention away from public expenditure cuts and the state's inability
to tackle the basic housing problems.

Jacobs concludes that Hackney has achieved considerable success
with respect to the changes in housing management. In addition,
partnership deals with the private sector and the Housing Corporation mean that diversification of tenure and ownership is taking
place but he stresses that new initiatives such as the CEI scheme
cannot be expected to be sufficient in themselves to overcome the
management difficulties. Local government continues to be con
strained by government policies and the state of the economy but the
experience of Hackney demonstrates that there is still scope to
maximise resources, develop partnerships and deliver a better service
to tenants.

Concluding comments

Housing management and ownership have been the pre-eminent
themes in the government's housing policy and flowed from an

agenda led by a determination to increase home ownership as well as an equally strong desire to contain investment and in due course, bring about the end of the council housing system itself.

Several chapters have emphasised the point that local authorities have experienced a historical evolution with respect to their management function which resulted in them being considered as bureaucratic and ineffective landlords. This failure was most clearly identified with the unpopular estates which were increasingly coming to light in the 1970s. This criticism was seized upon and extended to the whole of the council housing system in the 1980s, with the result that it was increasingly portrayed as completely incapable of providing an adequate landlord function. This was useful in legitimising the policy of reducing capital investment in this sector and increasing the incentives for council tenants to opt out of the system individually by exercising their Right to Buy. In the post-1987 period, the perceived inefficiency of local authorities as managers was picked up by the government once more in order to justify the more radical policies which were to enable tenants to choose to opt out of the council housing system *en masse.*

A number of chapters highlight the point that this blanket condemnation of local authorities was, to say the least, disingenuous on the part of the government. Whilst acknowledging the general critique of their housing management practices, especially where problem estates were concerned, the post-1987 Ministerial condemnation of the local authority housing system was overdone. It completely ignored the major changes taking place as a result of the impact of neighbourhood decentralisation, estates based management, customer care and a range of other developments taking place throughout the period from 1979. The experience of the DoE-led Estate Action initiative ought to have convinced government that local authorities were adapting their management arrangements, were bringing about major improvements in their very worst estates by working with their tenants and that a profound change was under way in council housing management practices. Government could certainly claim some credit for facilitating the process via financial inducements, though clearly this was not the only reason why local authorities were developing these management practices.

The independent public watch-dog, the Audit Commission, had talked of a 'crisis of serious proportions' in housing management

(1986) which might have prompted the government to resort to the assorted measures that were introduced, however, even that report stated that 'The most serious problems ... are thus concentrated in perhaps 30 local authorities out of the total [401]' (p. 7). Furthermore, the above study made it clear that public investment, combined with new management practices (a standard solution advocated by Estate Action) would reverse the trends even in the worst performing cases. The possibility that the government was choosing to deliberately ignore the mounting evidence that local authorities were not such deplorable landlords is underlined by its handling of the Centre for Housing Research report (1989).

This work was commissioned by the government to establish whether housing associations were indeed better landlords than local authorities. Although the research was carried out shortly after the Audit Commission's fieldwork it was only published in 1989, by which time the 1987 Housing White Papers and subsequent legislation were firmly on the statute book. The findings of the Centre for Housing Research contradicted the Audit Commission and by extension, the drift of government housing policy by alluding to the poorly informed views, impressions and prejudices which have come to prevail with regard to the effectiveness of housing management and then proceeding to conclude that:

This report sustains neither the proposition that there is a general crisis of resources for management nor the contention that there is a general organisational crisis. Our case studies revealed that 67 per cent of council tenants and 80 per cent of association tenants were satisfied with the services they received.

(1989, para. 9.2)

Such variance would not appear to justify the distinct policies towards the respective social housing sectors. Moreover, the report found good reasons for these differences:

in general, housing associations spend fifty per cent more per dwelling on management than do councils. This contrast in cost levels, however, arises largely from the extreme differences between the low costs of large councils and the high costs of small associations. Different capital financing arrangements have favoured associations. In short, from broadly similar rental levels, they spend double the proportion of rental income spent by councils. It is, therefore, hardly surprising that effectiveness measures incorporating tenants' view or tenant satisfaction scores place associations well ahead of councils who spend less. The key failing of many councils is that they spend, in comparison to associations, too little on management, rather that they are less 'economic' or 'inefficient'. This observation was particularly relevant to a number of very large councils.

(1989, para. 9.29).

The key finding was that 'overall [management] performance could be improved in both tenure sectors' (para. 9.1), however, this research which was of major importance to the debate was not released until it was far too late to influence the direction of government housing policy.

These general conclusions have recently been supported and supplemented by another major DoE-commissioned study undertaken by Bines et al. (1993) which is intended to provide a benchmark against which to compare subsequent studies on housing management. It demonstrates that significant changes have taken place since 1984/85, the most pertinent of which are:

• both authorities and associations have sought to improve their management performance by implementing a number of good management practice recommendations;
• use of recognised good practices in prevention and recovery of rent arrears has increased significantly;
• decentralisation of housing management functions have become even more widespread since 1984/85;
• there is no straightforward relationship between good practice and performance – in some areas, low performers were actually good practice organisations;
• the stock size, location and level of social deprivation is of importance, especially for local authorities and were particularly significant for London and metropolitan authorities;
• although district councils were overall more likely to be better performers, this was not necessarily because they were using better management practices;
• low performing authorities and associations were, on average, spending more on housing management than their high performing counterparts;
• there has been a distinct move towards systematic use of monitoring and targets in the social housing sector;
• however, there was a general lack of clarity about objectives; customer satisfaction surveys were undertaken but only as one-off exercises; and many landlords were collecting limited performance

and management information which does not bode well for
HMCCT preparations.

(Bines et al., 1993, pp. 161-164)

All the above testify to the effect that local authorities have taken
major strides in improving their management performance and that
both they and housing associations are suitable and competent social
landlords. All this evidence came far too late to influence the
legislation of the late 1980s. The 1988 and 1989 Acts set in place the
machinery which could, in principle, bring about the end of council
housing, and the policies arising from this legislation made clear the
government's continuing emphasis on management and ownership
of housing stock as the basis of its housing policy. The reliance on
housing associations and co-operatives rather than local authorities;
the options for councils to divest themselves of their housing stock
via voluntary transfers; the right for government itself to establish
trusts independently of local authorities and the tenants; and lastly
the tenants' right to vote to transfer away from council housing to
almost any other option, all point to the overriding concern with
management and ownership. This emphasis does not constitute a
balanced housing policy. The government has systematically avoided
tackling such issues as the:

• level of housing need and annual house building targets;
• need for adequate investment in the deteriorating housing fabric;
• imbalanced population structure in social housing (council and
  housing association estates);
• poverty and benefit traps in the social housing sector;
• lack of labour market prospects and social opportunities;
• need for fiscal neutrality between tenures;
• acute need for sufficient good quality private rented stock; and
• imbalance between owning and renting.

No doubt a number of other issues can be added to the above list,
but the point to note is that the promotion of home ownership and
the critique of council housing have substituted for a balanced
housing policy and have if anything, accentuated the housing
problems in Britain. The chapters in this book lead to a set of
conclusions which are likely to apply throughout the 1990s.

Despite the recent developments in home ownership such as the
collapse of the housing market, negative equity and two successive

reductions in mortgage tax relief, the government remains wedded to a belief in the inherent advantages of this tenure. The Right to Buy, Rents to Mortgages and Shared Ownership policies, combined with the indications of a housing market recovery and the British public's preference for this tenure, will all continue to push this tenure onwards and upwards. Murie argues that to the extent that council housing is sold off without replacement, these policies represent choices for the tenants making those decisions, but reduce the options for other existing as well as future tenants. This process will accentuate the residualisation and polarisation processes evident in council housing estates and may come to apply in housing association estates as well.

The recent successes in plugging the flow of housing away from private renting owes more to the collapse of the home ownership market than to government efforts to deregulate this sector. The tax breaks required to stimulate this sector appear to be greater than the government is prepared to contemplate, hence the phasing out of the Business Expansion Scheme at the end of 1993. Without new government efforts in the form of financial and tax incentives, this sector is unlikely to continue to recover, thus failing to providing sufficient furnished and unfurnished private rented accommodation.

With respect to the new government-approved landlords, Clapham and Kintrea argue that despite the many advantages presented by housing co-operatives and the apparent government support for this sector, a policy, legal and financial framework does not exist to enable this sector to grow rapidly, not even through transfers from council housing where Estate Management Boards appear to be better placed to benefit. Indeed, the new financial regime means that the rate of new co-operatives being formed in England has dropped significantly and will continue to diverge from the experience in Scotland. Despite its potential advantages as a form of management, it is unlikely that this sector will grow at a significantly faster rate under existing arrangements.

In her chapter, Harrison argues that the government has failed to provide house building targets for housing associations to aim at; that the new financial regime presents major affordability problems for those not eligible for Housing Benefits; and that it is leading to large-scale newly built estates which are already beginning to exhibit many of the features evident in problem council housing estates. The chapter also highlights the government's ambivalence to this form of social housing, which has resulted in housing associations being pulled in different directions with respect to their traditional housing role, as opposed to the new one offered by central government. This is most clearly illustrated in relation to the housing associations' extremely careful stance vis à vis local authorities as evidenced by their handling of the opportunities for rapid growth via Tenants' Choice and LSVT. The recent budget cuts in Housing Corporation funds mean that their favoured position is already being called into question, opening up the possibility that they may in due course be replaced by some other form of landlord as the future providers of social housing.

The experience of Estate Action, the developments in housing departments and the transition taking place in the London Borough of Hackney demonstrate that the council housing sector has made huge strides in responding to the academic, professional, political and tenant criticism of them as landlords. This is not to suggest that this has happened in every single housing department or that tenants are now all satisfied with the service they receive. Jacobs' chapter highlights the pressures, tensions and mixed experiences which have arisen from the process of change. There will always be good and bad local authority landlords as surely as such diversity will be also reflected in the other housing sectors, but the fact that tenants have not flocked to exercise the panoply of rights to transfer from council housing is indicative that they do not all perceive local authority landlords in the same light that the government does.

There has not been a single transfer under the Tenants' Choice option. HATs as originally conceived by government were a total failure. The new partnership-oriented HATs have been more successful, but the three which have been designated have turned out to be significantly more expensive than ever anticipated by government. This means that the Treasury is not keen on the idea of supporting many of these, not least now that tenants have won the right to transfer back to local authorities. The major success, though one not anticipated by government, has been in relation to voluntary transfers by local authorities themselves. This has resulted in 20-odd transfers but all were to a single landlord. As such they have not resulted in the government-expressed aim of generating a plurality of landlords. The new guidelines for LSVT make this diversity more feasible but reduces the financial appeal to local authorities and with it the prospect of major transfers of housing ownership from local authorities in the immediate future. A question mark hangs over the likely impact of HMCCT but if the government were truly motivated by the desire to improve the housing service to council housing tenants, it would remove some of the constraints and provide tenants with a much greater role in determining whether or not their housing service should be exposed to competition with the private sector, when to re-tender the contract and so on.

All of this tempers the arguments that the 1990s would bring about the complete demunicipalisation of local authority housing stock. The fact that the government has not been able to produce incontrovertible evidence of the advantage of other housing tenures as much more effective managers than local authorities; that housing departments have responded positively to the need to improve their management arrangements and enhance tenant involvement and empowerment; and that tenants themselves have largely proved loyal to local authorities, mean that rapid and total demunicipalisation is not likely. If the government were truly motivated by the need to increase choice, competition and tenant empowerment in relation to the housing service, it would recognise these developments and turn its not inconsiderable ingenuity to ensuring that council housing tenants really receive the housing service they desire. More generally, the quicker the government acknowledges the inadequacy of pursuing a housing policy which is, subject to economic circumstances, almost totally geared towards management and ownership to the exclusion of a range of other relevant factors, the better. It is difficult to see any sector of British housing which is in a robust condition and the consequences are set to reverberate throughout the 1990s unless the government develops the vision to progress beyond an ultimately inadequate fixation on housing management and ownership.

References

Audit Commission (1986) *Managing the Crisis in Council Housing*, London, HMSO.

Baker, R., Challen, P., Maclennan, D., Reid, V. and Whitehead, C. (1992) *The Scope for Competitive Tendering of Housing Management*, London, HMSO.

Bell, T. and PEP Consultants (1991) *Joining Forces: Estate Management Boards – A Practical Guide for Councils and Residents*, London, Priority Estates Project.

Bines, W., Kemp, P., Pleace, N. and Radley, C. (1993) *Managing Social Housing: A Study of Landlord Performance*, London, HMSO.

Burbidge, M., Curtis, A., Kirby, K., and Wilson, S. (1981) *An Investigation of Difficult to Let*

Housing: Vol. 1: General Findings; Vol. 2: Case Studies of Post-War Estates; Vol. 3: Case Studies of Pre-War Estates, London, HMSO.

Centre for Housing Research (1989) The Nature and Effectiveness of Housing Management in England: A Report to the Department of the Environment, London, HMSO.

Department of Environment (1994) Index of Local Conditions: An Analysis Based on the 1991 Census Data, London, HMSO.

Glennerster, H. and Turner, T. (1993) Estate-based Housing Management: An Evaluation, London, HMSO.

Minford, P., Peel, M. and Ashton, P. (1987) The Housing Morass: Regulation, Immobility and Unemployment, Hobart Paperback 25, London, Institute of Economic Affairs.

Murie, A. (1994) 'Researching Housing Management: Causes, Context and Questions', Paper presented at the Housing Studies Association Conference, University of York.

Page, D. (1993) Building for Communities: A Study of New Housing Association Estates, Joseph Rowntree Foundation, York.

Power, A. (1987) Property Before People: The Management of Twentieth Century Council Housing, London, Allen & Unwin.

Zipfel, T. (1989) Estate Management Boards: An Introduction, London, Priority Estates Project.

Index

Note: Page references in **bold** refer to tables

affordable housing 4, 61, 65, 72, 81-4
Association of Metropolitan Authorities (AMA) 125
assured shorthold tenancies 9, 37
assured tenancy 9, 37, 70-1
Audit Commission 21, 192, 196, 234, 253-4
    Managing the Crisis in Council Housing 186

Basic Credit Approval 31-2, 92
Birmingham Housing Action Trust 171
British Housing Associations 161
Business Expansion Scheme (BES) 9, 38, 39, 257

capital receipt 30, 31
Care in the Community 84-5
Castlemilk East 114
Census (1981) 74
Central Housing Advisory Committee 19
Central Reserve Fund 141
Centre for Housing Policy 194, 196
Centre for Housing Research 40, 193, 196, 237
Charles, Prince 213
Choice of Landlord scheme 159
City Challenge 30, 78, 140, 150, 220, 241
Clapton Park Estate 223
Commission for Racial Equality 113, 211, 251
Community Charge 209
Community Ownership Schemes 98, 107, 108

Comprehensive Estates Initiative 207, 213-14, 215-18, 224-5, 251, 252
Compulsory Competitive Tendering (CCT) 3, 12, 34, 91, 200-4
    favourable assessments 201
    limits of 204
    see also Housing Management Compulsory Competitive Tendering (HMCCT)
concierges 7
Conservative Manifesto (1987) 159
continuation funding 142
co-ownership co-operatives 97
cost and rent pooling systems 4
cottage estates 192
council housing 2
    building 6
    Conservative reasons for rejecting 17
    dissatisfaction with 4
    economic imperatives for rejecting 16-18
    erosion of 1
    expansion 16
    housing subsidies 193
    management
        criticism of 5, 8, 233-4
        problems 22-3
        transfer 9-10
    political condemnation of 5, 7
    rent increases 193
    repairs 20-2
    sales 34-6
    security of tenure 192
Council Tax 234

council tenants, characteristics of
    182, 195, 217

Dalston City Challenge Partnership
    213, 220
decentralisation 186-9, 197-8
    in Hackney 210-13
    management 5
    neighbourhood 24, 34, 55
deficit financing 26
demunicipalisation 168, 174, 259
Department of Environment 16, 21, 75
    Regional Offices 127
    Tenants in the Lead 102, 103
deregulation 9, 38, 61
Direct Labour Offices (DLOs) 127
Direct Service Organisation (DSO)
    200-1
Do It Yourself Shared Ownership
    (DIYSO) 76, 81

East London Partnership 219
enabling councils 9, 12, 45-6, 48,
    244
Enterprise Initiatives 149
equity-sharing co-operatives 100
Estate Action 2, 6, 7, 30, 34, 121-
    52, 169, 220, 233, 235,
    240-3, 258
    administration 132
    agents and policy content 128
    alternative management organisa-
        tions 147
    continuation funding 142
    criticisms 125, 149-50
    development of 39, 41-4
    finance 126-7, 143, 150
    future 149-51
    impact on run-down estates 133
    implementation and evolution
        127-35
        central-local interaction 129
        changing criteria and emphasis
            130
        deficient timetabling arrange-
            ments 129

    problematic administrative
        procedures 130
    response of EA Central and
        Regional Officers
        131-2
    tenant consultation 130-1
involvement of agents 127
national, regional and local
    assessments 133-5
    DoE Regional Officers and EA
        Central 134-5
    localities 135
    national postal survey 133-4
origins and aims 121-6
    DoE studies 122-3
    targeting, riots and privatisa-
        tion 123-4, 146-7
overall assessment 134, 137-49
    central-local relations 145-9
    financial issues 139-43
    housing policy issues 143-5
    impact 137
    management issues 136-9
    spending on improvements 102
    structure and organisation 126-7
    targeting 142-3
    topslicing 140
    underallocation 140-1
    underspending 141-2
Estate Action Central 127
Estate Action Housing Investment
    Programmes (EAHIPs) 30,
    140-3
Estate Management Boards (EMBs)
    102, 110, 139, 233, 239, 257

fair rent 63, 69
    abolition of 70
Faith in the City 22
Finance Act (1988) 38
flagship housing schemes 150
Flats Over Shops 81
Foyer schemes 81
Freeson, Reg 95, 97

Garden City Movement 96

General Household Survey (1991) 217
Glasgow Community Ownership
    111, 113-15, **114, 115**, 116
Glasgow co-operatives 98, 99, 115,
    187, 238
Granby and Canning Co-operatives 97
Greater London Council (GLC) 209,
    213
green field sites 19, 72
Greenwich 24
Guinness, Edward Cecil 60

Hackney 2000 213
Hackney, housing management in
    206-29, 187, 249-52, 258
  assessment 214
  attempt at restructuring social
    services 210
  decentralisation 210-13
  as focus of enquiry 207-8
  legacy of the 1980s 208-10
  management 215-18
  new initiatives 213-14
  partnership 219-23
  public relationship with DoE 212
  tenant participation 223-7
  unemployment 207-8
Hackney Housing Partnership 213
Hampstead Garden Suburb 96
hard-to-let estates 186
high-density flats 19
high-rise flats 19, 186, 192
Hill, Octavia 188
Holly Street Estate 220-1, 223, 224,
    251
Home Ownership for Tenants of
    Charitable Housing Associa-
    tions (HOTCHA) 66
Homelessness Review (1989) 11
Hostel Deficit Grant (HDG) 64
house building **68**, 257
house-price inflation 8, 11
Housing Act
    1957 61
    1961 62
    1964 62-3

1974 28, 63-5
1980 26, 35, 37, 65-6, 155, 192
1988 8, 10, 38, 41, 44, 45, 54, 55,
    66-73, 169, 183, 209, 235, 236
  main features 68-73
Housing Action Trusts (HATs) 3, 10,
    67, 81, 123, 125, 140, 150,
    151, 154, 181, 234
  development 44, 45-6
  failure of 258
  increased consumer choice
    through 72-3, 169-71
  limitation on 178
  in Scotland 107
  troublesome estates 245-6
Housing and Building Control Act
    1984 35, 66
    1986 9
Housing and Planning Act (1986)
    10, 46, 156, 159
Housing Association Grant (HAG)
    63, 67-70, 95, 97, 105, 107,
    235-6
  HAG Stretch 67
  Mini Housing Association Grant 76
housing associations 2, 39-41, 54-
    93, 235-8
  in the 1980s 65-73
  accountability 87-9
  assessment of 254-5
  budget 79
  completions 79-80, **79**
  confidence in 175
  effects of poverty and employ-
    ment 83
  ethnic housing 78
  historical development and
    changing role 60-5
  housing stock, physical standards
    71
  investment 1988-92 8
  management of registered 59-60
  nomination rights 85-6
  performance criteria 88
  Principal Development Agreement
    221, 222

provision of social housing 73-89
  access to housing 84-6
  need for social housing 73-5
  ownership, management and
    accountability 86-9
  rents and affordability 81-4
  units produced 75-81
  value for money 81
  relationships with central govern-
    ment 89-90
  as replacements for local authori-
    ties 91
  size of housing stock 40, 41
  special needs funding 58, **59**, 80
  subsidies 92-3
  tenants of 57-8, **58**
  types of organisations 55-6
  units owned by registered 56-7,
    57
  vacancies 87
Housing Associations Act (1985) 55
Housing Benefits 6, 68, 81-2, 83,
  237, 257
housing co-operatives 95-119, 238-
  40
  achievements of 108
  allocation policies 113
  committee 110-11
  co-ownership 97
  developing today 100-8
  equity-sharing 100
  financial regime 105-6
  funding 102-3
  future 116-19
  membership involvement 110-11
  par-value 97, 100, 102, 103
  resident control 109-11
  secondary 101, 104
  short-life 99
  start-up funds 104
  tenant management 97, 98, 99,
    109, 110
Housing Corporation 175, 176,
  251, 252
  Annual Development Programme
    75-80, **77**

funding of co-operatives 117,
  239
Housing Co-operative Strategy 103
  new build and 29
  responsibilities 56, 118
  role in tenants' choices 163, 164
  in Scotland 113
housing finance 26
  Basic Credit Approvals 31-2, 92
  capital account 27-30, **29**
  Housing Revenue Account (HRA)
    11, 21, 26-7
  recent financial legislation 30-3
  ring-fencing 32-3
  Supplementary Credit Approvals
    31-2
Housing Finance Act (1972) 63
Housing for Wales (Tai Cymru) 56,
  163
  see also Wales
Housing Investment Programmes
  (HIPs) 8, 28-30, 76, 124, 241
housing management 18-25
  changing nature and condition of
    stock 20-2
  criticism of 6-7
  managers 112-15
  organisation and evolution of
    housing departments 18-20
  problems confronting council
    housing 22-4
  political influence and weak
    professionalism 24-5
  style 4
Housing Management Compulsory
  Competitive Tendering
  (HMCCT)
  41, 47-9, 234, 246-9
  see also Compulsory Competitive
    Tendering (CCT)
Housing Market Package (HMP) 89
Housing Needs Index (HNI) 76
housing policy
  phases in 6-12
  themes 15-16
Housing Policy: a Consultative Document 28

Housing Policy Review 17
    1977 15
    1987 8
Housing Revenue Account (HRA)
    11, 21, 26-7
housing subsidy 27, **27**, 92-3, 193
Housing Trusts 243
Howard, Ebenezer 96

Index of Local Conditions 250
inflation 10
inner city developments 72
Institute of Economic Affairs 37
Institute of Housing 25
interest rates 10
Islington 24, 115, 187, 190, 210

Kingshold Estate 212
Kingston upon Hull Housing Action
    Trust 170
Kirklees 190
Knowsley's Cantrill Farm Estate 158

Lambeth Housing Action Trust 170,
    187
landlord-tenant interface 19
Landlords' Choice 165
Large Scale Voluntary Transfers
    (LSVT) 3, 34, 41, 45, 46-7,
    91, 123, 151, 234
    consent 166
    protection of existing tenants 172
    as tenants' choice 165-9
    transfer and 73, 199-200, 244,
        246, 258
Lea View Estate 212
Leeds Housing Action Trust 170
Letchworth 96
Lewis, Samuel 60
Liverpool and Holloway Tenant Co-
    operative 97
Liverpool co-operatives 99, 110-11,
    115-16, 238
local authority housing departments
    181-204, 246-9
    assessment 255-6

compulsory competitive tendering
    200-4
decentralisation 186-9, 197-8
difficulties with estates 191-5
failings 188-9
Government's role 199-200
Government's view 183-5
management and politics 189-90
problem estates 185-6
progress of organisational change
    197-8
role in Estate Action 127
support services and 187
unified housing departments 196-7
Local Government Act (1985) 209
Local Government and Finance Act
    (1989) 209
Local Government and Housing Act
    (1989) 8, 11, 31, 44, 183,
    232
Local Government, Planning and
    Land Act (1980) 28, 169
London co-operatives 99, 238
Low Cost Home Ownership 65

Major, John 10
    administration 11
management and ownership 3-6
management decentralisation 5
Merseyside Task Force 127
Metropolitan County Council 209
Mini Housing Association Grant 76
mortgage arrears 11
mortgage rescue schemes 11
mortgage tax relief 4, 8, 11, 35, 38,
    257

National Consumer Council (NCC) 20
National Federation of Housing
    Associations (NFHA) 22, 37,
    76, 83
    Inquiry into British Housing 22
National Federation of Housing Co-
    operatives (NFHC) 102, 117,
    118
negative equity 11, 256

neighbourhood decentralisation 24,
    34, 55
New Town housing 158
Nissan 202
North Hull Estate 170
Norway 99

Parker-Morris space and heating
    standards 29
par-value co-operatives 97, 100,
    102, 103
Peabody, George 60
Poll Tax 209
Portland Gardens 116
Priority Estates Project (PEP) 6, 7,
    34, 41-4, 104, 123, 169, 186,
    212, 233, 235
private rented sector
    need for 7
    stimulating 36-9
private sector leasing 81
privatisation 146-7
property market crash 233
Public Sector Borrowing Require-
    ment (PSBR) 6
Public Works Loan Board 96

Rachmanism 61
racial discrimination 113
Rate Fund Contributions (RFCs) 21, 32
Rates Act (1984) 209
Rent Act (1965) 63
rents 4, 70-1
    affordable 4, 61, 65, 72, 81-4
    arrears 5, 19
    collection 19, 194
    control 36-9
Rents to Mortgages scheme 9, 10,
    35, 232
repossessions 11, 36
Revenue Deficit Grant (RDG) 64
Ridley, Nicholas 160, 163
Right to Buy 3, 4, 10, 24, 32, 33,
    37, 45, 65, 90, 154, 155-9,
    178, 206
    aims 155

effects on council house estates 21
protection of existing tenants 172
sales to sitting tenants 156, **157**
in Scotland 99, 107
success of 35, 44, 232, 243
Right to Manage 3, 12, 45, 49, 106,
    107, 117, 118, 155
Right to Rent 38
Right to Repair 185
ring-fencing 11, 32-3, 45
Rochdale 190
Rough Sleepers' initiative (RSI) 78

Sainsbury 202
Sandwell Housing Action Trust 170
Scotland
    Housing Action Trusts 107
    Housing Corporation 113
    Partnership Schemes 171
    Right to Buy in 99, 107
    tenant's choice in 161-2
Scottish Homes 56, 178
    Community Ownership Co-
        operatives 107, 117-18
    housing co-operatives 98, 113, 240
    scrutiny role of 163, 164
    transfer 167
Shared Ownership housing 9, 35,
    65, 232
Shelter 62
shorthold tenancy 9, 37
Single Regeneration Budget (SRB)
    150, 152, 220, 222, 241
slum clearance 19
social housing policy, developments
    33-49
social landlords' charter 163, 164, 175
Southwark Housing Action Trust 170
special needs housing 57-8, 59
start-up funds 104
Stockbridge Village Trust 158
Sunderland Housing Action Trust
    170
Supplementary Credit Approvals 31-2
    see also housing finance
Sweden 99

Tai Cymru (Housing for Wales) 56,
    163
tax relief
    landlords 38
    mortgage 4, 8, 11, 35, 38, 257
Tenant Management Co-operatives
    (TMCs) 95, 97, 98, 99, 106,
    109, 110
Tenant Management Organisations
    (TMOs) 2, 49, 106-7, 233,
    240
Tenant Participation Advisory Service
    (TPAS) 104
tenants
    consultation 138
    contractual rights 176
    role in Estate Action 127
Tenants' Associations 127
Tenants' Charter 45, 66, 88, 154,
    243
Tenants' Choice 3, 44, 45, 81, 91,
    123, 159-65, 206, 234,
    243-6
    criticisms 176-7
    future developments 177-9
    Government objectives 173-4
    increasing consumer choice
        through 72-3
    in Scotland 107
    transfer and 67, 185, 199
Tenants' Guarantee 56, 82, 88, 176
Tenants' Incentive Schemes (TIS) 76,
    81
Tenants' Rights etc. (Scotland) Act
    (1980) 155
tenure patterns, twentieth-century **36**
Thatcher, Margaret 11, 209
    administration 123

third arm in housing 62
topslicing 125, 140, 241
Tower Hamlets Housing Action Trust
    46, 170, 171, 190
Training and Enterprise Councils
    (TECs) 150, 219
transfer
    management 9-10
    Scottish Homes and 167
    Tenants' Choice and 67, 185, 199
    voluntary 185, 234
    see also Large Scale Voluntary
        Transfer
Trowbridge Estate 223

Unwin, Raymond 96
Urban Development Corporations
    (UDCs) 46, 169
Urban Housing Renewal Unit
    (UHRU) see Estate Action
Urban Programme 72

vandalism 4

Waldegrave, William 101, 160, 163-4
Wales
    homes 56, 163
    tenants' choices 166
Walsall 24, 187
Waltham Forest Housing Action
    Trust 171
Waverley Housing Trust 167
welfare state 16, 27
    see also Housing Benefits
Wenlock Barn Estate 212

Young, Sir George 226